No One But Us

Personal Reflections on Public Sanctuary by an offspring of Jacob

Ted Loder

Foreword by Elie Wiesel

San Diego, California

LURAMEDIA™

© Copyright 1986 LuraMedia™
San Diego, California
International Copyright Secured
Publisher's Catalog Number LM-604
Printed and Bound in the United States of America

LuraMedia™
10227 Autumnview Lane
San Diego, CA   92126-0998

Cover by Bruce McNeel

Library of Congress Cataloging-in-Publication Data

Loder, Ted, 1930 —
    No one but us.

    Bibliography: p.
    1. Sanctuary movement — United States — Case studies.
    2. Church work with refugees — United States — Case studies.
    3. Refugees — Central America — Case studies.
    I. Title.
    HV645.L64   1986   261.8'32   86-7516
    ISBN 0-931055-08-3

===

"Who shall ascend into the hill of the Lord? or who shall stand for us in his holy place? There is no one but us. There is no one to send, nor a clean hand, nor a pure heart on the face of the earth, nor in the earth, but only us, a generation comforting ourselves with the notion that we have come at an awkward time, that our innocent fathers are all dead — as if innocence had ever been — and our children busy and troubled, and we ourselves unfit, not yet ready, having each of us chosen wrongly, made a false start, failed, yielded to impulse and the tangled comfort of pleasures, and grown exhausted, unable to seek the thread, weak, and involved. But there is *no one but us*. There never has been."

— Annie Dillard
Holy the Firm

===

From pages 56-57 of HOLY THE FIRM by Annie Dillard. Copyright © 1977 by Annie Dillard. Reprinted by permission of Harper & Row, Publishers, Inc.

For Joel, Gabriela, Lucy, and Joelito
The FUMCOG Public Sanctuary Task Force
The people of FUMCOG
all of whom are God's Sanctuary

CONTENTS

FOREWORD

I have know Ted Loder for years. He is a man of principles, a man of rare courage, a man whose sincerité is inspired by his love for the ancient prophetic message.

He is a man of compassion. This is why he wrote this book which is a call to compassion. I hope it will be properly understood. And widely read. Of course, his writing is personal. It ought to be. All moral issues imply personal involvement.

Ted Loder and I have participated in the first conference on the ideas and ideals that deal with Sanctuary. What he felt is in this book. What I said on that occasion may serve as a preface only.

— Elie Wiesel
New York, April, 1986

How could I fail to identify with refugees when I myself am one? Yes. I too was a refugee. Something in me is a refugee. In a strange way, a person who has been a refugee remains a refugee.

I'll give you two anecdotal examples. One is that whenever I travel abroad, I don't buy anything. God knows I have no patience, no interest, in buying anything in Paris or London. Yet whenever I return to the United States from abroad, before going through customs, I, quite literally, am afraid. There is nothing to be afraid of but I am afraid, because I am a refugee. As a journalist I crossed many borders, and whenever I had to cross a border, it was hell. I never knew whether I would get in or out of somewhere from somewhere else. Everybody was looking at me suspiciously, because everybody looks at refugees suspiciously.

"The Refugee" by Elie Wiesel. © 1985 by Elirion Associates, Inc. Originally presented as the preliminary address to the Inter-American Symposium on Sanctuary in Tucson, Arizona, January, 1985. Reprinted by permission of Elie Wiesel.

The second example is as anecdotal as the first, but more dramatic. I drive a car. I don't know how I do it, but I drive. And, believe me, when I got my driver's license, I was prouder than when I got an honorary degree. But when we have to make a U-turn in New York, I am so afraid of the policeman that I stop and let my wife do it.

There is a third beautiful anecdote that I remember from those times, and it is pertinent. In Europe during the war, the refugees passed their time waiting for visas. Always waiting for visas. They would wait for days and days and days, standing in line in front of all kinds of consulates, waiting for a visa to anywhere.

The main thing was to get out, out of occupied France, out of Europe, and to go. Two Jewish people finally managed to get into different consulates, and when they met, one said to the other; "Did you get a visa?" "Yes!" "Where to?" "I'm going to Brazil." "Good." The other person then asked, "And you also got a visa? Where are you going?" The answer was in Spanish: "Tierra del Fuego." So the other person then said, "But that is so far!" And the first replied, "Far from where?"

That, to me, describes the state of mind of a refugee. Far from where? Suddenly geographic distances no longer matter. One can live a mile away from the border, and it's not a mile, it's a lifetime. Those French people who, during the war resided at the Swiss border, for instance, saw Switzerland day after day; they saw people who live freely. I could never understand them and still cannot ...what did *they* think of their freedom?

Permit me to turn the question around. I could never understand and I cannot understand now how those people in Switzerland, who were free, could remain free and eat in the morning and at lunch and at dinner while looking at the other side, at occupied France. After all, they lived in the same time, and yet, time itself had its own divisions.

If ever time was a metaphysical notion, that was it: when good and evil were separated by a man-made frontier. Any frontier is man-made, and yet, on one side people died, while on the other they went on living as though the others didn't die.

Those who know me will confirm that I am not a political person. I have never been involved in anything political. I don't understand politics; to me, it is something extremely obscure. I come from a tradition that aims at conferring an ethical meaning on anything a person does or does not do.

I would like, therefore, to see this problem in its ethical perspective. And from the ethical perspective, it is impossible for human beings today, especially for my contemporaries, who have seen what people can do to themselves and to one another, not to be involved. We must be with those who have suffered, and we must be with those who have tried to prevent others from suffering. This is the real community: it does not deny the differences, but rather enhances and transcends them. Because I am a Jew, and profoundly a Jew, I have to be a part of that community.

I have been asking myself where the whole concept of sanctuary comes from. First I went back to the Bible, and I discovered that there the word *sanctuary* somehow is not what we think it is.

The sanctuary concept in Scripture is rooted in what we call in Hebrew *arey miklat*, meaning "cities of refuge." However, we cannot draw a direct parallel. For a refuge-city, according to the Bible, is a place for guilty people, as distinct from refugees fleeing from Central America. A person who inadvertently was guilty, who unwittingly, unknowingly, committed a crime, would flee to one of the designated cities for a safe haven from revenge. Why? We are told in the Bible that it is natural to want to avenge a relative. It is an instinctive reaction. But there is one place where that avenger cannot enter. It is the refuge-city.

So I said to myself, that principle doesn't apply in your case, because surely not one of you has committed any crime. If you are here, my friends, it is because you want to live far from crime. It is because you want to renounce a society that may, in its foolishness, believe that violence is the answer. That is why you are here. And therefore you deserve another kind of sanctuary. Not the biblical kind.

I went to the Talmud, and there I realized that the entire problem, the entire theme of sanctuary, is always linked to war and peace. So what is a sanctuary in the biblical sense? It is an outgrowth of violence. For this reason, we are totally opposed to war, not only war against peoples but also war against individuals. When a state declares war on individuals, that means that something is wrong with that state. Then we have to find another concept of sanctuary.

What is it? Here again I come to my Jewish tradition, and with delight I discover that when we speak of sanctuary in the Jewish tradition, it refers to human beings. Sanctuary, then, is not a place. Sanctuary is a human being. Any human being is sanctuary. Every human being is the dwelling of God — man or woman or child, Christian or Jewish or Buddhist. Any person, by virtue of being a son or a daughter of humanity, is a living sanctuary whom nobody has the right to invade.

I have seen the opposite. I have seen the invasion of obscurity into light, of violence into wisdom. I saw it forty years ago. Most of you have studied the Bible. As you know, in the Bible forty years make one generation — which means we are one generation away from those times.

I remember *when* I became a refugee. Of all things it was on a Saturday, on the Sabbath. The gathering took place in the synagogue because the enemies, in their perverted imagination, tried so to hurt us that they sought to commit the worst crimes in our holiest place. Therefore they gathered the Jews in my town, Sighet, into the synagogue. And it is there that the first humiliation occurred.

We stood in line; there was a table with many gendarmes, feathers in their hats. We would come and give our papers. We were so naive. We thought that we were protected by our papers. Therefore proudly we took out our citizenship papers certifying us as citizens of Hungary. May I tell you, my good friends, what we had to do in order to obtain those papers? I cannot begin to tell even you. I remember the pain and the anguish that some of us had to go through to prove that our great-great-grandfather was born in a particular village, or town. Finally, we got the papers, and we felt good about them. We felt safe. But then, when I approached the table, in the synagogue courtyard, the officer didn't even look at the papers. He took them, tore them up and threw them into the wastebasket. I thus became a refugee. That feeling of being a refugee lasted and lasted for many, many years — in fact, until I came to this country.

You who are so-called illegal aliens must know that no human being is "illegal." That is a contradiction in terms. Human beings can be beautiful or more beautiful, can be right or wrong, but illegal? How can a human being be illegal?

I was in France for many years, always as a refugee. Only here did I become a citizen, and I must tell that I feel nothing but gratitude to this country, the first country that offered me a home and a refuge. I can tell you, my good friends from El Salvador, from Guatemala, and other places, that I hope you will soon feel what I feel. The twentieth century has created so many symbols, so many new concepts. It has also created a new human species: the refugee.

Now what is the characteristic of a refugee? It is that she or he has no citizenship. Hundreds of thousands, if not millions, of human beings have felt — overnight — unwanted. Now nothing can be more painful than being unwanted everywhere, undesired, and this is what a refugee is.

What has been done to the word *refuge*? In the beginning the word sounded beautiful. A *refuge* meant "home." It welcomed you, protected you, gave you warmth and hospitality. Then we added one single phoneme, one letter, *e*, and the positive term *refuge* became *refugee*, connoting something negative.

What I hope this century will achieve before it reaches its end is to get rid of this species. No more refugees. Wherever people come, they should be accepted in every society with friendship, they should be given a new way and a new measure of hope by becoming citizens of that country, our brothers and our sisters.

How does one achieve this? I know that American public opinion has political influence. If the American public were made aware — through newspapers and through television — of what is happening, if they were shown the suffering of the refugees, they would move Congress to act.

After, Congress is our best ally. I am pleased to hear that Senator DeConcini has introduced a bill. I think we should work with all our friends in Congress so that the bill passes in the House and the Senate. I think that is the way we must follow. I think it can be done. It can be done because humanity is contagious. We have seen it.

I'll give you an example. A few months ago I was in St. Louis with my friend Harry Cargas. I spoke for Christians and Jews; it was just a day or two after we heard and saw what was happening in Ethiopia.

Well, we tried to alert people, we spoke, we mobilized sympathies, and the American people responded beautifully. I know that in the places where I was, every child in every school gave a dollar. Communities galvanized their strengths, and there too, Jew and non-Jew came together. For it was unbearable to see men and women suffering, dying in front of us. I literally couldn't take it. Nor could the American people.

No comparisons should ever be made between tragedy and tragedy. Every tragedy is *sui generis*. It's only for you — I mean you, victims — to find the name for your tragedy. I have no right to give it a name, but I will accept the name that you give me. The least I can do is to accept your testimony, the testimony of the victims, and give it full credence, because you are both victim of and witness to your own cause.

I believe, therefore, that those men and women who decide to leave a country because they are hungry, because they cannot see their children die, or because they cannot see their parents die of hunger, deserve our respect; they deserve our friendship; and they deserve our support, just as do those who flee the very same country or others for political reasons.

Not to be hungry is part of our human right. How to feed his children is the obsession of every father. When a father cannot feed his children, the humiliation of that father or mother or sister, the torture of that family, is something that we here in America should not be able to tolerate. And we cannot tolerate it. We must speak and we must act as one human being to another. We must show that we care.

A few months ago we had a conference in Washington, which we called Faith in Humankind, a conference of rescuers of Jews during the war. It was devoted to what we called the righteous Gentiles. The idea came to us because I wanted to understand what made some people care and, secondly, why there were so few. We brought seventy-five righteous Gentiles to Washington; we brought scholars and philosophers and moralists, and we met together and we tried to understand what it was.

One of the great surprises for me was to realize that those people who cared — or as we put it, who had the courage to care — were not people of high stature. They were not generals, ministers, university professors, or industrialists. Most of them were simple people who didn't even know that what they were doing was courageous; they didn't even know that their acts were heroic.

They did it because it was the thing to do. And I felt then, woe to our society if to be human becomes a heroic act. Today, the times are different; therefore, please never compare, never. But as long as people suffer, I think there must be other people, and more, who should come to help them.

It doesn't even take that much. A gesture, an invitation to dinner, a smile, a meeting here tonight or a conference, or simply an idea that some young and old people come together for the best and most human cause in the world: to alleviate human suffering and to prevent humiliation.

My good friends, having received your calls and letters, how could I not come to be with you?

I am not sure that I can help you very much. I have no political power. All I have is a way of putting some words together, that's all. I represent my words, but these words come from ancient legends and laws, and after all, those legends and laws are not only mine, they are yours as well. To make you feel better, I will tell you a story: Who was the first refugee? Moses? No. Abraham? No. Adam.

Adam was our grandfather. And Adam was our first refugee. I'll tell you when and how it happened. It had something to do with his wife, but if not with his wife, it had to do with a serpent. The serpent was actually very good, because later, I imagine, the Bible knew that a certain Sigmund Freud would come along. I remember how it happened, we all remember that one day Adam fled; he committed a sin and he fled, at which point God said to him, "A*ifo ata*" — what beautiful words in the Bible — which means "Where art thou?" Adam, "Where art thou?"

The specific story tells us that one day a great Hassidic master, the founder of the Lubavitch movement, was in jail. He too was a refugee. The warden of the prison came to see him and said to the rabbi,

"I know that you know the Bible, maybe you can answer me. In the Bible it's written that God asks Adam, 'Where art thou?' Is it conceivable that God didn't know where Adam was?" And Rabbi Meyer Solomon answered: "God knew, Adam did not."

Do we know where we are? That is, do we know our place in history? Do we know our role in society? I can tell you of my experience and of my learning, again, which I have inherited from centuries of sages and disciples.

My place is measured by yours. In other words, my place under the sun, or in the face of God, or in my own memory, is measured by the distance it has from you. In other words, if I see a person or persons suffer, and the distance between us does not shrink, oh, then, my place is not good, not enviable.

Where am I? I am where you are, and if not, who knows where or whether I am at all?

In conclusion, what is a sanctuary? The sanctuary often is something very small. Not a grandiose gesture, but a small gesture toward alleviating human suffering and preventing humiliation. The sanctuary is a human being. Sanctuary is a dream. And that is why you are here, and that is why I am here. We are here because of one another.

Elie Wiesel is a survivor of Auschwitz and Buchenwald. He lived for many years as a stateless person. His books include novels, an autobiography, plays, and philosophic essays.

Jacob sent messengers before him to Esau his brother in the land of Se'ir, the country of Edom, instructing them, "Thus you shall say to my lord Esau: Thus says your servant Jacob, 'I have sojourned with Laban, and stayed until now; and I have oxen, asses, flocks, menservants, and maidservants; and I have sent to tell my lord, in order that I may find favor in your sight.' "

And the messengers returned to Jacob, saying, "We came to your brother Esau, and he is coming to meet you, and four hundred men with him." Then Jacob was greatly afraid and distressed . . . so he . . . took from what he had with him a present for his brother Esau, two hundred she-goats and twenty he-goats, two hundred ewes and twenty rams, thirty milch camels and their colts, forty cows and ten bulls, twenty she-asses and ten he-asses. These he delivered into the hand of his servants . . . He instructed the foremost, "When Esau my brother meets you, and asks you, 'To whom do you belong? Where are you going? And whose are these before you?' then you shall say, 'They belong to your servant Jacob; they are a present sent to my lord Esau; and moreover he is behind us.' " . . . For he thought, "I may appease him with the present that goes before me, and afterwards I shall see his face; perhaps he will accept me." So the present passed on before him; and he himself lodged that night in the camp.

The same night he arose and took his two wives, his two maids, and his eleven children, and crossed the ford of the Jabbok. He took them and sent them across the stream, and likewise everything that he had. And Jacob was left alone; and a man wrestled with him until the breaking of the day. When the man saw that he did not prevail against Jacob, he touched the hollow of his thigh; and Jacob's thigh was put out of joint as he wrestled with him. Then he said, "Let me go, for the day is breaking." But Jacob said, "I will not let you go, unless you bless me." And he said to him, "What is your name?" And he said, "Jacob." Then he said, "Your name shall no more be called Jacob, but Israel, for you have striven with God and with men, and have prevailed." Then Jacob asked him, "Tell me, I pray, your name." But he said, "why is it that you ask my name?" And there he blessed him. So Jacob called the name of the place Peni'el, saying, "For I have seen God face to face, and yet my life is preserved." The sun rose upon him as he passed Penu'el, limping because of his thigh.

— Genesis 32: 3-7a, 13-18, 20b-31, RSV

Begin somewhere in the middle, which is where we begin anything whether we acknowledge it or not. Fresh starts are a gift of grace to individuals but apparently not to history, and history is always where we are. So even fresh starts don't mean simply beginning, but beginning again . . .

The time has some bearing on the event. It was Friday, April 12, 1985 — one week after Good Friday, five days after Easter. Five of us arrived at the airport in Managua where we were scheduled to catch a plane for Guatemala. We were going to observe a human rights demonstration by the Mutual Support Group. We were part of a Congressional Delegation of thirteen persons on a fact-finding trip through Central America. Of the five going to Guatemala, two were the congressmen who headed the delegation: Bob Edgar (D., Penn.) and Ted Weiss (D., NY). The others were William Sloane Coffin, Senior Minister of Riverside Church in New York City; Phillip Berryman, who had lived and worked in Guatemala for four years with the American Friends Service Committee; and myself. I was included because I am the Senior Minister of the First United Methodist Church of Germantown, in Philadelphia, which had declared itself a Public Sanctuary church for a family of Guatemalan refugees.

As we entered the small, unpretentious room which served as a lounge for arriving and departing dignitaries at the airport, we were met by the political officer from the United States Embassy. With the smooth efficiency of a funeral director, she escorted the two congressmen into a corner where she began to talk to them as if they were the immediate family of the deceased. While the rest of us waited, we drank the small cups of coffee which the young Nicaraguan attendants served to us with a watchful pride that softened the plastic and pine wood plainness of the room, yet somehow added to my sense of unease. Shortly, Jody Williams, the project director for the trip, sauntered over to me and said, "There might be some trouble that would keep the congressmen from going. What would you do then?"

"Go anyway," I said quickly. I wonder why I am so quick to posture like that, what I'm forever trying to prove? I didn't even ask what the trouble might be. Or what Bill and Phil thought. Maybe for me what's worse, after all, is not being a hawk but being a chicken. Or having someone find out how easily I can become one.

After a few minutes which seemed much longer, Edgar and Weiss called us into private session and explained what was happening. *Prensa Libre*, a major Guatemalan newspaper, carried stories of death threats which had been made against them if they came into Guatemala to "participate" in the demonstration. The threats included the whole delegation and, in light of Guatemala's human rights record, had to be taken seriously. That we were only going to observe didn't persuade the Guatemalan government — the most repressive in this hemisphere. Apparently observation meant participation. Actually, the Guatemalan government has a point, depending on what you observe, and what you say about it, and to whom. In any case, tyrants are nothing if not cunning, and the United States State Department did not want the congressmen to go to the demonstration. If they became involved in even a minor incident while in Guatemala, major and embarrassing consequences might be provoked for the United States and its support of the government of Guatemala. Under that great pressure, Edgar and Weiss reluctantly decided not to go. The question that remained was whether Phil, Bill and I would go. We had twenty minutes to decide before the flight to Guatemala City left.

Embroidered on the personalized stole I wear when leading worship is an outline of Jacob wrestling with the Stranger at midnight by the River Jabbok. I chose that symbol because I relate to it so powerfully. Who was that Stranger? An angel? God? Some shadow side — or light side — of Jacob? Whoever it was, after the match Jacob limped for the rest of his life, and he had a new name: Israel. I sensed that this time in the Managua airport was like Jacob's wrestling match for me. I knew it was a time I would remember always; a time that in some way I understood, and in other ways I didn't at all. So much of me — of who I was and would be — depended on the outcome of the struggle which this decision triggered in me.

Whether or not we went — and why — might not matter (or matter much) to history, though no one ever really knows things like that. But to me, the decision would matter in some very specific ways I couldn't escape, ways which would shape me from then on. Intuitively I knew that. I suppose there are moments like this for everyone, lots of them, all the time, whether we recognize them or not. Scrape away all the diversions and denials, and such moments are probably more than half of what life is about. At least that's the theory, the topic of numberless sermons. Still. . . damn the Stranger who grabbed and twisted my gut, my soul, in those sweaty, short-breathed moments in that Jabbok of a lounge.

It was clear that the threats were real, and all the more frightening for their vagueness. No one was sure who had made them. The probability was that they were prompted by a speech in which Guatemalan Chief of State, General Oscar Mejia Victores, had called supporters of the Mutual Support Group "subversive elements." If we went, there was a risk, however small, that we might be killed or simply "disappear," as do so many persons who are labeled subversive by the military rulers of Guatemala. Fear wafted over me like fog off a slow river. I began to grope around for a plausible, face-saving excuse not to go.

I thought of Jan, the woman I love beyond all telling of it and with whom I wanted to spend my life. I thought of each of my children whom I love so fiercely. And as quickly as came those thoughts, came

19

the intuitive realization that any excuse which saved my face would cost my heart, because an excuse would betray something essential about love. Or perhaps it would be more accurate to say an excuse would betray something essential about a person who *attempts* to love — in this case, me. Even more curiously, an excuse would betray something essential in the persons I loved. I won't argue the logic of those intuitions, only report the experience of them. Indeed, to apply an explanation as structured as logic, or even argument, to those moments would require a far stretch. But, even if not immutable truth, these intuitions came with unshakable conviction. The Stranger I wrestled with was slippery, and the match went on.

Time was ticking. We talked. Can any of us, short of Dostoevsky, begin to tell why we make the decisions we do? I suspect, like Jacob and the Stranger at midnight, we wrestle and decide most important things in something like the dark, so that shadows and shades, the snap of a twig, a slight shift in the wind, a sliver of reflected light are decisive, not detailed maps and surveillance reports. Bob Edgar told us that the United States Embassy in Nicaragua didn't want us to go and that the Embassy in Guatemala couldn't guarantee our safety. "You're adults and you can do what you think best," Bob said, "but I don't think you should go."

I was ambivalent. I was startled by my awareness that something in me strongly wanted to respond to the offered "out." At the same time, I knew I wouldn't take it. Partly, because to do so would mean some small complicity in what I considered to be the misguided and unjust State Department policies being implemented by the very embassy which didn't want us to go.

Mixed in with the morality of my refusal to take the "out" were less noble motives. I knew if I took it, I would be ashamed to face my friends who shared my objections to United States policies in Guatemala; and, most of all, ashamed to face my congregation and staff colleagues who had declared Public Sanctuary. I also knew that, personally, Bob wanted to make the trip and was angry at the circumstances and the way they had come about — circumstances which made it necessary for him, as a congressman, not to go. I knew Ted Weiss felt the same way. Bob had given us an "out" if we needed it to salve our consciences, but I felt I'd let him down if I took it. Avoiding shame surely isn't a very noble or moral motive, though the Stranger we wrestle with does have sneaky ways to try to pin us. In any case, the making of personal decisions apparently is more corporate than we realize...to say nothing of the consequences.

But a twig had snapped and a shadow moved when Bob pointed out that we were adults who were responsible for our own decisions. I smiled. Though I knew that intellectually, in those moments I also felt the tug of the wish to have someone else protect me and tell me what to do. Of course, I realized no one else really could tell me what to do; I was responsible for myself.

Still, the less-than-mature wish was undeniable, and confronting that wish in myself was critical. As I reflect on it, I came to understand viscerally the appeal of authoritarian religions and governments: it is safety! Safety from loneliness, from uncertainty, from responsibility, ultimately from death and damnation. Yet here we were, one week after Good Friday when we meditated on the life of a man who risked all those and knew that safety was an illusion. But wrong and insidious as I believe authoritarian religion and governments are — for keeping their adherents in a state of childish dependence with assurances of the sort of safety and security even God doesn't give — the wish for safety was in me.

That's the insidious thing about the appeal of safety: it is so seductive. The danger is that the gift we'll give to gain safety is our self! Still, the twig had snapped, and I knew I could not decide for safety and take the "out." But knowing now how deep the wish is in me, I will be more on guard against — and more challenging of — the siren songs of authoritarian religion and government. I will also try to be more gentle with that wish, somehow. I really do fight in others what I'm afraid of in myself.

All through the discussion Bill Coffin kept insisting, "I'm going, even if I have to go alone. I'm not going to be intimidated. That's an old ploy they tried to use on us in the civil rights days to keep us out of the South. You can't let them get away with it." Phil Berryman was more quiet. He'd lived in Guatemala and had been forced to leave. He, more than any of us, knew what it was like and the dangers involved, since he was already *persona non grata* there. But, he seemed equally determined to go. I knew I was going, too. And I kept saying so, punctuating my insistence with questions which only had the effect of provoking Bill into repeating, "I'm going even if I have to go alone," to which Phil would respond, "That's fine, Bill, but Guatemala isn't Alabama."

It was almost funny: we were like three boys screwing up their courage to jump off the railroad trestle into the river, knowing people had broken their necks doing it, but believing we'd be okay if we did it right. I tried to figure out why I wasn't about to let Bill go alone. Was it competition in which I somehow didn't want him to get ahead of me . . . or any *further* ahead, since he'd always been far ahead of me in everything? Or was it because I really loved this old friend from Yale Divinity School days? Was it because he had a way of making me feel guilty for even *thinking* of doing otherwise? Was it because I trusted him? Was it because I felt we all belonged inviolably together — Bill and I and Phil (though we'd only known Phil for a short time)? Was it all of these? Would I ever know? Did it matter, really?

Jody Williams told us the plane was about to leave. Almost as if it was an impulse — which maybe finally it was — I jumped to my feet, said, "Hell, let's go," grabbed my bag and went out the door toward the plane. Jody finally caught up with me just as I was about to go past the soldier guarding the gate.

"Hey, you have to wait for the attendant to escort you." I was flustered. Bravado can get you in trouble. But then, so can timidity. "I'm glad you're going," she said.

"Yeah, so am I," I said. And I meant it! My motives, my reasons for going were certainly not all pure or noble or simple. But I was glad, honestly and freely glad! And maybe that's as close to being blessed by the Stranger as I, or anyone, has any right to get. Anyway, it's about the wrestling — the processes of deciding, and the struggle of learning and loving, and so of finding out something of what faith might be about, and growing even a little in it — that I am writing this book.

Not that my fear is gone, just subsided. Sometimes I just get it in a better perspective. Sitting on that plane in the moments before take-off, I thought hard about the people who had been on my mind the whole time. I thought about Joel and Gabriela and their five year old daughter Lucy — the refugee family from Guatemala who are in Public Sanctuary at the church I serve. About two years before, they had had to flee for their lives from the country into which I was about to fly. Joel had been on two death lists in Guatemala, a country in which the military rulers have created a nation of widows and orphans. (Amnesty International reports that some twenty thousand people were killed between 1966 and 1977. According to the most recent study, based on Guatemalan Supreme Court figures, an additional fifty to seventy-five thousand people have been murdered between 1978 and 1985.) Joel had been tortured by a death squad and lost hearing in one ear. On his body were scars from that torture. Gabriela's brother had "disappeared," as have unnumbered thousands of Guatemalans in recent years. The "disappearances" are an especially cruel way of intimidation: the family never sees the missing person again, and they have no way of knowing whether the missing person is dead or alive. And it was to observe a protest by families of these "disappeared" people that we were going to Guatemala now.

The United States government supports with economic and military aid the government of Guatemala. In fact, the CIA helped overthrow an elected civilian government and put the military government in place in Guatemala in 1954. That government, though suffering a series of coups, remained for thirty years a military dictatorship which has been systematically oppressive and capriciously violent. Guatemala is the only country which, as an entire nation, Amnesty International has cited for flagrant human rights violations. A report entitled Bitter and Cruel,[1] issued by the human rights delegation of the British Parliament, concludes that evidence points directly to the state security apparatus as responsible for the disappearances and killings of Guatemalan citizens. Yet, the United States govern-

[1]BITTER AND CRUEL is the October 1984 Report of the Central American Human Rights Committee, of the British Parliament Human Rights Group. It was published with the support of War on Want, with financial help from *Christian Aid*. Copies can be ordered from British Parliament Human Rights Group, 20 Compton Terrace, London N1 2UN, England.

ment supports the Guatemalan government, offering as its fundamental justification the belief that this government is anti-communist! It doesn't seem to matter that any group or person who questions the Guatemalan government — or raises issues of economic or political justice or human rights — is considered by that government to be *ipso facto* a communist. It doesn't seem to matter that the Guatemalan government is a facist tyranny. It is enough that it is simply anti-communist.

I knew these facts about Guatemala before this trip. I had heard chilling accounts of torture and violence in Guatemala from Joel and Gabriela. I had seen in their eyes the pain, the suffering, the fear and the smoldering anger of their experiences in their homeland which they loved and to which they wanted desperately to return. By declaring Public Sanctuary, our church was giving this family of illegal aliens — as our government calls them — a place where they would be safe for a time. We were providing them with legal assistance, so they could not be deported automatically and through which they could file for political asylum. And more, we were making it possible for them to tell their story, to inform people about what is going on in Guatemala — information which the United States government doesn't want spread, because it contradicts the Administration's "official" version.

The plane was taxiing toward the runway for take-off. In the last few minutes I experienced just a fraction of the fear Joel and Gabriela knew so well. I had to look that fear in the face. I knew that Joel and Gabriela were an urgent, yet somehow mysterious, reason why I was on that plane going where I was. The mystery was how the trails of our lives — mine beginning in a small Nebraska town, their's somewhere in Guatemala — had become woven together in Philadelphia. Who except God could have looked at us those long years ago and calculated the odds on us ending up — or better, beginning again — as we were through Public Sanctuary? I was going to Guatemala because of Joel and Gabriela. In a way, I was going for them. Or was this going really some form of the limp that constituted the blessing of the Stranger? I supposed it might be, except the wrestling still goes on. But who knows, that might be a part of the blessing as well.

Then we were in the air. Off in the west the sun was setting in a silent explosion over the Pacific Ocean. The colors flowed liquidly from the fiery ball of maroon out into scarlet, gentling into a quieter orange which melted into a shade close to muskmelon, then thickened into an elegant gray which deepened into purple and finally into a bottomless black, pin-holed with stars. I gulped back the tears and the longing. Suddenly I was aware once again that I, too, am always looking for sanctuary, looking for a place — or is it a dimension that hovers, attends — a sanctuary where I am accepted, where there is peace, an ease for my spirit, a trust, a grace, something like healing, the sniff of resurrection. I sensed again that Public Sanctuary and personal sanctuary are somehow inseparable, just as Jacob's wrestling was all of a piece (or all of a peace) with his upcoming confrontation with Esau and finding his way home to become Israel.[2]

Slowly the plane banked, and the sunset was lost behind us. We droned into the darkness. I looked at Phil and Bill and realized we hadn't talked for some minutes. We were lost momentarily in our thoughts. I tried to imagine how Joel and Gabriela must have felt — running for their lives through the night, carrying their baby, making their way in fear and in faith toward us, whom they knew not, as we awaited them, unknowing. Shadows, a slight shift in the wind, a sliver of reflected light. I grapple and hang on and gasp, "O God, bless me ... Bless all us wrestlers who limp toward the dawn ... and resurrection."

[2]Genesis 32:3-31

Innocence

It was a Saturday night in late August, 1984, when I first met Joel and Gabriela and Lucy. A wedding at which I'd officiated had caused Jan and me to arrive quite late at the home where the welcoming picnic for the refugees was being held. I remember walking around the side of the house in the darkness and feeling awkward. In addition to our church's Public Sanctuary Task Force, I knew that people from Riverside Church in New York City were going to be there. Riverside Church also had declared Public Sanctuary, and the refugees going to that church were close friends of Joel and Gabriela. In fact, they had come out of Central America and traveled across the United States together. We had agreed to care for both families for a few weeks until Riverside Church could complete its preparations for their refugees' living situation.

NO ONE BUT US

Since I had known their Senior Minister Bill Coffin for years, part of my feeling of self-consciousness stemmed from wanting to make a good impression on those visitors. I don't like that about me, but the feeling was palpable. Bill is the Pavarotti of Protestant preachers, and I'm lucky to make spear carrier in the chorus. By what perversity do I insist on comparing myself with him, our church in Philadelphia with his church in New York? Why am I so competitive? It torments me. What am I competing for? What does this son of Zebedee[1] want? I don't know. What I do know is that I felt a certain pride that our church had declared Public Sanctuary before Riverside Church had, and that there now was this new link between us.

As we came around the corner of the house, the first thing that struck me were the colored lanterns hung around the yard. They gave the setting a festive and fanciful quality, separating little islands of light from the surrounding sea of blackness which, by contrast, seemed deeper and more seductive. The wilt and smudge of an August growing weary had disappeared under the cosmetic of night. The shapes and faces of people appeared blurred in that deceptive light, and it was hard to identify the particular individuals who were there, squint as I did. The effect was of something like a fantasy, a movie set, a space out of time, an anywhere/nowhere kind of party in which the cares of the world — if not the world itself — had been suspended. It felt, at most, only a step east of Eden.

Somehow the setting was fitting. As we gathered that night, we were innocent — not by being without fault, but by being without knowledge. We were ignorant, and I think ignorance is about as close as we can ever get to whatever "innocence" might mean to us. There really are times when, like Adam and Eve, we haven't eaten of the tree of the knowledge of good and evil. At least that night, I was innocent by virtue of ignorance.

There are, of course, many varieties and variations of ignorance, and I am subject to enough of them not to be qualified to explicate many of them. But four varieties do occur to me as relevant to my state

[1]Mark 10:35-41

that August night. The first is *ignorance from lack of information.* Everyone suffers some degree of this ignorance, because there is always more information about anything than anyone can ever gather. That's why, finally, truth is interpretive, not factual; partial, not absolute. That's why decisions about anything that matters much are always risky.

Still, I had learned enough information about Central America — about its repressive governments, the persecutions, the death squads; about the forced dislocation of large segments of the civilian populations; about the circumstances of Archbishop Oscar Romero's martyrdom in El Salvador — to know that something was radically wrong and terribly unjust in those neighbor nations. I had learned enough about our own nation's foreign policies there — about how those policies helped create conditions of political persecution and large scale suffering among the people of those countries; about our own country's Refugee Act of 1980 and the discriminatory application (or non-application) of that law to refugees from Guatemala and El Salvador by the Immigration and Naturalization Service — to have strongly supported the group of our church members who advocated that we declare Public Sanctuary for refugees from these countries. Our government puts these refugees in double jeopardy: we support governments which brutalize them, and then refuse them asylum when they flee to this country to save their lives.

When our church finally made the decision to declare Public Sanctuary, it may have been risky, but it was far from whimsical. The knowledge we — or I — lacked that made us innocent that August night was *not* lack of information (except in the sense that this lack applies to everyone). The irony, however, is that it is precisely this sort of ignorance, and "innocence," of which the government accuses people in the Public Sanctuary Movement when they call us "misguided and misinformed." (I wonder if their accusations of our innocence will hold up in court!)

No, our innocence — my innocence — derived from ignorance of other varieties. One such variety is the *lack of knowledge which results from some hidden — or nearly hidden — desire not to know something, because the knowledge might be intimidating.* Was it the Goths who went over their battle plans twice: the first time when they were sober, to be sure those plans were somewhat realistic so they could have confidence in them; the second time when they were drunk, to be sure the plans weren't based on so much reality that they would lack the courage to engage the enemy? It's that kind of innocence that the youthful David must have had when he determined to take on Goliath, even though more seasoned, knowledgeable warriors had backed down. If David had let himself know too much about Goliath, if he had considered too long the formidable strength of this giant, he might have dropped off his brothers' lunch and gone back to tending sheep instead of going off to find stones for his slingshot.[2]

So that night, while I felt good about what we were doing — and "drunk" with that — I simply was ignorant of the full implications. The refugees had arrived! Months of talk and preparation became incarnate in this Guatemalan family. Exuberant and brash as David, I didn't want to look too closely at the Goliath government we were taking on . . . or even think of the government of the country I loved as being a Goliath.

I really can't explain how ingrained is my love for my country. Maybe it comes from all those hours when George Washington and Abraham Lincoln peered unblinkingly down on us in those little South Dakota schoolrooms where I learned to read and add. I grew up believing this country is dedicated to the proposition that all people are created equal, that we are pledged in heart, as well as voice, to a flag that stands for liberty and justice for all. Something in me, even now, believes that people in this country — that our government — will respond to truth, to an appeal to conscience, to a call to justice, to a summons to the things that make for peace. I still believe, somehow, that this country might come to recognize and honor the rightness of the cause of Public Sanctuary, that the government will not callously continue to deport these refugees to almost certain death or imprisonment. I suppose my belief is naive, but I don't really want to know that the contrary might be the larger reality. At least on that lovely August night I didn't want to know. That is something of what I mean by innocence.

[2] I Samuel 17

But my innocence derived from an even deeper level of this second variety of ignorance, for there was something else I lacked knowledge of that night: knowledge of myself. And I don't think I wanted that knowledge much either. Our church was daring to challenge authority by what we were doing. I certainly don't have any qualms about challenging authority, especially when that authority is acting in an immoral way — as I certainly think the government was, and is, acting in the issues to which Public Sanctuary is addressed. Nothing prophetic is ever done, or said, without challenging authority — or at least without challenging one authority in the name of another, higher one.

I often think of what Albert Camus wrote to a Nazi soldier who had been his pre-World War II friend. Camus told him that Germany "has received from its sons only the love it deserved, which was blind. A nation is not justified by such love. That will be your undoing."[3] Unless we hold our country's feet to the fire of God, or to a higher moral standard, we betray both God and our country.

And yet, there is something else, some self-ignorance, in the challenge. It is exciting and morally energizing to take on authority, to face the Goliaths of the world. But there are dangers in it, too. You can begin to think that you, as David, have some special favor with God, and that Goliath is anyone, or any institution, you don't like who has power. You can begin to be afflicted with a certain knee-jerk, anti-authority response to every authority around, everyone with any power you butt against. That's an affliction not entirely unknown among us so-called "liberal" or "prophetic" people. The psychological term for it is counter-dependence, which simply means we are dependent on some authority figure who defines who we are by providing a presence against whom we can rebel. It's probably no accident that David was a teen-ager when he went up against Goliath, and no denying that I manage to act like a teen-ager at many inappropriate times and in many awkward ways.

[3]From page 11 of RESISTANCE, REBELLION AND DEATH by Albert Camus, translated by Justin O'Brien. Copyright © 1960 by Alfred A. Knopf, Inc. Reprinted by permission of Alfred A. Knopf, Inc.

What's missing, and painful to come by, is self-knowledge. I like to avoid self-knowledge when the knowledge may not be good, when the truth of me probably won't measure up to the image I've been taught and tried to project. I suppose I'm a little like a pharisee who prefers being a hypocrite to being humiliated. So, it's much easier to see the justification for my *challenging* authority than it is to see the justification for my *being challenged* by authority. To really honor the challenge of authority — not just of power — means having to look as honestly as you can at yourself, and to come to some painful self-knowledge that you didn't have before.

I didn't have that kind of self-knowledge that August night; and neither, I think, did many of us present there. We were innocent. The subtle danger of challenging authority in the name of a higher authority is the ease with which we can forget that the higher authority also challenges us. David may have defeated Goliath because he challenged him in "the name of the Lord of hosts," but David didn't come to know himself by the same challenge. So David, minus that self-knowledge, later betrayed Uriah in order to gain Bathsheba and consequently lost peace in his kingdom.[4]

I wonder if the heart of religion isn't in discerning how the challenge to self-knowledge comes — and from what authority. I suspect truth, as it comes to us, is seldom as lopsided as we might like it to be, and often more painful. It didn't occur to me that lovely backyard night to wonder what truth was going to confront me — confront us — as we moved ahead in Public Sanctuary. That night we knew only the truth which we were confronting: people in Central America were dying because of political persecution, and we were helping to save at least three of them. We were innocent, because we were without deep self-knowledge.

The last two varieties of ignorance are simple, and they also applied to us. The third variety is the *ignorance that comes with being time bound*. Some things you simply cannot know ahead of time, before you experience them. You may know them in your head, imagine them,

---

[4] II Samuel 11

pre-enact them. But you cannot know them existentially, so to speak, in your gut. You cannot know them through the wounds or the joys they bestow.

And the fourth form of ignorance is irremediable, though God knows there are hucksters of remedies in church, state and market place. Still, there are some things it simply is not given to mortals to know. There is *knowledge which resides only in God*. Wise are they who acknowledge their ignorance of that knowledge, and confess that innocence. For those who assert that they have that knowledge are not innocent of the inquisitions they initiate in their arrogance. The terrible threat is that arrogance is easily spotted in individuals, but very difficult to see in governments and nations. It is when finite creatures — and their institutions — claim God's knowledge, that exercising power takes precedence over seeking truth.

On that August night, as we welcomed the refugees, little did I know. Little, I think, did *any* of us really know. We were in a state of euphoristic innocence. In that state we greeted one another, put onions on our hamburgers, piled potato salad fatteningly high on our paper plates, and skittered around at the edges where the darkness and conversation were shallow enough to negotiate with such loads. Finally we came to them. "Jan and Ted, I'd like you to meet Joel and Gabriela and Lucy."

Two impressions struck simultaneously. The first was how small they were physically. I don't know why, but that surprised me, even came shockingly close to disappointing me. Why? Later I tried to sort it out. I think, being raised an American and being an ex-basketball player, I unconsciously identify size with strength and, by some circuitous slight of mind, with value. Oh God, the chauvinism of size to add to all the others! I wonder how big Jesus was.

The other impression, even in that shadowy half-light, was of their eyes. Gabriela's were enormous and childlike, conveying an ingenuous quality that belied her being a tough and disciplined mother who had escaped her pursuers and, with her baby and husband, had overcome tortuous obstacles to find safety in this country. Joel's eyes were deep set and sad, watchful — as if looking for someone, something, to trust, but wary of finding them. This man, who had been on two death lists in his homeland and had been tortured until he had lost the hearing in one ear, had seen things which seared him, yet strangely gentled rather than embittered him. You don't forget Joel's eyes.

I put out my hand and said, "I'm glad to meet you, and I'm very glad you are here." I would have gone on except I realized that Joel and Gabriela had looked away from me toward a woman standing next to them. The woman was a member of our church's Public Sanctuary Task Force. I had known she was going to be there to translate for the refugees, but my experience with translators is quite limited. I was caught off guard when she began to speak to Joel and Gabriela in Spanish. That brief interruption was disconcerting to me. Obviously, she was telling the refugees what I had said, after which she turned to tell me their reply, though I understood their soft, "Bueno, bueno."

But somehow during that necessary intrusion of the translator, I felt as though the refugees had receded out of hearing. It was as if some silent earthquake had opened an enormous canyon between us and we were on opposite sides. The quick sense I had was that I would be forever yelling things to them across this yawning gap, then waiting to find out what they had heard — and how much — while they would be doing the same with me. There was the mock of impenetrable loneliness in it, and a cramp of foolishness. What had I expected? Immediate rapport? Easy friendship? Collegiality in a cause? Whatever it was, it wasn't this!

I became aware that no one was talking; they were waiting for me to say something else. I felt flustered, stupid. I'm not sure what I said, but I am reasonably sure it was totally banal. I realized I didn't even know what questions to ask these refugees, or what they really needed to know, or even what I was to listen for — or how — in their words, inflections, pauses, gestures. Of course, it was a language barrier traceable in part to my coming through an educational system which gives only marginal, if any, attention to teaching a second language — a lamentable lack complicated by my own clumsiness in the languages I did try to learn.

Yet, it was more than a language problem. Even with excellent translation, there was still the barrier of not being at all sure of the reality the words were straining to convey: the culture, the roots, the symbols, the fears and longings and loves, the scars and odors and caresses, the sweaty, moon-washed experiences of these human beings. Would I ever know who they were? Would they ever know who we were?

Do we ever know who anyone is, even the self we give our own familiar name to? That was the question I finally came to later that night, sitting outside our home watching the sheet lightning do its rain dance in the sky and listening to the rumble of distant thunder. I knew my question wasn't a new one or even a particularly intriguing one any longer. Philosophers have been dicing that one up a thousand ways for more than a thousand years. Still, the question seemed, and seems, to me.too grimy and urgent for philosophical abstraction. Is it possible for people who live in the United States to really *know* Central Americans...or any Third World people? Is it possible for conservatives to know liberals and vice versa, or men and women to know each other, children and parents, black and white and so on and on and on? Can we tell each other even a fragment of who we are and what we mean? Will we ever trust one another? Who can help translate us to each other? Who can shrink the canyons between us? Or, if it is possible, do we really *want* to? Maybe we prefer the gaps because they protect us. Maybe the word which most fascinates us — and which we understand most easily, or think we do — is power, not truth or love. Maybe this is so for me as well, else why the self-consciousness, the concern for impressions, the compulsion to compete?

The thunder was getting louder. Part of my torment was that religion, of all the human enterprises, claims — or perhaps is assigned —the task of translating us to each other and ourselves, telling us what we mean. So what am I doing as one of its spokespersons? More critically, how do we translate — and trust — a God whose language and culture is apparently as different from us humans as was Joel and Gabriela's from those of us who had gathered to welcome them that August night? With that final question, I found myself smiling. It occurred to me the question itself was a clue to the answer...as I suppose most questions really are.

The wind had risen. I stood and watched the trees sway wildly, creating a frenzy of shadows and shifting shapes. Earlier it had seemed as if we had gathered only one step east of Eden. At some profound level that was an accurate feeling, for we probably are always at once further from and closer to paradise than we know. I sensed that already I was losing the innocence I'd had a few hours before. The loss was probably good, for even a short step away from innocence may be a long step toward yourself and those you walk the earth with. The storm broke. It started to rain.

Pride

Most people are curious about those who do unusual, controversial or apparently dangerous things. So from the beginning, questions were asked of our church: How did a congregation of nearly one thousand members come to declare Public Sanctuary? Wasn't it divisive? Weren't many members against such action? Weren't they leaving the church? What was the effect of declaring Public Sanctuary on the budget, on church attendance, on morale? Didn't potential new members shy away from identifying with a church engaged in such activity? Those of us most invested in our church's Public Sanctuary work would answer, with just a hint of a swagger, that it was quite the contrary. Everything at the church was up: attendance, budgets, new members, morale. Yet, whenever I heard that statement, or said it myself, part of me grimaced. Both the swagger and the grimace testify to the subtleness of pride.

I wish I could remember who said, "All idolatry springs from a desire for order." No matter where I ran across the words, the thought embedded itself like a sliver in my memory. It seems especially true, if the desire for order is understood as involving a desire for success. When we first broached the idea of declaring Public Sanctuary, only *one* of my questions was about the morality of the action. The rest were precisely those questions other people asked after we made the decision to declare Public Sanctuary. I didn't want the church to suffer loss of membership or money *if it could be avoided.* Essentially, I felt that the risk of such an action was more professional than personal. This discomforting insight signaled yet another round in my endless struggle: how to keep from forfeiting my humanity to my ministry. It's a struggle accentuated by people's expectations of ministers — what they should be and do — and the ease with which I could accede, if I don't stay watchful, to those expectations out of my desire to succeed.

The intensity of my desire to succeed professionally still startles me. But then I guess you don't sell your soul in one grand, Faustian bargain; you nickel and dime it away. The church of which I am Senior Minister was close to becoming — if not actually being — my idol. The church might seem less obvious and less self-serving than more mundane and lucrative idols, but it is just as insidious and just as demanding, since all idol worship requires some form of human sacrifice. When I am quiet long enough to tune to such signals as children and Orion, I find myself wondering what it would mean to be successful as a *person*, rather than as a professional. In any case, I did not rush to declare Public Sanctuary with unbridled enthusiasm or moral zeal. It was a struggle, with order and with pride.

Still, to be human at all, you — I — have to make moral choices and take moral actions. The evidence, incomplete as it may be, is persuasive that some things are simply wrong. Injustice, exploitation, oppression, tyranny are unarguably real in our common life, even if the solutions are arguable. The whisper — or scream — of conscience can be ignored only at peril to one's humanity. There are some acts that cannot be avoided, no matter how much you squirm, even at risk of members and money. At last there is no place to run, no direction to go but to ford whatever is your Jabbok; nothing to do but confront what you owe to your brother and sister and to yourself; no one to fight with but the Stranger. It's just that, as with Jacob, the problems persist — maybe even intensify, or at least take different forms — when you win. Whatever winning means. For Jacob, it meant a life-long limp and a name he didn't deserve. For me, the limp is hidden in the swagger, a name in the grimace.

Over the years, I and the church whose ministry I've shared for twenty-four years have won. We are one of the few churches in the urban Northeastern United States which has managed to go through significant transitions and emerge with a strong, vital congregation of young, seeking, talented people. We have won a reputation as an innovative church with excellent music, creative preaching and liturgy, outstanding programs in drama and the arts, and, perhaps most critically, an effective commitment to justice and peace in our city, our nation, and the world. We have been involved in the civil rights movement: I had marched with Dr. Martin Luther King, Jr., on several occasions; and Andrew Young had spoken from our pulpit shortly after Dr. King's assassination. We had been part of the movement to end the Vietnam War. Bill Coffin had visited to alert us to the terrible consequences of the nuclear arms race, and we had joined the "Peace In Search Of Makers" effort to reverse that race. We have begun and spun off major community-based, non-profit corporations in health care, housing and education for people in our section of the city. We have invested in and made outright financial grants to organizations committed to meeting human need and making our community more just and humane. We have won, as it were, and I have been the Senior Minister for sixteen years, a Co-Minister with Robert Raines for eight years before that.

So there was a swagger about me, about us, however modestly affected. Our pride in being "different" — which I shared, if not generated — was not only self-promoting, an advertisement for our special quality, but bordered on being judgmental of churches of allegedly lesser moral and/or creative stature.

But the limp hidden in the swagger became ever more pronounced, at least to me. Pride has an underside which is compulsion: the compulsion to avoid possible humiliation, to prove something to yourself and to others, to make good on the brag and then top it the next time. I recall Liston Pope, Dean of Yale Divinity School, telling of a certain professor who called his autobiography, *Glimpses of the Cosmos*. Now that is compulsion, pride, run wild. But, I suppose everyone of us who writes — or preaches or does anything public —suffers from from this kind of pride. We assume, despite denials, that what we have to say is at least a glimpse of the galaxy, if not the cosmos.

In any case, the compulsion for me has to do with proving my value, my worth. If compulsion is hooked on moral action, on prophetic witness, then that action becomes addicting, whatever the cost. Then you *have* to make the stand, take the risk, give the gift to prove that you are good, that you are worthy. This is the compulsion which has fueled much of my ministry, indeed much of my life. It is the energy of my competitiveness, and it is a torment. It is a limp.

Why? I'll try to tell you, but first I feel constrained to emphasize that the people I am compelled to try to help, in my moral competitiveness, often *are* truly helped. And they don't give a damn for my motives, any more than I care much what the motives of my doctor are, as long as she cures me when I'm sick. Let her get rich as long as I get well. The beaten man on the Jericho Road didn't probe the motives of the Good Samaritan. The Samaritan's goodness was measured by his behavior.[1] Motives didn't count. . .except Jesus told the parable as an example of loving your neighbor. So maybe there is, or can be — perhaps even *must* be — a limp in love, and at least a pinch of torment.

So, why the limp? What's the torment? It's because the issue isn't solely one of love; it also has to do with faith, or with the lack of it. If you're out to prove your worth, your goodness — even your love — to yourself and to others, you don't much need God except, perhaps, to receive your deposits of virtue and to compound the interest on it. Operationally, existentially, God becomes irrelevant, not really required to do anything — in fact, required *not* to do anything. If God did something, you couldn't claim the credit and, therefore, you wouldn't have proved anything about your worth. If, in your view, your right-

[1] Luke 10:30-37

eousness and your value depend on your works and your accomplishments, then calling on God would be a crib.

From that point it's but a weary sigh to the nagging sense that there just might not be a God to do anything anyway. So, when you scrape away all the preaching and posturing, most of what's left is that it's up to me, but I'm not up to it.

In one of his columns in *The New York Times*, William Safire says, "The only thing we have to fear is fearlessness — nameless. . . unjustified overconfidence. . . "[2] I'm learning enough about myself to agree with his statement, except I don't think the fearlessness is nameless. Its name is pride, and it really isn't fearlessness, but *pretense* of fearlessness, which is empty. Most of what I've won in my compulsion has turned out to be nearly hollow victories.

Well, that's half or more of me, and that's my limp: knowing that the awful longing of my soul — the haunting uncertainty I feel, the desperate need of me — can never be satisfied, or satisfied for long, by any act I do or any gift I give. Yet I keep acting and giving compulsively. When the twigs snap and the shadows move, I jump and tremble. Yes, I wrestle in the dark with the Stranger. But the Stranger does not tell me his name, nor am I sure of what her blessing is. Yes, of course, I pushed for declaring Public Sanctuary, and we did, and three refugees' lives will be saved because of that, and that's enough . . . No, not enough, but very much. And I'm proud to have done it. Proud! O God. . .

But, I began to discover that the grimace is as much a part of my pride as my swagger, and perhaps more subtle, and certainly paradoxical. Whenever I heard members of the Public Sanctuary Task Force claiming that it was the declaration of Public Sanctuary that somehow accounted for the health and vigor of the congregation, I wanted to protest and claim more credit. It felt as if they were dismissing everything else the church — and, of course, I — had done prior to that. But I didn't express that protest, because I didn't like myself for feeling that way. The bells of piety had conditioned me to

[2]From William Safire's column in THE NEW YORK TIMES, Sunday, August 22, 1985, page A23. Copyright © 1985 by The New York Times Company. Reprinted by permission.

believe it was wrong to feel that way. Therein is the grimace and the paradox of pride for me.

On the one hand, it is a terrible thing not to like yourself. Under the dislike is a wish to be something else or someone else. What? Who? Someone not afflicted with such ignoble traits? Someone perfect, yea, someone more than a flawed human being. More and more it occurs to me that to want to be more than human is the genesis of being inhuman. What you don't like about yourself, you don't like about others. And you flail away at them for it one way or another, just as they — and you — flail away at you for it.

Perhaps I'm beginning to understand a bit more about the story of the fall. Why did Adam and Eve want to eat of the tree of the knowledge of good and evil? Because armed with such knowledge, they could avoid flaws and failures and be like God...who is a pretty good candidate for the "someone else" you'd like to be when you don't like yourself. When they had eaten, they knew — or at least felt — they were flawed, which is precisely what a mere mortal feels when he or she wants to be perfect. So, out came the fig leaves for Adam and Eve. They covered themselves. They hid from each other and from God. I suspect it was the *hiding* more than the eating that constituted their fall. Even so, I hide what I don't like about myself behind fig leaves of humility. Even to write about not liking myself has that fig-leaf-stickiness about it!

On the other hand, one of the things I am re-learning for the umpteenth time through Public Sanctuary (and will no doubt be re-learning all my life) is that honest pride, open pride, is better than false humility. That is the paradox of pride. If the "underside" of pride is compulsion, the "alongside" of it is daring. If you are out-front proud, you dare to do things that might cost you, probably *will* cost you. In this case, if being the minister of a church declaring Public Sanctuary didn't cost me professional damage — potential loss of members and money — then it could cost me a fine and imprisonment, plus legal fees and reputation fighting those penalties. And if it didn't cost any of that, at the very least it would cost me involvement in controversy, which inevitably includes ridicule and likely forfeiture of professional advancement in the ecclesiastical system.

But, I think it was just this kind of daring which Jesus demonstrated at the beginning of his ministry when he dared to turn water into wine and lepers into leapers. What if he hadn't pulled off those miracles he so audaciously attempted and for which, if he was fully human, there were no guarantees? It's that kind of daring which he demonstrated on through to the end when he challenged the religious and civil order of his day, and lost...at least insofar as it cost him his life. But without that daring — that *pride* — he wouldn't have risked anything. So, in that sense, Jesus was a proud man.

Honest pride seems spiritually and psychologically preferable to pretended humility. The paradox is that pride generates daring, and daring leads to the kind of action which could — and probably will — bring humiliation. Thus, the rack I'm being stretch on is the growing realization that *true humility is the willingness to risk being humiliated*. That is why humility is so hard to come by and why I think it is the way of Gethsemane and the cross. Humility is not being deferential and unctuous and avoiding confrontation, which is easy. The willingness to be humiliated is quite another matter. It takes daring. It takes pride. Maybe what is so winsome about Jacob is that he had the kind of pride that enabled him to go back and confront Esau, and wrestle with a Stranger who could bring him to his knees, and still demand and get a blessing from that Stranger. Daring to assume the risks of declaring Public Sanctuary is a kind of wrestling with the Stranger, and part of the blessing is that it is teaching me something I desperately need to learn about honest pride and true humility.

So where's the truth in all this? I think it is both the limp hidden in the swagger, and the name hidden in the grimace. The limp accompanies the personal wrestling, but the name is Public, as in Public Sanctuary. The name is corporate, it is community. It is people linked in a common act, a moral witness, trying to express a religious vision in whatever way they can. Marc Chagall said, "To preserve the earth on one's roots or to re-discover other earth, that is a true miracle."[3] I am

---

[3]From page 123 of CHAGALL BY CHAGALL, edited by Charles Sorlier. Copyright © 1979 Crageur Editeur. Reprinted by permission of Harry N. Abrams, Inc., publisher.

finding that the earth is community: not only the present community in which I live and work, but also the community I inherit; the community that shaped the stories and was shaped by the stories of Abraham and Sarah, Jacob and Rachel, Moses and Miriam, Isaiah and Mary and Jesus. Their stories give me hints of who I am and what I can do to be true to my identity. Without the earth of community, my roots, my personal story, my limp wouldn't mean much, would probably shrivel up along with my life.

As contemporary off-spring of that ancient community, our church, aided by the Public Sanctuary Task Force of the Christian Social Concerns Committee, spent a year talking and studying the issues of Public Sanctuary. We gathered information and shared it in every possible way with the congregation. When questions were asked for which we didn't have information, we got it. Step-by-careful-step we moved toward the meeting of the membership at which the vote for the declaration of Public Sanctuary would be taken.

As we moved, the awareness grew in me of the formidable adversary we were taking on. Shakespeare wrote, "O, it is excellent to have a giant's strength; but it is tyrannous to use it like a giant."[4] More and more it seemed our government was using its enormous strength in tyrannous ways: justifying its military support of oppressive governments in Central America by saying they are anti-communist, while denying that they are also right-wing dictatorships; justifying its violations of the 1980 Refugee Act by calling refugees from Central America "economic" refugees rather than admitting they are "political" refugees. If our government acknowledged their political refugee status, it would be tantamount to admitting that U.S. policies in Central America are partially responsible for causing the very problems from which these refugees are fleeing.

Under the 1980 Refugee Act, *forty to sixty percent* of refugees from communist countries (seventy-eight percent of Russian applicants) are given political asylum. In contrast, such asylum is given to fewer

---

[4]From MEASURE FOR MEASURE by William Shakespeare, Act 2, Scene 2, line 90.

than *four percent* of refugees from right-wing dictatorships in Central America. But, people in the United States don't know that part of the story. The information they get — and tend to believe — comes from an Administration which is selling a policy by managing the news. A government that has the will and the where-with-all to distort and dissemble news — and to insist that we, not it, are breaking the law by declaring Public Sanctuary — is formidable and frightening. Such a giant gives me a terrible sense of impotence or a case of laryngitis. Public Sanctuary would be a way of finding a voice, of trying to tell the other side of the story. It might be futile, but it couldn't be avoided.

In a conversation with me, Barbara Krasner, a superb family therapist, said, "Feelings are important, but they just aren't enough. You have to turn feelings into choices." Even so, faith has to be turned into faithfulness which is choice, act, living out. Faithfulness might then, just might, be transformed into faith. Or to put it as personally as I can, what matters most is not what the state of my personal faith struggle might mean to declaring Public Sanctuary, but what declaring Public Sanctuary might mean to my personal faith struggle. In many ways, that is a more frightening risk than the professional risks, or the risks of fines and imprisonment. The risk is in finding out who you are and whether or not the story that claims you — and you claim — is authentic. You can't really feel your way into that. You have to choose.

On May 20, 1984, our congregation met to vote on the declaration of Public Sanctuary. The vote was unanimous with three abstentions. So it was done. For me, for many, it was done in a tumble of motives, out of compulsion, yet with daring. We were proud; I was proud. As I sat there, an old Hungarian proverb echoed in my head: "God writes straight with crooked lines." Those words sustain me often when I wonder about being a minister — a minister with doubts; a minister who struggles and often feels uncertain, hollow, phony; a minister who mostly feels God and he are strangers, but who wrestles mightily in the hope it might be otherwise. Yet again...and again...you have to choose.

So, as a church, we chose. Our name became Public, which is really another version of the name "Israel" which the Stranger bestowed on Jacob. We chose to declare Public Sanctuary because human lives were at stake, and still are, and refugees are not abstractions or arguments. They are people and are part of the Public which we chose as our name, if that name means anything at all. We chose, because *not* to choose would have made our name something other than Public, somehow. It would have made it Personal . . . or Private or Indifferent. And, as Elie Wiesel has said, indifference, not hate, is the opposite of love.[5]

We closed the meeting with Holy Communion. As I helped serve the elements, I felt my longing for faith being accentuated. "Draw near with faith and take this sacrament to your comfort . . ." were the words our District Superintendent David Fife read as the traditional invitation. I drew near, but not with much faith, and the sacrament didn't hold much comfort for me. Yet I deeply loved these people, and therefore was glad for the church's assurance that the efficacy of the sacrament doesn't depend on the state of the server. "To preserve the earth on one's roots . . . that is a true miracle." If "God writes straight with crooked lines," who am I to insist on being a straight line? And yet . . .

The line to receive the elements grew shorter. There were children in it, wide-eyed as always, giggling quietly. The shutter of my subconscious snapped, and the image of Orion flashed in my mind. I found myself wondering about two things: what this action was going to mean to us, and to me; and why, when I take communion by intinction, it always tastes like a jelly sandwich and makes me feel like a little boy. I couldn't help giggling, too . . . quietly . . .

[5]Reported in THE PHILADELPHIA INQUIRER, Saturday, April 20, 1985, page 6-A. From Wiesel's remarks on receiving the Congressional Gold Medal from President Reagan.

Excitement

There is something about the slant of light in September that triggers in me an odd blend of anticipation and nostalgia. Maybe it is the longer, softer reach of the sun's fingers, or the subtly paler blue tint of the air through which the sun runs those fingers. In any case, there is change in the touch of light, and the hint of something new, as well as a remembering of what came before. I wonder if it was autumn when dusk drew itself around Jacob camped alone there by the Jabbok.

In autumn come football and school — in that order, at least in my younger years. Early in my life, my attention was somewhat unequally divided between classroom and locker room, with locker room getting the largest portion — especially in high school when I was certain not even girls mattered quite as much as my football and basketball teams, and the winning and losing of games. In college the classroom necessarily got more of my attention, and I decided to play only basketball, my first love in sports. I remember the game days, the

smell of liniment in the trainer's room, the taping of ankles, the nee-
dling and banter in the dressing room, the growing tension, the fre-
quent visits to the urinals, the coach's pacing and talking, the team
finally pounding up the stairs and trotting down the corridor onto the
court. . .and then the roar of the crowd, the surge of adrenalin, the
addictive high produced by the insistent enthusiasm of the band, the
incantations of the cheer leaders, the pontifications of the public address announcer. Then the strain and grace of the game itself, which
always had about it (especially if it was a major game) the faint — or
not so faint — warp of Armageddon.

And sometimes during the game, there was a state of euphoria, a
sense of being blessed, somehow, a shifting into another plane of ex-
istence where everything works as if by magic so that the ball doesn't
hit the floor, passes always hit the open man, shots hit nothing but
net. The power of it was some mysterious alchemy of dreams and
sweat which turned me and four other young men into a thing of grace,
a moment out of time, a gig of laughter. The next day, the following
weeks, the memory of it always left me strangely unsatisfied, hungry
to find it again. As long as I can remember, there's been in me an in-
satiable hunger for the mysteries of. . .of what? Of skill and courage,
of battle and some sort of resolution. . .of whatever the mysteries of
gracefulness might be about.

Maybe that hunger is actually something of what the nostalgia
and anticipation of the fall season is for me. I've often wondered if, in
a some way past unraveling, my ending up as a professional minister
is related to the experiences of my days as an athlete — related not
only to performing for the crowd and the pay-off in cheers (and
boos?), but to that hunger for the mysteries of struggle, of resolution
and meaning, of rare moments when the experience of gracefulness
touches on joy.

If there is some relationship, I suppose there might be something rather questionable about the parallel motives. They are, after
all, motives of one used to getting attention for one's own talent, and
obviously wanting that. But then, what am I to do. . .disqualify myself
from this profession? Aren't most public figures, including most ministers, motivated to some degree by the desire for attention? At least

most ministers aren't in it for the money! And if they gussy up their motives by claiming they are doing it all for God (which, when you come to think of it, probably everyone is, whether they *believe* they are or not), then it should be pointed out that perhaps they want the biggest hunk of attention of all: namely, God's attention. That reminds me of something Francine du Plessix Gray wrote: "...indulging in that greed for personal salvation...might be the most obnoxious greed there is."[1] She has a point, surely! Besides, how is it so many religious people profess to know so much about God and salvation, when actually they know so little about themselves?

All of which brings me circuitously back to autumn, 1984, and the planning of the worship service to officially welcome Joel, Gabriela and Lucy into Public Sanctuary at First United Methodist Church of Germantown. Maybe the connection to what I've written about athletics and motives is the excitement of the occasion — the crowd of people who would be coming from all over the city, plus television and news media people who would be at the welcoming.

Two factors became more clear as we planned the service. The first was that in any public appearances, especially those in which pictures might be taken, the refugees would have to wear bandannas over their faces to protect their identity. If the government of Guatemala were to discover — or be told by our government — that Joel, Gabriela and Lucy were in the United States and speaking out about their experiences in their native country, the family members left behind in Guatemala would be in extreme danger of being picked up and "disappeared" or simply killed outright. (This is also the case with refugees in Public Sanctuary from El Salvador.) Seeing the refugees wearing those bandannas, pulling hats down over their foreheads until only their dark eyes peered out, was a dramatic and terribly disturbing testimony to the utter seriousness of the situation with which we were dealing.

Yet, there was something ludicrous about the wearing of ban-

---

[1]From page 225 of WORLD WITHOUT END by Francine du Plessix Gray. Copyright © 1981 by Francine du Plessix Gray. Reprinted by permission of Simon and Schuster, Inc.

dannas which gave the whole thing the appearance of some kind of childish game. It wasn't! Still, why were the bandannas necessary? Why was our government in complicity with such oppressive tyranny? What did the eyes peering over the bandannas express? Fear? Anger? Or simply sadness? Whatever it was, it was difficult to hold their gaze for long! Our symbol for Public Sanctuary became a small piece of colored cloth folded in a triangle like a bandanna and pinned to the lapel of coat and blouses.

Even so, my initial reaction to the refugees wearing bandannas was negative. I was surprised to discover some anger and embarrassment about those masks. I tried to sort out why. It turned out to be something quite simple. I wear masks, too, though less obvious ones. Everyone does! We hide from each other and from ourselves. What would I do if others found out who I *really* am: all those motives, fears, drives, lusts, greed, ambitions; and my softness, vulnerabilities, needs, longings, and loves as well? What would they do to me? Would they make me "disappear?" Would they kill me in some polite way, kill my spirit. . . as people often to do to nonconforming children? In turn, what would I do to them if they exposed themselves to me? Of course, those are childish fears, but they are undeniably real and operative in us, else why all our masks?

So the refugees' masks touched a nerve of my psyche, my spirit. "The danger with any mask," says Francine du Plessix Gray, "is that it may force one's true features to emulate it, it's urgent that we remove masks before it's too late, before our features have hardened into them irreparably."[2]   I agree; it is urgent, but I also know it is painful. I've had enough, and done enough, psychotherapy to know that — and enough praying. But how else are we ever going to forgive and love each other as we love and forgive ourselves?

In an interview I once read, poet e.e. cummings said that what we really want is to tell each other who we are, not what information we have. Well, to do that takes courage and wrestling with yourself. Surely a piece of the Stranger whom Jacob wrestled with was his other side, his hidden side. Maybe it wasn't only that his thigh got put out of

[2]*Ibid.*, page 280, 281. Reprinted by permission of Simon and Schuster, Inc.

joint in that struggle, but that his mask got torn off. *And there, under the mask of Jacob was...Israel!* Now that's hopeful! I wonder if the whole Public Sanctuary enterprise is about getting peoples' masks off: the refugees', because justice makes it no longer necessary for them to wear bandannas; and ours, because we've learned what love requires. In fact, maybe that's most of what the faith enterprise is about. At last, how do you tell anyone who you are except by words made flesh, and flesh made into honest words?

The second thing that became clear as we planned the welcoming service was how much all of us who were working on Public Sanctuary wanted from it for ourselves. I don't think any of us could have articulated what we wanted or even admitted that we had such desires. Perhaps that inability is what makes many of us so compulsive. It would have helped if we had been able to admit our needs. It would have at least been a step toward unbuckling our masks. But we never talked much about our own expectations and needs, our own wants. So those things seemed to come out indirectly: in the prickly ways we often related; in the kind of jockeying and posturing we sometimes got caught up in as we discussed leadership issues, who would get credit for what; and in the diverting intrusions of other personal agendas each of us attached to this cause. Ironically, we hadn't yet learned how to be much sanctuary for each other.

Still, we shared a sense of excitement as we arranged what would happen at the welcoming service on Sunday evening, September 9, 1984. Most of the members of our Public Sanctuary committee had attended a similar welcoming service at Tabernacle Church — a Presbyterian and United Church of Christ church in Philadelphia which had declared Public Sanctuary before any other Philadelphia church and which had refugees from El Salvador. We had some ideas from that service, but we felt that, as a larger church, we should do something on a somewhat larger scale. So the committee decided to invite several prominent figures to speak: the resident Bishop of the United Methodist Church, F. Herbert Skeete; the Congressional Representative from our district, William H. Gray III; and the Executive Secretary of the American Friends Service Committee, Asia Bennett. Of course, Joel and Gabriela would speak, there would be music and liturgy and, since we wanted the service to be ecumenical, several religious leaders in the community would participate.

Without being too direct (there's the mask), I indicated that I thought I should have some part in the service as Senior Minister. The committee suggested that I should be liturgist and make a brief statement introducing the main speakers. I was deflated. It was like being asked not to play much in the championship game, even though I thought the team they'd put together was an excellent one. I looked around the room, weighing their proposition. A breeze stirred the curtains and shadows played across the ceiling. A horn honked somewhere off in the night. Damn this Stranger who keeps sandbagging me! I felt all I could do was agree. But I continued to wrestle with myself about it.

And it was on my mind the morning of September 9, 1984, when we introduced Gabriela and Joel and Lucy to our own congregation during the regularly scheduled worship service. As part of that service, I repeated words which Joel used, when he was a union organizer in Guatemala, to persuade workers to join the union: "One twig alone can be broken, but the twigs standing together cannot be broken." The late night before, when I was out walking and wrestling, I had gathered some twigs and bound them together. I held up those ten twigs and put them on our altar, under the cross. They've been there ever since.

Often, when I look at those twigs bound together, I find myself thinking of what a team is: that alchemy of dreams and sweat, that moment out of time, that gig of laughter, that experience of gracefulness close to joy. I detest simplistic analogies like this, but such analogies are something of what human relationships are about as well. I ache over how much we need each other's love and support, mercy and challenge...and how rarely we admit and ask for it. Maybe Public Sanctuary will teach us both our need and our reluctance. Maybe something like that is really what all of us want from Public Sanctuary for ourselves.

In any case, the service that evening was superb, if a bit long. Each speaker emphasized the injustice of the application of the 1980 Refugee Act which excludes Central Americans as political refugees, and commended us for the moral stand we were taking. Bishop Skeete spoke of the action taken by the United Methodist Church at its 1984 General Conference endorsing the action of local congregations in declaring Public Sanctuary and urging other local churches to consider doing so. Congressman William Gray, himself a Baptist preacher, stressed the racism implicit in the policies of the Justice Department and the Immigration and Naturalization Service which keep the Statue of Liberty pointed toward Western Europe, but not toward Central America, or Haiti, or South Africa. Asia Bennett shared her personal observations on the conditions in Guatemala and El Salvador which have forced people to flee the civil wars there.

As they spoke, I found myself feeling increasingly frustrated that more people weren't hearing what these outstanding leaders were saying, that the media didn't give these views equal time and space with those of the Reagan Administration. It felt both flattering yet ridiculous that this church should be considered in any way special for doing what it seemed obvious that thousands of churches should be doing if they were to be faithful to the gospel, faithful to the commandment to "love your neighbor as yourself," faithful to the kind of neighbor love that doesn't stumble at national borders. Where were the other churches? Where was their courage? I recall Fred Craddock, in his Beecher Lectures on Søren Kierkegaard, saying that too many Christians are victims of " . . .the illusion of participation where none exists, an illusion created by the power of sheer numbers to overcome private judgment and personal decision."[3]

" . . .illusion of participation . . ." What a telling phrase, not only for individuals overcome by the inertia of public opinion and the seductions of "the good life," but also for churches which, by what they do and don't do, cautiously nurture that illusion in the name of a Christ who was himself a refugee given no sanctuary by religious and government institutions in his time. Whose side are Christians and the church on in the battle for justice and mercy? Where are their dreams and sweat, their gig of laughter, their explorations into the mysteries of gracefulness? God save me, save us, from the "illusion of participation."

[3]From page 31 of OVERHEARING THE GOSPEL by Fred B. Craddock. Copyright 1978. Reprinted by permission of Abingdon Press.

When Joel and Gabriela spoke, their voices were soft, their words firm. What they stressed was their faith as Christians —she a Roman Catholic, he an Evangelical. Joel said it was his faith that made him try to help people in his country through his student and union organizing. It was his faith in God that gave him strength and led him and Gabriela through their struggles and brought them to this church. He thanked us and prayed God's blessing on us. But, even in that moment, it was dawning on me that this Guatemalan man and woman and child were God's blessing on us; that Joel was thanking us for simply being what we had the audacity to call ourselves: a Christian church. Obviously, the deeper truth was that we owed thanks to him and Gabriela for helping to save us from an illusion.

The service closed with everyone singing a slightly amended version of the Holly Near song, "It Could Have Been Me." In part the words went:

> "It could have been me, but instead it was you.
> So I'll keep doing the work you were doing
>   as if I were two.
> [I'll be a student of life, a singer of songs,
> A sharer of food and a righter of wrongs.
>
> It's gonna be me and it's gonna be you.
> And it will be us, dear sisters and brothers,
>   before we are through.
> 'Cuz if you can live for freedom —
>   freedom, freedom, freedom,
> If you can live for freedom, we can, too.]"4

After the service I went back into the sanctuary alone and sat for a long time in the not-quite dark and not-quite quiet. Light from passing cars bounced through the stained glass windows and chased across the walls. The great, old beams creaked, and the big radiators under the floor grates pinged as they cooled. I wondered what was

---

4From "It Could Have Been Me" by Holly Near. Copyright 1974. The words within brackets were adapted for the occasion of the welcoming service for the refugees. (See page 2 for the original lyrics.) Reprinted by permission of Hereford Music.

going to happen and, of course, there was no way of knowing. I thought about the psychological truth that a child desires to conform to the people and environment who protect her. That conforming is such a mixed bag, and everyone bears both the gifts and the wounds of it. In a way, wanting to conform to the power that protects us explains the reluctance of Americans — and American Christians — to challenge the authority or the information of government. But what happens when the protection demands paying the price of integrity, of conscience, or of personhood? When that happens to children, hopefully they find their way to therapists who can help them. But what happens to the people of a nation — or of churches — when that happens?

I shifted in my pew. What if Joel and Gabriela began to subconsciously desire to conform to our environment and so lose their uniqueness? What if we subconsciously wanted that conformity from them? Isn't there something in the privileged position of Americans that tends to give us the expectation that others should bend to our will? Isn't there something in the mission enterprise of the church that insists that our religious "truth" is something to which others ought to convert?

Many years ago a black man spoke to a group in our church and used the story of David and Goliath. He called attention to something in that story which I've never forgotten. When David went to fight Goliath, Saul offered David his own armor and sword, but David refused them because they didn't fit him. They weren't his weapons. I'm not sure this black man would have said it this way, but I think he was saying to that white audience that one gift blacks could give to whites was to refuse to assume their weapons. And that one gift whites could give to blacks would be not to expect them to assume the same weapons. (If that wasn't his point, it's still a good one and never mind whose point it is. Maybe it's the Stranger's point.) Anyway, it came to me quite strongly as I sat alone in the not-quite dark and the not-quite quiet. Maybe our accurate choosing of weapons and letting others choose theirs touches on something else of what Public Sanctuary would teach us, hard as it would be to learn.

I remembered that, instead of Saul's armor and sword, David went and found five smooth stones for his sling. Five stones, but only one did the giant slaying job. I went over what amounted to our stones in Public Sanctuary: information, organization, motivation, finances...What was the fifth stone, the one that might slay the giant of injustice? I suspected it might just be integrity — assuming the truth, the weapons, that fit you and allowing, yea encouraging, others to take the same option. Ten twigs, a team...different gifts, the battle, the mysteries of gracefulness.

As I got up to leave at last, I realized I'd been sitting where I usually don't sit: off-stage, back pew. In a sense I'd been sitting on the bench. I smiled to myself and remembered not being one of the featured speakers earlier in the evening. I realized I'd never spent much time on the bench at any stage of my athletic career. I'd always been a starter and a star, and so I'd never learned the grace of sitting on the bench. It takes courage to sit on the bench. It takes courage to let others have a chance; to support them and their gifts; to join their gig of laughter, their experience of the mysteries of gracefulness.

In fact, the truth I keep forgetting is that whatever the alchemy was that turned young men into a thing of grace on the basketball court, it wasn't just five but twelve young men who were a team — not just the players on the floor, but the players on the bench. And where did the team end? With the trainers, the coaches? Was there an end to it, really? I don't know. I only know the team extended beyond the boundaries my ego had set. It always does.

I remembered watching Joel and Gabriela at the service earlier, doing a native Guatemalan dance to a tape of Guatemalan music. We had watched — a Bishop, a Congressman, an Executive Secretary, and a Senior Minister, along with about eight hundred Americans from a cross-section of professions and businesses. And we were entranced, inspired, as close to joy as most of us ever get. Maybe it's a parable: Americans sitting on the bench for Third World people. I wonder if we — if I — can ever learn that parable and that joy. I locked up the church and drove home, and found myself singing softly:

"It's gonna be me and it's gonna be you.
And it will be us, dear sisters and brothers
before we are through...
If you can live for freedom we can, too."

Shock

The telephone rang once...twice...

It was Monday morning, January 14, 1985. My feet were propped up on the desk in my study. I was drinking coffee and reading the morning paper. One major story was about the upcoming Inauguration of President Reagan for a second term, which I skimmed quickly. Another major story, in which I was absorbed, was about the Super Bowl to be played the next Sunday between the Forty-Niners and the Dolphins — an event which "unofficially" caused the observance of the Inauguration and the public swearing-in to be postponed until Monday, January 22nd (though the law requires the swearing-in to be held on January 21st). Official spokespersons for the Administration were saying that the public observance was being delayed because the legal date for it fell on a Sunday. But the fact that I, and probably several million others, read every word about the Super Bowl, while skimming the Inauguration news, made the "unofficial" reason for a postponement more likely. This Administration is skilled at public relations and the use of the media to create attractive images. Why would they compete with the Super Bowl? Bread and circuses!

The phone was insistent...three rings...four...

About half the time I hate jangling telephones. I want them to shut up, go away and leave me alone. This was one such time. It was early Monday morning! I was tired. The day before had been an emotional high, but exhausting. As usual on the Sunday closest to January 15th, we'd celebrated Dr. Martin Luther King, Jr.'s birthday. Dr. Constance Clayton, the black woman Superintendent of Schools in Philadelphia, had given the sermon at the morning service and done a fine job linking the claims of justice and freedom to the need for renewed commitment to public education, especially in urban areas with large populations of poor and blacks. And the weeks before had been frantic. The Christmas season had been full of wonder and weariness, extraordinary moments somehow tucked into the familiar whirl of frantic preparations for what cannot be frantically prepared for. In early December a book of my prayers had been published[1] — my first book ever, a dream I never thought would come true...and private fantasies are always easier to deal with than public realities. I wanted the book to sell a million copies, but I was sure no one would like it, that it would be buried a pauper in a field of criticism. The uncertainty kept my shoulders ear-high. Plus, the church was still working on trying to get the 1986 budget in place and make final plans for Lent and Easter. It was a Monday morning in January — bleak, cold. I hadn't even had a chance to read the Sunday paper.

Whoever was calling didn't care...five rings...six...

"Hello," I barked, the paper sliding in sections onto the floor.

"Ted, this is Bill," came the response. "I'm down at the church office, and Flo Huber from the nursery school just called for you. She said some man in a brown car with government license plates is parked outside the nursery school. She's feeling very nervous, and she wants you to call the school."

If pride goes before a fall, what comes *during* a fall is shock — shock because you're caught off-guard; shock because somehow you

---

[1]GUERRILLAS OF GRACE. San Diego: LuraMedia, 1984.

58

didn't really believe it would happen at all; and if it did, it certainly wouldn't be in this quite banal way. But suddenly it was happening, and that is how it began — the arrests of Gabriela and Joel that cold Monday morning, January 14, 1985.

Bill Ramsden is one of the Associate Ministers of our church. Flo Huber is a teacher at a nursery school several blocks from the church buildings. After Joel and Gabriela and Lucy had lived in the church for nearly three months, the Public Sanctuary Task Force had arranged with Marion Brown, the director of the nursery school and a member of the church, for the refugee family to live in the little apartment on the second floor over the nursery school.

I called Marion. She was also nervous as she told me about the man who was parked in the small lot outside the school. He seemed to be getting something out of his trunk. "He looks very suspicious to me," Marion said. "I think you or someone should get right over here." I told her I would call our attorney, Ted Walkenhorst, and talk to him first. I did, and Ted immediately called Marion back on another of his office lines. For about ten minutes we had an awkward three-way conversation, Ted serving as the relay and adviser. The knot in my gut was tightening all the time, my palms sweating as the information we pieced together indicated the probability that the man was an agent of the Immigration and Naturalization Service — the INS.

"You'd better get over there," Ted Walkenhorst suggested to me. "If Joel and Gabriela are arrested, call me. I'll meet them at the Federal Building."

Five minutes later I was in the nursery school parking lot introducing myself to the man Marion had described. He was, in fact, an INS agent and told me that he and the other agents were there to arrest the refugees. That he was a black man accentuated my sense of shock. I guess my naive assumption was that people who have a history of being oppressed would somehow be sympathetic to other victims of oppression and not throw in with the oppressors. Of course, it's an illogical assumption, but the force of it for me was undeniable.

The feeling of shock was reinforced when I climbed the outside stairs and went into Gabriela's and Joel's apartment. One of the other two agents was a woman, which also felt morally incongruous. I wonder what would happen if people who feel the weight of discrimination or exploitation, because of race or sex or nationality or religion, ever got together to change the system that dehumanizes them. I understand something about the entrenchment of power — being white, male, and American — and how difficult it is for those who have power to share it without feeling they are losing their identity and, for men, their masculinity. But how is it that the system itself is so deftly able to turn victims of discrimination against each other?

In 1965 at the end of the march from Selma to Montgomery, Alabama, I recall hearing Dr. King say that poor white people and poor black people might one day discover they are natural allies in the struggle for justice. There were tears in my eyes as I stood there in front of the capital of Alabama over which flew the Confederate flag as well as the American flag. With 25,000 other marchers I listened to Dr. King:

> "Our aim must never be to defeat or humiliate the white man but to win his friendship and understanding. . . the end we seek is a society at peace with itself, a society that can live with its conscience. . . How long will it take? . . . Not long, because the arm of the moral universe is long but it bends toward justice."[2]

Twenty years may not be long, but that many years later, a society at peace with itself — a society that can live with its conscience — is a discovery still waiting to be made, like a treasure buried in a field of prejudices. What is there about us that needs victims or needs to be victims? I always believed, and believe still, that alliances for justice are what this country is about — alliances that cut across class and race, religion and sex, and all the rest. In any case, such alliances are certainly close to the core of the prophetic character of our Judeo-Christian inheritance.

[2]Excerpt from OUR GOD IS MARCHING ON!, March 25, 1965, by Martin Luther King, Jr. Copyright © Martin Luther King, Jr. and the estate of Martin Luther King, Jr. Used by permission of Joan Daves.

The agents were going through the little apartment looking for whatever they look for in such instances, even to the extent of the woman agent going with Gabriela when she went to the bathroom. It felt like such a violation, but I could think of little to say, nothing to do, though I kept thinking I should. Shortly after I arrived, Anne Ewing arrived. Anne is a capable, bright, tough woman who is a member of our Public Sanctuary Task Force. Usually vocal and articulate, she had little to say, either. Gabriela looked very frightened, her large eyes grown even larger as she dressed little Lucy for the ride to the Federal Building. Gabriela's English is limited, and the circumstances didn't permit any private conversation.

Joel was not present. Very early that morning he had gone to work with a local carpenter with whom he had made friends. (Carpentry had been Joel's trade in Guatemala.) No one knew where they were working. Later we found out that the agents had presented themselves to Gabriela as participants in the Sanctuary Movement in Tucson. They had claimed they were carrying messages from people whom Joel and Gabriela had met when they passed through Tucson on their way to Philadelphia. The agents had pressed Gabriela to call Joel and have him come home to meet them. Trusting their introduction, she had tried to locate Joel, but had been unsuccessful. It wasn't until after Gabriela had asked the agents to leave and come back later that they revealed their true identity.

Why was such subterfuge necessary when the essence of Public Sanctuary is that it is *public*? Joel and Gabriela had circulated and spoken in dozens of public gatherings openly announced. The whole covert procedure of arrests seemed to subvert the dignity of everyone concerned — certainly that of the refugees, but also, curiously, that of our own government and its representatives. Their method seemed close to a knock on the door in the middle of the night.

Anne and I gave reassurances to Gabriela that lawyers would meet them when they arrived at the courthouse, that she shouldn't worry because we were prepared for this to happen, and that everything would be all right. She nodded, but her eyes radiated disbelief. We watched as they got into the government car and drove away. Somehow it all felt unreal, as if things were happening in slow motion

— a family movie of a gathering of cousins, nieces and nephews who didn't know each other and so were acting very awkwardly.

I felt helpless and a bit ashamed that I hadn't been able to intervene in some way to protect the refugees. Helplessness is a very disorienting feeling and must go along with the experience of shock. What can you do when the government moves against you with all the powers it has at its command — including the law as it interprets it? For the first time I felt the bitter gag of fear and rage that must be the ferment of helplessness which, from time to time, ignites explosively in our ghettos or in Third World countries. How to turn those feelings into creative choices was — and remains — the test we faced following the arrest of the refugees.

I stood for a moment in that nursery school parking lot, aware of the cold and the clear blue sky, and the sounds of children playing in the school room behind me. They were oblivious to the seriousness of what had happened outside their play room. Or maybe they just assumed that, whatever it was, some "big person" would make it okay. I thought of Lucy, reflecting her mother's fear as she climbed into the Immigration and Naturalization Service car, yet somehow trusting that the "big people" would take care of her. Where it had eluded me before, the powerful symbolism of the setting now struck me: the refugee family was living over a nursery school. Children always seem to be right in the middle of things, daring to be exactly who they are and trustingly making their demands. I remember my mother calling me an "itch" when I was a kid. Maybe all children are an itch. If so, I suspect they're God's itch — an itch to remind us of the rightness of certain demands and to teach us what it means to be trusted. I wonder if we "big people" ever will realize that and not betray their trust.

We drove to Anne's house and made some calls. As I dialed, I noticed on the wall opposite the telephone a poster showing an ostrich with an even more compressed head and tighter bill than usual. The legend on the poster read, "Don't tell me to relax! My tension is all that's holding me together." I laughed at the accuracy of it, and then I prayed for something other than tension to hold me and the rest of us together. Without putting it into words, we knew we'd entered another stage of our Public Sanctuary effort. Anne agreed to try to locate Joel and get him down to the church office. In turn, I would go to my office to keep in phone contact with our attorney.

When I arrived at the office, a crew from one of the major network stations in Philadelphia was already waiting. From the crew reporter, Kate Larsen, I learned that the Justice Department had made a nationwide "sweep" of Public Sanctuary people that morning, and that the Federal Attorney in Phoenix would be making a statement later in the day. Our refugees were among approximately sixty refugees nationwide who had been arrested. At the same time, indictments were served against the ministers, priests and nuns who were the leaders of the Public Sanctuary Movement in Arizona. I told Kate that we wouldn't have a statement until later, but they were welcome to wait in one of our offices if they wanted to. They did, to my surprise. The enormity of what was happening hadn't yet dawned on me.

Then the calls started coming in from media people and from others around the country. It was heady stuff, all that attention. It didn't take long for me to begin feeling very important. If power is the ultimate aphrodisiac, as someone has said, then attention is the poor person's generic substitute. Power is seductive! I can understand, though not approve, how Secretary of State Haig could have gone on television shortly after President Reagan was shot in 1981 and told the nation "I am in charge here." It's easy to lose perspective when people pay attention to you. Maybe that's why Jacob's decisive wrestling match happened when he'd sent everyone else on ahead. Maybe that's why Jesus kept going off alone to the wilderness. Attention has an effect similar to shock: it's disorienting and distorting.

In the midst of the telephone calls, we had a series of meetings in which we tried to sort out what had happened. Several months earlier, while the refugees were in a temporary living space in the church, there had been a break-in and, along with a radio and tape recorder, some letters and other documents had been stolen. The break-in was suspicious, but most of us didn't believe our government would operate that way. But it was beginning to be evident now that, in fact, our government *had* operated that way. Several Sanctuary churches had been similarly burglarized. Slowly the truth came out that someone who had posed as a friend to Joel and Gabriela while they were in Phoenix in early summer, 1984, had managed to get their Philadelphia phone number, had called them and, on the pretext of sending Lucy a Christmas present, gotten their address for the INS agents.

Gradually we began to piece together the information that the government had used undercover agents to infiltrate church gatherings in Arizona — including worship services, prayer and bible study meetings — and to indiscriminately record such meetings. This was the first time in American history that covert agents, under Federal authority, had infiltrated houses of worship. Those tape recordings — obtained without warrant and in violation of the principles of the First and Fourth Amendments — would later be a large part of the prosecution of the Sanctuary workers indicted on January 14th. Indeed, the refugees — including Joel and Gabriela — were arrested to serve as government witnesses *against* the very people who had helped them.

The evidence covertly obtained by illegal means supported our information that the Immigration and Naturalization Service would not *openly* force its way into any church property to arrest refugees, because they didn't want the adverse publicity that would result. But clearly, the government did not have similar concerns about sending covert agents into churches without warrant and without probable cause — namely, that there be established a compelling state interest to protect endangered Bill of Rights liberties of its citizens before such a breach of First and Fourth Amendment rights can begin to be justified. My shock — and the shock of many of us that day and since — is that I could not conceive of our government doing such things.

In the early afternoon, word came that Joel would be coming to my office within the hour. We had already consulted with our attorney, Ted Walkenhorst, and knew what was at stake. In any case, the final decision on what to do was Joel's. Should he move back into the church and avoid arrest, or turn himself in?

When Joel arrived, a few of us gathered — including Efrain Cotto, a young Puerto Rican United Methodist minister who had served as a translator on many occasions; and David Fife, the District Superintendent who was my immediate superior in the United Methodist Church. Understandably, Joel was shaken and frightened. It was hap-

64

pening to him again: arrests, threats of dire consequences. Nevertheless, he did not hesitate in making his decision to turn himself in. We assured him that he would have good legal representation, that under the law he would not be detained long, and that this country was different from Guatemala. Of course, the insidious but unspoken threat was that, while he wouldn't actually be imprisoned or killed in the United States, our process could result in his deportation back to Guatemala — which would mean the strong likelihood that both he and Gabriela would be killed shortly after their arrival. We all knew the danger, but still Joel was clear about his decision. Finally, it was a very human one: he belonged with Gabriela and Lucy.

We called Ted Walkenhorst at the Federal Building. He was consulting with the legal people of the Immigration and Naturalization Service. We interrupted and told him Joel was coming in. Ted told us what to do, where to go, where to wait. When that call was completed and the information shared, we stood and had a prayer. Efrain translated my words, and I smiled, thinking, "Someone had better translate us to God." Then Efrain added his own prayers. We hugged each other. Then Joel and his driver left for the Federal Building.

After the office had cleared, I picked up a batch of phone messages from my secretary and told Kate Larsen we would probably be ready to make some statement for the five and six o'clock news, if they were willing to televise it live from the church. She agreed. I'd just walked into my office and partially closed the door when there was a timid knock. I opened it, and there stood Jack, one of the men who comes in on Mondays to count, record and deposit the money from the pledge envelopes received in Sunday's offerings — a crucial, thankless job he and two others do so faithfully.

I invited him in, but he only entered a few steps and then stood awkwardly. "What is it, Jack?" I asked.

He looked at his hands and answered softly, "I know you're really busy and that it's awfully important, what you're dealing with. . . .I mean, you're probably too busy for this, but. . .I just wanted you to know that Gladys is pretty sick. I mean, the doctor wants her to have another series of chemotherapy, but she won't . . ." He choked on his words and his tears. I choked on the sudden lump in my throat and my exaggerated self-importance. All I could do was put my arm around him and stand with him for a few moments.

Finally, we talked a little. A few years earlier, Jack had been severely beaten by some men who'd broken into his home to rob him. He'd almost died, and it had been a long, painful struggle back, not only from his physical injuries but from the emotional trauma. When his wife Gladys had become ill, he'd taken over managing the house and caring for her. Now the fears were back. I asked him how he thought I could help. He asked if I'd come and talk with Gladys. I said I would. I asked him if there was something I could do for him. "Pray," he said. We did, and I told him I would keep praying for him and Gladys.

When he'd gone, I stood and looked out my office window for a long time. It was late afternoon, and already the winter darkness had wrapped itself around the city. The street lights were on, looking a bit forlorn through the leafless, curbside trees. Early homeward traffic was beginning, and a crowded bus crawled up the Avenue between a line of cars. Every vehicle carried people like Jack, I thought, people struggling with hard problems. "Probably you're too busy for this . . ." The words kept echoing in my head. "O Christ, what is the Jabbok doing running through my office?" I muttered to myself as I watched the lights and shadows play outside my office window and heard the bus roar away from a stop on the corner. Too busy? How about too inadequate!

At five and six o'clock, I made statements on the evening TV news. It was telecast from the outside of the church chapel where the reporter, Kate, and I stood, the noise and headlights of traffic pouring up Germantown Avenue in the background. About seven o'clock, Joel and Gabriela and Lucy returned to the office. Arrangements had been made for a certified check to be delivered to the Federal Building by the treasurer of our Public Sanctuary Task Force, and Joel and Gabriela had been released on $3,000 bail. Joel, sitting in my office, carefully concealed in indirect light, made a statement for the eleven o'clock news, and sitting behind my desk in glaring light, I made another.

When I got home after a church Administrative Board meeting, the late TV news had just begun. The story of the arrests started with the announcement that "a smugglers ring of illegal aliens has been uncovered right here in the Delaware Valley." I wonder what sensational distortions our modern media would have made of the Underground Railroad during the Civil War? Fragments of Joel's and my interviews were shown, along with a supper gathering of our Public Sanctuary Task Force with Joel and Gabriela and Lucy. The final statement of the reporter was that "the people of First United Methodist Church have vowed to stand by their refugees." Amen to that!

Tuesday morning began as had Monday, only earlier, with a telephone call — this time from Senator Arlen Specter (R., Penn.) He voiced his opposition to the action of the INS the previous day and wondered if we could bring the refugees in to see him by ten o'clock that morning. I said I'd try, but we had to arrange for lawyers to be there as well. By the time we arrived at the Senator's office, which is also in the Federal Building, he had had to leave for another appointment, but wanted to meet us for lunch at one of the hotels in Center City. In the meantime, one of his aides interviewed Joel and Gabriela and assured us of the Senator's determination to call for an investigation of INS policies and procedures in the matter of Central American refugees.

During a break, I had to make a phone call to check on the arrangements for a press conference scheduled for Joel and Gabriela at one-thirty that afternoon at the church. I sat at the Senator's desk and looked out at Independence Hall at the far end of the mall. It really is a beautiful Georgian building. I watched the people going to and fro on the streets six floors below. It all felt detached. I decided no public official should have an office you had to take an elevator to reach.

We managed to spend about ten minutes with the Senator at lunch before he had to leave for another appointment. He wanted us to wait, but we were already late for our press conference. The frantic pace and cursory meetings seemed to trivialize what Joel and Gabriela were confronting. Yet, the possibility of the Senator's support was important, because justice is about half determined by politics.

At the church we found over a hundred people waiting for our arrival — many of them media representatives; the rest, people from the church and community. When Joel and Gabriela walked in, they were greeted with a standing ovation. After a few welcomes and introductions, I was supposed to make an opening statement. The TV lights came on, and the press photographers snapped away. Ah, the glitter of the temptress! The only thing was that, for some reason, I felt like a freshman on his first date. I was completely unprepared, but I managed to ramble on for a couple of minutes. Then, before I'd even thought about it, I said, "If the INS is going to send Good Samaritans to jail, then let us pack and go." People applauded. Where had that line come from? What a mouth! Of course, some of us were in jeopardy with the government, subject to fines and imprisonment for "harboring illegal aliens," but it was Joel and Gabriela who had been arrested, not me or any of the Public Sanctuary Task Force. Besides, even at my very best, who am I to compare myself to the Good Samaritan? I was a little embarrassed by my own brashness, but the line stuck and got picked up and used by the press. I sat down and Joel spoke; then our attorney, Ted Walkenhorst; then it was over. I hadn't heard much of what was said, because I was thinking of Jack.

The rest of the week was similarly frantic. There were television interviews and long distant calls, and an interview with U.S.A. *Today* in which I said I thought that if a refugee came to the White House and asked for help, probably Mr. Reagan would not turn the refugee away, especially if it meant the refugee would lose his life because of that rejection. "Then why," I concluded, "is Mr.Reagan's administration pursuing policies that cause the same deadly result for those same refugees?" Unfortunately, the only part of the comment that was quoted in the paper was that if a refugee came to the White House, I was sure Mr. Reagan wouldn't turn him away. Actually, unless the whole quote is used, I'd have to say I'm *not* at all sure Mr. Reagan wouldn't turn the refugee away. The Oval Office is like being six floors above the blood and sweat of life, or sixty floors above it.

Congressman Bob Edgar called on Friday, and I was eager for him to schedule a time to talk with Joel and Gabriela. We set a date for them to go to Washington to meet some other members of congress and have a news conference in the Capital. In the course of the conversation, I asked Bob if he was thinking of going to Central America any time soon. He said he was going in April and asked if I wanted to go along. I said that's why I had asked. He told me he'd like me to go and would arrange it.

Sometimes my audacity surprises me. Maybe I really am more like Jacob than I like to admit; I mean, like him *before* his wrestling match with the Stranger — when he had cheated his brother out of his birthright and his father-in-law out of his sheep. But then, maybe audacity is the bubbly of faith — the sparkle that gives it punch and makes it move. What the hell, I was finding out that declaring Public Sanctuary really was audacious.

Sunday, January 20, 1985, was brutally cold. We had scheduled a public service of Celebration and Recommitment for eight o'clock that evening, knowing we were competing with the Super Bowl. (I thought again about the decision of the Administration pros *not* to compete with the Super Bowl.) That morning in our regular worship service, Joel spoke to the congregation. He told us that the last thing his father had said to him before leaving Guatemala was always to remember Joshua 1:9:

> "Have I not commanded you? Be strong and of good courage; be not frightened, neither be dismayed; for the Lord your God is with you wherever you go."

Those words were an enormous gift to us.

Later in the service, I spoke a little about the Good Samaritan. I said that maybe we needed to see that Joel and Gabriela are Good Samaritans to us. Maybe it is we Americans who are half-dead by the side of the road, and it is our arrogance and insensitivity to what is going on in the world that deadens us. Then somebody like Joel and Gabriela comes and begins to take care of us . . . telling us that we are half-dead for want of our brothers and sisters in the world, as well as them being half-dead for the want of us. Joel and Gabriela give us the chance to be the church again.

That night, nearly five hundred people came to the service we had had so little time to promote, came in spite of below zero weather and the Super Bowl. The bulletin cover quoted the plea that had come out of the camps of Central American refugees: *"If you knew the truth, then surely you would help us."* How could we make the truth known — at least our part of it, the part that all the mechanisms of government seem geared to suppress?

We had walked the first mile by declaring Public Sanctuary: by confronting the discriminatory way the 1980 Refugee Act is applied by this Administration, and by challenging the foreign policy of this country which supports oppressive governments in Central America out of its obsessive anti-communism. Now we were being challenged to walk the second mile: to defend our refugees in court and to expose the questionable means used by the INS in arresting refugees and indicting the Public Sanctuary Movement leaders. The government's fear had summoned us to battle: its fear of the truth of the refugees' stories which it would silence; its fear that the national conscience would be aroused if those stories were heard; its fear that our appeal to justice would find resonance in the American people, because that appeal to justice is the best and truest God has put in us. Fear had summoned us to battle, and love would respond. We would walk the second mile, and the third, and as many as were necessary. That was the spirit of the service that cold night as we shared communion together and renewed our commitments.

By the time I got home, the Super Bowl was over. It had been something of a blowout anyway, the vaunted duel between Montana and Marino never developing. The old pro had given the young one a lesson. But at noon, the legal swearing in of Mr. Reagan for a second term had happened, and the next day the public celebration of the Inauguration would take place, although the arctic weather was forcing them to move things indoors and cancel the parades. That was small consolation. We faced four more years of the Administration of an extraordinarily popular President whose script for Central America simply was not based on reality or on the highest principles of this nation. What would that mean to Joel and Gabriela and Lucy — and to thousands of refugees who had fled for their lives and who were, in truth, being turned away from the White House door and sent to probable death? Maybe that old pro could give us young ones a lesson in public relations, but what about the truth?

*"If you knew the truth,
then surely you would help us."*

I pulled off my clothes and sat at the edge of the bed. I looked at Jan, already asleep. My love for her is absolutely central to my life, and yet our time together keeps shrinking. The cost of this battle is time, and I have so little. So little! And what I have is spent doing things that take me away from the one I love most. What is this all costing her, too? Tears started rolling down my cheeks. I thought again of Jack, standing there, looking at his hands, speaking so softly, "Probably you're too busy for this . . . but Gladys . . . " Yes, yes, but Jan! But Mark! But Karen! But David and Tom and Chris and Jon and . . . and . . . and . . .

What's important? That's the damn trouble . . . everything! Or everyone! Freedom and justice and love and beauty are all abstractions, finally, except they bear on people, express people, bless people. I know I have to choose. It's the mature, adult — finally, faithful — thing to do. Okay, turn feelings into choices. But whom do I turn away from my door? I crawled into bed and hugged Jan. I am simply inadequate, and that's the truth, too. It really is all too much for me.

If pride goes before a fall, and shock comes during a fall, then what comes after a fall . . . and over and under and around it? Grace, surely. Grace, please. God's grace! God's grace on Gladys and Jack, on Joel and Gabriela, on Ronald and Nancy, yes . . . and on Jan and me. God's grace on us all! I fell asleep praying.

Renewal

The United States is an incredibly beautiful country. When I was a boy, I lived in small towns on the prairies of Nebraska and South Dakota. It is no wonder that the wagons on which the pioneers crossed those lands were called schooners, for the prairies are as elemental as the sea and, in their own way, just as awesome. There is mystery and perspective in the wind speaking in its own kind of tongue, in the interpretive creak of a windmill; in the sturdy thrust of a cottonwood tree, in the quick devastation of a hail storm; in the sun sinking in a wondrous conflagration on a winter night and leaving you with the same sort of lonely longing you feel sometimes sitting before the fire late at night.

During my high school and college days we lived in Portland, Oregon, nestled in the evergreens and damp wood smells of the Willamette River Valley. That valley, pinched lovingly by the majestic Cascade Mountains and the mighty Pacific Ocean, blushes a thousand shades of roses and azaleas and rhododendrons and every sort of fruit tree. My Cornhusker parents were amazed: my dad reveling in the flowers he grew so easily now, and my mother touching the blossoms gently with her fingers and saying to me, "Teddy, can you believe this?" I'm not sure she ever did, and I had to get older before I really understood her question.

Then it was the East Coast for graduate school, the beginning of my own family, and the unfolding of my professional life. Here I've rooted and been watered: by the sheer vitality of New York City; by the history written in streets and buildings in Boston and Philadelphia; by the quiet riot of New England in the fall; by the parable of scrubby trees clinging to the rocks stubbornly mocking Maine's pounding surf; by the long view of the rolling hills and hex-protected farms of Pennsylvania; by the somehow larger-than-life buildings of Washington, D.C. (which express the dignity of democracy while, unfortunately, I think, disguising its nitty-gritty humanity).

Reinhold Niebuhr expressed that nitty-gritty best: "Man's capacity for justice makes democracy possible; but man's inclination to injustice makes democracy necessary."[1] Finally, it is our utter, awkward, eloquent humanity that is the most beautiful quality of this beloved country. What is most deeply attractive about this nation is its tapping of our capacity for justice which, at its best, plugs our inclination to injustice. The struggle between justice and injustice is ongoing and critical, and should never be hidden or snuffed by the cosmetic of noble buildings and clever rhetoric. It is our human capacity for justice — which is to say, our ordinary, yet for that reason extraordinary, humanity; our honest, and for that reason inclusive, humanity; our

[1]Reinhold Niebuhr, quoted from THE CHILDREN OF LIGHT AND THE CHILDREN OF DARKNESS. Copyright 1944 Charles Scribner's Sons; copyright renewed © 1972 Ursula M. Niebuhr. Reprinted with the permission of Charles Scribner's Sons.

humble, but for that reason accurate, humanity — that we religiously need to be nurturing and demonstrating.

On Tuesday, January 22, 1985, I was sitting in an airplane 30,000 feet over this country on my way to a Public Sanctuary Symposium in Tucson, Arizona.[2] I was looking down on the quilt of the country below — the squares of farmland, the roads stitching them together, the decorative clumps of trees, ponds, creeks, little towns. I was with Louise Spiker, a leader in the First Baptist Church of Wayne, Pennsylvania, which had declared Public Sanctuary; and Elaine Wahl, a member of our own Public Sanctuary Task Force. We'd made a connecting flight in Kansas City, and now people from other Public Sanctuary churches and denominational agencies, who had made the same connection, were moving in the aisles, talking to each other as if they were old friends. Maybe they were, maybe they weren't.

In any case, I always feel terribly uncomfortable in such circumstances and am sharply reminded of how hard it is for me to meet and be with people I don't know, or people I consider better educated or more experienced than I. Perhaps that shyness has something to do with my small town boyhood. Or maybe it's a nearly universal human trait. I suppose it doesn't matter much, because the real question is, "What is it I feel embarrassed about, anyway?" Is it my humanity, all the gurgles and growls and giggles of it? Why is it I am often embarrassed to admit that I am a minister, as though that made me a second-rate professional, if not a truncated person? Maybe Jacob had to wrestle on one side of the Jabbok with his embarrassment at regularly tripping over his facileness, while Esau had to wrestle on the other side with his embarrassment at constantly falling into the trap of his gullible impulsiveness, before they could meet again as brothers. I wonder if it was embarrassment, as much as anything else, that made the Israelites go chasing the skirts of other gods, like Baal, who were apparently more acceptable and reputedly more attractive than

[2]Inter-American Symposium on Sanctuary, January 23-24, 1985, Tucson, Arizona. Sponsored by the Tucson Ecumenical Council's Task Force for Central America.

their hard-nosed, desert-weathered Yahweh. Is it possible that we commit untold sins out of a fear of embarrassment? Is it possible that one of the struggles of faith is wrestling with the embarrassments that inhibit our taking leaps of either passionate commitment or unrestrained joy?

Often, when I begin to feel shy and embarrassed, I recall a scene in William Inge's play, The Dark at the Top of the Stairs. The mother is talking to her daughter, Rennie, about Sammy, one of Rennie's classmates who had committed suicide. Rennie had gone to a dance with Sammy but had run to the girls' room when someone had ridiculed Sammy for being a Jew. Then she'd come home alone, stranding Sammy. Later Sammy had jumped out a window to his death. Finally, the mother says to Rennie:

> "You ran off and hid when an ounce of thoughtfulness might have saved him . . . Tears aren't going to do any good now, Rennie. Now, you listen to me. I've heard all I intend to listen to about being so shy and sensitive and afraid of people. I can't respect those feelings any more. They're nothing but selfishness."[3]

Well, I don't think my shyness is of that proportion — or its consequences as devastating and dramatic — but you never know! Maybe it's some sort of shyness that keeps more congregations from declaring Public Sanctuary. I forced myself to get up and move around the plane.

I'd only made my way forward about six rows when I looked over and saw my old friend, Bill Coffin, engrossed in writing something. I'd missed him when we boarded in Kansas City, so that's what my shyness had gotten me! I whooped, and he greeted me as he invariably does: "Theo — dosius: gift from God." It's a charming and disarming greeting which I'm sure he means as an affirmation as well as a

---

[3]From page 95 of THE DARK AT THE TOP OF THE STAIRS by William Inge. Copyright 1958 by William Inge. Reprinted by permission of Random House, Inc.

---

spoof. He invited me to sit in the vacant seat next to him, and we animatedly talked our way on to Tucson.

I've always had enormous admiration for Bill, much like that of a small town boy for a city cousin versed in the ways of the world. So I am always both pleased and nonplused when I'm with him; glad to be his friend, while at the same time surprised that I am; benefiting from the friendship, but not at all certain I contribute anything to it. I suppose it's something of a contemporary version of the old Catholic "treasury of merit," where the extra merits of saints who didn't need them could be drawn upon by those who did — a sort of "grace by association." Maybe if you don't press it too hard or too far (and are ready to argue a little with Luther over five percent of his objection to the notion), you might say grace by association is something of what the church is about. At least I've occasionally felt it to be. It certainly is what my marriage is about . . . and a few friendships. And maybe the relationship of refugee and congregation in Public Sanctuary is partially grace by association. Perhaps the promise of grace by association is God's sneaky way of luring us out of the shadows of shyness. Anyway, my encountering Bill was a great pleasure and the first of a series of surprises that renewed my heart on this brief trip.

What Bill had been writing was his keynote address to the Sanctuary Symposium the next day. The fact that he was so typically confident that the muse would sing to him so close to the time he had to speak typically boggled me! He wanted to read parts of his speech to me and, sure enough, the muse had sung! The most memorable section, for me, was:

> " . . . foreign policy . . . reflects a government's attitude toward its own people . . . Our foreign aid today to Central America is making the rich richer, the poor poorer, and the military more powerful. Isn't that exactly what is happening in our own country?"[4]

[4]From "The Tasks Ahead" by William Sloane Coffin, page 180 of SANCTUARY, edited by Gary MacEoin. Copyright © 1985 by the Tucson Ecumenical Council Task Force for Central America. Reprinted by permission of Harper & Row, Publishers, Inc.

Apart from a momentary flicker of envy, I was delighted at Bill's ability to see and say things so memorably. What he had done in such a decisive stroke was to make clear that what happens in El Salvador and Guatemala and Nicaragua involves *everyone* in the United States. What our government does in *those* countries is directly reflected in the military budget, the tax policies, and the domestic programs that bear on the lives of citizens of *this* country — perhaps particularly those of poor people, blacks, and women. Hence, Public Sanctuary and all it symbolizes is not a peripheral issue, because justice is indivisible! Human welfare is indivisible! Humanity is indivisible! Perhaps the clearest, if not most moral, argument for reversing the arms race is that fratricide/sororicide is suicide. A nuclear exchange between two parts of the planet probably would destroy life on all of it.

The rest of the way to Tucson we swapped jokes. I'd been clipping things from magazines and papers I'd brought and, wanting to give Bill something, I passed along some choice quotes which he jotted down in an old notebook he carries for that purpose. In turn, he told me an old Ebo saying I've since used in a sermon: "It is the heart that gives, the fingers just let go." He told me that he'd try to arrange for me to stay with him at the home of the prominent family who was hosting him. But when we got off the plane in Tucson, the press and TV people rushed him off for an interview for the early news show, and his last words to me were, "I'll see you later." My fingers let go, if not my heart, and I went off with the others from Philadelphia to get my baggage. I think maybe I'm more like plodding old Esau than dashing old Jacob after all.

Since the Sanctuary Symposium opened with a banquet in the dining room of a large inn several miles from the downtown motel at which we were staying, we were bussed to the location. When we arrived, there were already long lines waiting to get in. Most people, including us, did not have tickets. Registration at the Symposium had tripled in the one week following the indictments of Public Sanctuary workers and the arrests of refugees, and the result was mild chaos. But, since Elie Wiesel was to be the main speaker, everyone wanted to attend, tickets or not. Non-ticket holders were asked to put their names on a waiting list and take their chances at getting tickets at the last minute. I signed us up and then, with a certain bravado, told the others in the Philadelphia contingent to go on into the dining room and sit at a table as if they had tickets, as others seemed to be doing. I'd stay by the crowded ticket table and bug the people on our behalf. Actually, while standing there insistently waving money and questions at the poor ticket people — and wondering if we'd miss the event because my friends would be asked to leave, since they didn't have tickets — I felt anxious, stupid and very lonely. I was surrounded by people I didn't know, awash in the din, being pushed this way and that by official-looking people going that way and this. I kept breathing in — as deeply as I could — the breeze that occasionally blew in through the entrance and wondering what I was doing here anyway. Then the "blessing" began...and I hadn't even known I was wrestling!

Elie Wiesel came through the door escorted by several people. There is something in the expression of his enormously sad, compassionate face that makes him look surprised to be where he is. I suspect it is the look of someone who has survived what he has. It would be impossible to relate how deeply his words and his presence have influenced me. I had first met Elie Wiesel nine years earlier when he had come to Philadelphia to speak at an event jointly sponsored by our church and our neighboring Jewish synagogue. Before then, I had read his books and felt their spiritual power. When I had shaken his hand and spoken to him that afternoon nine years ago, I had had the overwhelming sense that he was a holy person, that his eyes had seen what no human being should see — the face of the demonic and the backside of God.

That long ago evening, before he returned to New York, we'd had dinner together in the rabbi's home. Just before dinner, the rabbi's daughter — a passionate woman who has since become a rabbi — said to me very angrily, "In light of the holocaust, I don't see how Christians could feel anything but guilt." I said I did feel guilt, even anguish, over the holocaust and what it meant. Elie looked at me and said softly, "The more anguish and guilt a person feels, the closer I feel to him." I've never forgotten those words. Since that night, I've written perhaps three letters to Wiesel, and gotten gracious replies, and been in his home one afternoon for a conversation. In truth, many things he's written or said I carry around with me like a tin of hot coals to keep my spirit from growing cold. One of his statements explains a little of why I am committed to Public Sanctuary: "If someone suffers and he keeps silent, it can be a good silence. If someone suffers and I keep silent, then it's a destructive silence."[5]

It had been several years since I'd seen him, but without thinking, I approached him now and said, "Elie Wiesel, you probably won't remember me, but my name is Ted Loder." Without hesitation he said, "Of course, I remember you. You're from Philadelphia. I want you to come and see me. I have missed seeing you." I could scarcely believe it, scarcely stammer out the words, "I'll come soon. I've missed seeing you. I am really glad to see you now." He nodded, and then his hosts ushered him off toward his table. I was ecstatic. Elie Wiesel was a reminder, a connection with something holy which was finally what this Movement was about, what life is about. That he would remember me was like being given...a name!

I was still standing there in a daze when another friend I hadn't seen for many years — almost since our days together at Yale Divinity School — came in. It was Ralph Waite. "My God, Ralph," I gasped. We looked at each other like long lost brothers — Jacob and Esau, surely — and hugged and pounded each other. What serendipity! People around us looked cross-eyed at us. We laughed. (So much for shyness, at least temporarily.)

Most people know Ralph as Pa Walton from the popular television series, "The Waltons." I knew him in my heart as one of my oldest, closest friends. He had come to this Sanctuary Symposium to explore the possibilities of making a movie about the Public Sanctuary Movement, and a director/producer friend, Michael Jaffe, was with him. Since Ralph had to check in with a few people quickly, he and I promised to meet after the dinner. Several times in recent years I had tried unsuccessfully to contact Ralph through artists' agents or media

[5]From page 7 of HARRY JAMES CARGAS IN CONVERSATION WITH ELIE WIESEL. Reprinted by permission of Harry James Cargas.

---

people I knew. Then, suddenly, there he was! There was glee in my blood as I went back to the ticket table. I wonder if Jacob — or the Stranger, for that matter — felt at all exhilarated during the wrestling match. In any case, my evident glee apparently out-flanked the ticket people. They gave me tickets. I was on a roll!

Surely all prophets don't thunder. That evening Elie Wiesel spoke in his intense, insistently reverent, probing style which, rather than evoking wild cheers, sears the soul with burning coals, as did the seraphim to Isaiah.[6] Of the many memorable things he said, two were particularly poignant to me.[7] One was the story of a prison warden who was troubled by the account of the fall in Genesis in which Adam and Eve had disobeyed God's commandment. The warden posed this question to a rabbi who was in jail, himself a refugee: "It's written that God asks Adam, 'Where art thou?' Is it conceivable that God didn't know where Adam was?" The rabbi answered, "God knew, Adam did not." Then Wiesel asked quietly, "Do we know where we are?" By implication (though I was so moved I could have missed him asking it directly), the question was inclusive: "Where is the religious community of this nation, the citizens of this land vis-a-vis loving our neighbor — the stranger, the refugee — as ourselves?"

The other memorable moment was Wiesel's telling of a conference called Faith in Humankind, a conference of people who had been rescuers of Jews during the war. They met to explore why some non-Jews had risked their lives to help Jews during the holocaust. They especially sought to understand two things: What had made these people care, and why were they so few? Their exploration revealed some surprising things. Those who cared about the suffering of the Jews were, for the most part, simple, common people. They didn't consider what they did to help Jews as being at all courageous or heroic. They did it simply because they believed it was the human thing to do. Wiesel concluded, "Woe to our society if to be human becomes a heroic act." Once again, profoundly and unmistakably, it

[6]Isaiah 6:6

[7]Refer to the Foreword, page 6 for the complete text of Wiesel's address.

had been made clear for all with ears to hear that Public Sanctuary, for all its political implications, is fundamentally a spiritual issue — perhaps the the profoundest of spiritual issues: "What does it mean to be human?"

After dinner I encountered several people who were disappointed in Wiesel for what he'd said — or more exactly, for what he *hadn't* said. They thought that he had evaded the issues; that he should have made a much stronger statement; that he should have added his considerable stature and influence to condemning the Reagan Administration for its policies, which largely were responsible for the injustices Public Sanctuary was trying to redress. My immediate reaction was to defend Wiesel. But quite quickly I realized that Elie Wiesel needed no defending by me. Then I wondered why I felt I had to defend him; and whether my gratitude for his friendship was blinding me to some truths I should hear. Was I guilty of idolatry in my reverence for Wiesel? Probably, some. Yet, Wiesel is a man through whom I see God, while idols are people, things, groups, nations who are substitutes for God. The difference is critical for everyone who takes an uncompromising stand on one side of any cause or commitment. Still, the torment is that I envy the certainty of people who take those uncompromising stands. That's my constant dilemma! I think what made me feel defensive was having the button of that tormenting dilemma pushed by the criticism of Wiesel.

Of course, our government can be morally indicted, and rightly so, for the injustices of its Central American policies. But somehow to do that too easily seems immorally arrogant to me. I'll never be much of a prophet, because the complexities are always there for me: the complexities not only of issues and interpretations, but of how those interpretations are made. I realize that when all the facts are in, the truth is still out, because, finally, truth is always interpretive, not self-evident. To me, that's something of what Reinhold Niebuhr was getting at in his insight about democracy: our capacities which make it possible and our inclinations which make it necessary. *Prophets, however, are monarchists.* But their blood isn't in my veins, only the desire. Ah, to be able to pronounce, "Thus says the Lord . . ." and then be in undisturbed agreement with what the Lord says.

The issue is always how to take a stand when the issues are complex. If simplicities distort, complexities paralyze . . . if you allow them to, as a majority of people do. "Woe to our society if to be human becomes a heroic act." So, I think you take a stand as a human being, not claiming too much for yourself, but with agony and humility. Which is to say, you stand with the willingness to be humiliated, accompanied by a realistic expectation that the humiliation *will* happen, maybe even *should* happen — since perhaps the greatest temptation of all is to idolize your own ego without realizing it. At least that's the temptation I find myself easily into, arduously out of.

So you choose. I find myself making choices on the basis of who has no voice and so calls me to lend them mine; who has little power and so needs the little more I have; who is oppressed and so needs me to take the foot of my indifference off their necks. I might be seduced, or intimidated, by the wealthy and powerful, but when push comes to shove, I can be claimed only by those who disturb my conscience and deliver my humanity.

One of my sons, who is a lawyer, sometimes becomes the ardent devil's advocate about issues I espouse. When he has finished pointing out the inadequacies of my positions, he'll smile and say, wistfully, "I know, Dad. Someone has to represent that side." I'll smile back, grateful for his struggle with justice. For me, and now for him, the struggle is never simple, never easy, and always has its price. While disclaiming the masochism of a fanatic, I do think the price required by a stand is one sign of its moral authenticity.

Still, I am disturbed by the easy arrogance of any advocacy — including my own — that is so single-minded it quickly becomes incapable of thinking two thoughts at once, especially if one conflicts with the other. But my wife Jan says, "Loving your enemies doesn't mean being afraid to make them." She's right, and she also means, "Loving your enemies doesn't mean dismissing them, either." It is hard to dare to make enemies by taking a controversial stand, and equally hard not to dismiss them when they don't stand where you do. So you choose, and pray, and try to develop a silver ear to go with your supposedly silver tongue.

And as often as you can, you seek a friend. Few plays have impacted me more powerfully than Peter Shaffer's magnificent *Equus*. There is a telling line almost buried in it. It's when Dysart, the doctor, is describing the pain of the seventeen year old boy who is his patient. Dysart says, "[He has] no friends. Not one kid to give him a joke or make him know himself more moderately."[8] To make you know yourself more moderately is an invaluable gift from a friend. More moderately...with some sense of proportion and humor, and perhaps of peace; your urgent sense of self-importance moderated, like letting the air out of an overblown tire. Thank God for friends! They're indispensable and rare. I met Ralph in the hotel lounge about an hour after the opening dinner of the Symposium.

When the cocktail waitress came, Ralph ordered coffee. So I began to catch up with his life by learning that he is a recovering alcoholic and is deeply involved in Alcoholics Anonymous locally and nationally. I told him about the years I'd been in psychotherapy. That sharing of scars seemed to stitch us together again across the years and miles of our separation. At the same time, I realized we — Ralph and I and Michael Jaffe (who was also with us) — were being ogled by some of the women in the lounge and, at one point, three of them approached us, ostensibly promoting a local golf tournament. Ralph and Michael dealt with them smoothly. It was my first exposure to public attention showered on celebrities. It was both heady — people assuming I must be someone famous as well, since I was with Ralph — and humorous, since I knew the person Ralph Waite was not the same as the persona Pa Walton. I also understood how such attention would become irritatingly intrusive in a very short time. But, I confess, while I was bumming around Tucson with Ralph, it was fun. I wonder who all those fans thought I was?

We hadn't been in the lounge long when John Fife came in. John, along with Jim Corbett, actually began the Public Sanctuary Movement, so Ralph was eager to talk with him about the possibility of making a movie. Since I'd met John earlier, I went over and told him

---

[8]Peter Shaffer, quoted from EQUUS AND SHRIVINGS. Copyright © 1974 Peter Shaffer. Reprinted with the permission of Atheneum Publishers, Inc.

about the movie project and invited him to talk with Ralph. Fame has its assets. John was surrounded by people, but Ralph's name got his attention, and shortly he came over with his wife and teen-aged son. For the next two hours we got the inside story on Public Sanctuary from the man who'd been at the center of it from the first day. It was fascinating and enlightening!

John Fife must be 6'6" and weigh no more than 170 pounds, and he's a chain smoker. But he radiates energy, is articulate, innovative and bright, clearly an extremely competent, professional minister. He has kept his roots in his local parish while growing into a leader of national stature. When you listen to him, you quickly get the impression that God put the right person at the right place at the right time.

One of the most interesting tidbits of information he tossed off was that the Sanctuary Movement actually began with the help of the Immigration and Naturalization Service. In 1981, INS agents had called John at the Southside Presbyterian Church in Tucson and asked if the church would assist some Central American aliens whom the INS had just arrested. They had found the aliens abandoned in the desert in a locked, closed truck, left to die by a coyote who had been smuggling them in as migrant workers. Several of the aliens had died, and those who hadn't were in bad shape. John and the people of Southside Presbyterian Church responded, and that was their introduction to the tragedy of the refugees from Central America. Members of the Southside Presbyterian Church even re-financed their homes to provide over $700,000 legal assistance and other aid to hundreds of refugees. Finally, they instituted the notion of Public Sanctuary in order to provide haven for the refugees and to enlist the aid of other religious bodies. From that seed grew the Public Sanctuary Movement. At the same time, the Reagan Administration was increasingly accentuating a military, hard-line policy in Central America, as well as denying political refugee status to its victims fleeing into this country. But the irony of the INS's part in the origins of Public Sanctuary surely testifies to the sneakiness of God and the deep ambivalence of this country on this issue.

That ambivalence was underscored during our conversation with John Fife when someone he knew came and sat with us. It turned out to be William D. Clarke — a businessman from Canton, Ohio, who had been quoted in the *Wall Street Journal* months earlier as a staunch Reagan supporter, but who also was a leader in trying to get his church to declare Public Sanctuary because it was the moral thing to do...and morality cuts across political allegiances. Clarke told us that he was taking a leave from his electrical contracting company to devote more time to the Public Sanctuary Movement. I was about to ask him how he could support Public Sanctuary and still be for Reagan, when I gagged on my own dogmatism. Good God, apparently I was the one who couldn't think two thoughts at once.

About two o'clock in the morning, the talk broke up, and Ralph was going to drive me back to my motel. We were about to leave the lounge when I suggested that, since we were going to have breakfast together back at his hotel, I drive his car over and back, so he wouldn't have to make the trip. He smiled and said, "Sure. I'll show you where it's parked." I assumed he'd flown in from Los Angeles and rented a car. When we got to the car, it was a 1985 Jaguar! He'd been in Palm Springs and driven to Tucson in his new car which, he laughingly explained, he'd gotten mainly at his step-son's urging, since the old, beat-up cars he usually drove around in were a standing joke among the people he worked with. I told Ralph I'd never even *been* in a Jaguar, let alone *driven* one. He said, "There's nothing to it. Enjoy the ride."

So there I was, attending a Symposium for refugees, tooling around Tucson in a Jaguar. I felt like the minister who played hooky from church one Sunday on the pretext of illness, played golf instead, and got a hole-in-one. Whom could he tell? I'm not sure whether I was more afraid of being seen or not seen. Actually, I did feel a little guilty. Then a line came to me from a poem I'd read once (I think it's by Seamus Heaney) in which there is a description of a seminary student who is "doomed to do the decent thing." I can't forget that line, because it fits so many of us clergy. What a pale-cheeked, rattle-breathed, fluttery-eyed, shrivel-scrotumed thing to be: "Doomed to do the decent thing." What the hell is the *decent* thing? If you're doomed to it, it must be about as juiceless as not swearing in a Ladies Aid meeting. Why do we talk so much about love, so little about fun? How about "picked to do the daring thing" or "tickled to do the exciting thing?" Anyway, "decent" would be a prissy and inadequate way to describe what Public Sanctuary is about. I took the long way back to my motel and honked every chance I got.

At the opening session of the Symposium the next morning, Bill Coffin was to give the keynote address. As Ralph and Michael and I walked down the aisle of the synagogue in which, with accurate symbolism, the Symposium was held, another surprise leaped up to greet us. Herb Reinelt was at Yale Divinity School with us. He and Ralph and I played on the same intramural basketball team — and won every year! We drank gallons of coffee together in the snack bar (paid for by I.O.U.s), studied and talked together for endless hours, were like brothers. Herb now teaches philosophy and religion at University of Pacific in Stockton, California. Herb and I write about three times a year, telephone each other about twice a year, see each other about once a decade, yet somehow remain inseparable. Neither Ralph nor Herb nor I had known either of the others would be at the Symposium, but something of what made us inseparable had also drawn us to be there. Our being together just then, just there, seemed to us at once improbable and inevitable, and the mystery of it excited yet puzzled us. Ralph kept saying that maybe our meeting, after all these years, would be the hook to hang his movie on, or at least to write a play about; Herb referred repeatedly to coherence related to chance and probability (I think); and I kept pounding on their backs and saying, "Can you believe this?" (with the same delighted wonder as my mother about Oregon roses).

As I reflect on it, I think we were each a bit flustered as well as intrigued by our feelings, because they touched on the mystery of love — not just our's for each other, but a larger love which had nurtured us and somehow brought us to this place in some way, for some reason past coincidence. It was a gift. It was grace.

So we listened to Bill speak and then pulled him off into one of the rooms in the synagogue school where we drank coffee and talked, as we had so many years before. The rest of the Symposium was something of a blur to me. Of course, I remember some of the exposition of the history; the theological underpinnings of sanctuary; all the political and social and economic analyses of Central America and the policies of the United States in that region; all the barbed criticisms of the Reagan Administration and its covert, unjustified methods of infiltration of churches by the Department of Justice agents, and the repugnant implications of such actions.

But mostly I remember the slivers and shards. I remember Felipe Ixcot, a Guatemalan refugee, speaking with pride of the sophisticated Mayan civilization of his forebearers, and ending with a Mayan blessing: "May all arrive; may none be left behind; may all be one."

I remember B. Davie Napier — my Old Testament professor in seminary and another friend who influenced me profoundly — telling of going to worship at Jerry Falwell's church in Virginia just to experience the spirit of the Moral Majority. When he didn't hear a single reference to justice or righteousness or compassion, he realized that Falwell was a Marcionist — a position the church in its formative stage had decided was heretical because it tore the gospel away from its Old Testament, Jewish roots. Somehow I felt reassured by that reference to "the earth on [our] roots."

I also remember Napier referring to a quote from Jeane Kirkpatrick, former Reagan Administration Ambassador to the United Nations, in which she'd said, "Marxism is the enemy, and *any action* taken to defeat it is moral." [Italics mine][9] *Any* action? Including the strafing and bombing of civilians, death squads, the murder and torture of people who demand justice and human rights, the invasion of countries we don't like, covert operations to overthrow governments whose politics we disagree with, even nuclear war? That position is appalling, yet apparently Kirkpatrick expressed the official position of the Reagan Administration which appeals to the knee-jerk, unexamined fears of many people in this country.

The inherent tragedy is that historically, as a democratic society, we have insisted that the ends do *not* justify the means. That's what the Constitution and the Bill of Rights are about! That's what our pledge to "liberty and justice for all" makes clear. Are we now negat-

---

[9]Jeane Kirkpatrick as cited by George Black, "Unmanifest Destiny," in THE NATION 239 (October 20, 1984). (Quoted by Davie Napier in his address to the Sanctuary Symposium, "Hebraic Concepts of Sanctuary and Law").

---

ing those laws, those commitments? Or are we only forsaking them when it comes to dealing with other nations — particularly weaker, Third World nations, where we can act with relative impunity? But do we really think we can treat others differently from ourselves, if, in fact, a nation's "foreign policy...reflects [its] attitude toward its own people" and inevitably, therefore, the way it treats its own people? As a powerful nation — and a self-indulgent one — have we actually come to believe that our ends *do* justify our means?

I remember Dick Shaull, a retired Princeton professor who lives near me in Philadelphia and has given our church counsel on Public Sanctuary, analyzing what he termed "the systemic nature of evil." He suggested it results from an economy which serves profits, not people; from a government bureaucracy which distances decision-makers from the people affected by those decisions; and by the attempt to smother dissent, or even questions, with appeals to national security.

During the Symposium, I felt a growing anger, frustration, discouragement...familiar and growing feelings since our declaration of Public Sanctuary. I don't get much satisfaction over rehearsing the problems or booing the enemy. I want to win the battle, or at least feel I have a chance to win. But when you're battling the government, it is, at best, an uneven fight. What do you do in an uneven fight? How do you keep on with it, find energy for it, remained focused about it, faithful to it? Those are the questions that wrinkle my sheets at night, that lurk in the shadows and pounce when a distant siren wakes me in the darkness before dawn. I guess you look for the small blessings along the way, the little miracles — like bread and wine — and sometimes remember that the Stranger was more powerful than Jacob, too.

So mostly I remember Ralph and Herb — and Bill, too, though he wasn't with us much. I remember the jokes, sneaking off for lunches and snacks, and practicing our "shell out falter." I remember the long talks as we hurried to fill in the gaps our absences had created, comparing experiences in careers, what had happened in our marriages. Ralph and I had both been divorced, and Herb's wife had died, and all of us were remarried. Ralph and I were exploring the territory of step-parenting. We talked about our faith and doubts, how they had changed and, mostly, simplified over the years. "Fewer beliefs, more belief," someone put it. I remember sitting one night in a fast food place (which Ralph knew about because it served a terrific hot fudge cake) and hearing the waitresses ask him for his autograph. Then slowly finishing our coffee, we came again, all those years later, to that sort of ease with each other that permits silence. After many moments of quiet smiles and watery eyes, Ralph broke the silence saying, "You know, there's a definition of heaven which is that when you finally get there, God motions for you to look back. And when you do, it hits you and you say, 'So that's what it was about.' "

The next morning, I was the first to leave for home. Ralph and Herb gave me a ride to the airport. More coffee and more talk in the small snack bar. Then, standing in the wide corridor in front of the metal detector, a long, three-man hug and a promise to stay in touch. The last thing I said to them was, "I love you guys." And the last thing I heard was, "I love you, too."

It felt like a short ride home. As I sat there on the plane, some words of Marc Chagall kept echoing in my head: "I know that the road of life is eternal and short."[10] I had learned again something of what makes life eternal. Old Qoheleth is right: "A faithful friend is a sturdy shelter. He that hath found one has found a treasure."[11] I had learned that, in some elemental way, Public Sanctuary has something to do with friendship — just as does personal sanctuary, and therefore, the church as well.

I felt good. I was glad to have gone to Tucson and found my friends. They renewed me. Now I was glad to be going home to Jan, my best, most intimate friend, and to friends in the church, and to Joel and Gabriela and the Public Sanctuary battle. I had been given a glimpse of heaven, and I could say, with a somewhat clearer perspective, "So that's what it's about." I'd been blessed! Who cares about the limp?

[10] From page 201 of CHAGALL BY CHAGALL, edited by Charles Sorlier. Copyright © 1979 Drageur Editeur. Reprinted by permission of Harry N. Abrams, Inc., publisher.

[11] Ecclesiasticus 6:14

Perseverance

The gray, pre-dawn light disguised what the late February day's weather would be. I stared out the bathroom window as I brushed the tracks of the retreating night from my mouth. Streaked against the sky over the neighbors' rooftops was an undulant wingprint of geese, headed north. It seemed early in the season for them. I cracked the window and listened to them honk through the cold air, imagining the faint wake of vapor trails those sounds might be leaving. Strange longings were churned up in me. My grandfather told me — or perhaps I read somewhere when I was young — that old barnyard chickens jump up and flap their wings, trying to fly, when they hear geese going over. I know the feeling! I turned and was actually startled to find my face in the mirror. My whiskers, reaped by the razor, matched the color of the sky. Time passes. It's the dailyness of it that slowly accumulates to suddenly catch you off guard. Yet . . . almost dawn . . .

NO ONE BUT US

In the early 1970's, I saw Ingmar Bergman's movie, *Scenes From A Marriage*. It did not seem to me as powerful or moving as other Bergman films, yet a single sentence in it struck, and I've not been able to dislodge it from my mind. It is near the end in the "Sixth Scene," when Johan and his divorced wife Marianne meet and she asks him how he is doing. Part of his answer is, "If anything, I've found my right proportions."[1] Those few words, and the feelings accompanying them, frequently get tugged into my consciousness. Sometimes the feelings translate into a sense of being judged, other times unleash a sense of longing...and now that I reflect on it, maybe experiences of judgment and longing are actually very similar.

In any case, Johan's words usually come to me as to an old barnyard rooster who thinks he can fly, and tries to, and so becomes overextended out of his compulsiveness and need. Still, flying — or some performance level akin to it — seems to be exactly what the church is forever exhorting us to achieve. Or is it just something some ministers, such as I, feel driven to do in order to prove we're as good as people who *work* for a living? I suspect our true proportions — or mine, at least, — are somewhere between the illusions of grandiosity and the seductions of mediocrity. Easily said! But how do you find those proportions?

I'm beginning to think you find them in the long slog of the daily, when the spotlights are off, the crises past; when you march to an inner drum, not a outer drum major. Perhaps that's when you find out who you are, what you can really do, what your talents and commitments come down to. Maybe that's why Isaiah added a third image to the strengths of those "who wait for the Lord." *Wait*? Yes, that's the word! And the strengths? We've all heard them. First, "They shall mount up with wings like eagles..." Okay; and second, "They shall run and not be weary..." Right; and finally, "They shall walk and not faint."[2] Ah, yes, prophets are sneaky, aren't they? Walking and not

---

[1]From page 195 of SCENES FROM A MARRIAGE by Ingmar Bergman, translated by Alan Blair. English Translation copyright © 1974 by Alan Blair. Reprinted by permission of Pantheon Books, a division of Random House, Inc.

[2]Isaiah 40:31, RSV

fainting — not copping out — that's the test, isn't it?

Maybe that's why impetuous old Paul says — surely as much to himself as to anyone — that the first characteristic of love is patience.[3] It's not exactly the first thing I would have said love is. Or the first most of us would have said, probably. I doubt that Paul would have said it either, except surely it began to dawn on him, over those long years of his mission, that the Second Coming wasn't going to happen on his schedule. So, whatever else he had to learn if he was going to love, it had to include patience (which, it must also have occurred to him, is one critical quality of God's love).

So, February. So, back from Tucson and on with the dailyness of our Public Sanctuary commitments. So, the slog began, and with it the resumption of my search for my right proportions (which may be another way to think of a limp!). That search is probably a lifetime proposition, and always the longing of it tugs. But then, the wrestling match with the Stranger went on all night, didn't it? I'm sure it was a very long night. Apparently, the Stranger is too elusive — or gracious — for knockouts or quick decisions by either side.

Occasionally, I began to resent the claims of time and energy the Public Sanctuary work made on me, and on the discretionary time and energy of volunteers in the church. Our congregation is extraordinarily active and is engaged in a wide variety of program and outreach. In addition, the great majority of people who belong to this church are young, energetic women and men who have significant commitments to careers, to family, and to numerous causes and groups in which many assume leadership responsibilities, most often as a corollary of their faith. It is not an easy or simple matter to sustain the wide range of the church's program and mission. But I believe that such a range is needed both to minister to a pluralistic society and to resist the temptations to idolatry — which perhaps are strongest in a homogeneous, single emphasis congregation, especially those with rigid measures of either belief (orthodoxy) or practice (orthopraxis).

While our commitment to Public Sanctuary was viewed by me and others as a natural outgrowth of the faith, history and spirit of our congregation, it was important, to me at least, for us not to become a

[3] I Corinthians 13:4

Public Sanctuary church rather than a *church* which had declared Public Sanctuary. In principle it was not too difficult to keep clear on that distinction because, except for the crises which temporarily were almost totally absorbing, Public Sanctuary fortunately was just one of the many things we were doing as a congregation.

But, unfortunately, though Public Sanctuary did not represent an "added on value," it was an "added on project" to a schedule already overcrowded — in my case with meetings, counseling, weddings, funerals, a benefit concert series arranged by one of our members (renowned pianist Natalie Hinderas), upcoming programs for Lent, sermon preparation, denominational responsibilities, speaking engagements, plus all the etcetera "business" which Qoheleth, the grandfather of all preachers, said God has given us to be busy with.

One complication of that personal and institutional "busy-ness" was that it frequently obscured the fact that it was the entire church which had declared Public Sanctuary — not just the group of most heavily involved persons who constituted the Task Force and, naturally enough, tended to think of the project as primarily theirs. Dealing with that emotionally charged complication was a test of diplomatic skill which I did not always pass. The constant struggle for me, professionally, was to negotiate the way to accurately emphasize that our's was a *church* which had declared Public Sanctuary. The personal struggle was to determine with integrity what I owed of time and energy to what I perceived to be a variety of legitimate, if not highly worthy, claims on me — and, as a corollary, what real or imagined affirmation I got from trying to meet those claims.

But talking about priorities is easier than setting them, and then re-setting them daily according to circumstances. Judging from Jesus' life, faith surely involves caring responses to ongoing interruptions and the adjustments they require. Yet, how do you apply a tourniquet of "noes" to staunch the flow of time and energy toward more claims than you can meet? That's my dilemma, commonly shared. I remember, once, leaving for a vacation on Nantucket and being asked by my daughter to bring her back a shell or stone from that island because she loved it so. One afternoon I walked on a Nantucket beach to collect the token she wanted and found myself picking up another stone, another shell, and then another, and another, and another, each time thinking this one, or the next, or the next, would be the right one, the most beautiful one. I collected a bagful...and she had asked for one! Priorities are like that for me. They're determined not only by the perceived value of a certain options in relation to other options, but more critically by the *confidence* — or lack of it — with which I do the perceiving. Confidence must be the sunny side of faith.

Therefore, part of what makes the daily so difficult, for me, is not just accepting my limitations, my right proportions, but *trusting* those limitations. Trusting not only that a Power is at work beyond those limitations, but that I am accepted and loved in, and in spite of, them. My struggle to trust goes on. In my own way I keep demanding that the Stranger who has me in the hold of those limitations bless me with some confidence...having not yet learned that the blessing may only come by my letting go of my expectation that *the* right, *the* true cause is one I can grasp. Until I can let go of that, at least a little, probably I'll go on picking up stones, shells, causes, activities — and frustrations.

Paradoxically, one factor that helps me to continually reaffirm Public Sanctuary as a high priority is the willingness of others in our church, who are equally busy, to invest themselves in it. I know that this decision is no easier for them than it is for me. I think of John, a computer expert and young father whose son has a severely cleft palate that requires a continuing round of surgery; George, a utilities executive whose passionate concern for Central America first alerted us to that situation, and who has gone alone to visit a priest friend in a Nicaraguan village; Dick, a foundation officer who signs his letters "Peace with Justice" and lives accordingly; and his wife, Julie, who, along with Dick, spent a year of her life working among the Native Americans in the Southwest; Anne, a high powered, amazingly efficient organizer who, in addition to caring lovingly for her family, gives uncounted hours and enormous energy providing brilliant leadership in our church and community; Lynne, compassionate and compelling in her commitments to justice and to living her faith, who believes in including her children fully in her activity, as part of what it means for her to be a mother; Celeste, a single parent who works long hours and yet always has tough love and probing insight to contribute to making the human community more just and humane, because she is a battler of the sixties who remains clear-eyed in the eighties; Claire, who teaches school in a depressed area, comes home in her VW bug drained, yet writes beautiful poetry both with words and deeds, and who gave the humorous, steady-handed, trusted leadership that made Public Sanctuary possible for us; Elaine, whose language skills and love for the refugees enables her not only to translate words but nurture their lives; Barbara, who quietly takes on the thankless scut work without which nothing happens, and who does it with grace and effectiveness; Ted, a young attorney who gave the first years of his professional life to Community Legal Services, who almost single-handedly managed to negotiate a federally funded rehabilitation project for an abandoned apartment house in the city, and who now freely gives thousands of dollars worth of the legal counsel necessary to protect Joel and Gabriela legally and to sustain them emotionally; Karen, a public defender attorney whose wide-eyed delight over nearly everything is accompanied by a stubborn determination to fight for the underdog victims of injustice; Virginia, whose ethical commitments are bone-deep, and who gives all her working hours living and quietly working out her convictions, in part through her professional leadership of an area ecumenical organization dedicated to a just community; Wally, Director of the Wholistic Health Center, who engages in living a wholistic life day by day; Marianne, representative from the St. Vincent's Roman Catholic Peace Center, for whom a life of faith means a life of risk unflamboyantly, but unflappably, taken; my staff colleagues, Michele, George, Bill and Noah, whose deep dedication to our common ministry, whose steady support of Public Sanctuary, whose leadership in church and community, and whose counsel to me has been wondrously sustaining; and so many others who do so much in so many critical ways to accomplish the simple, compelling task which is the heart of Public Sanctuary: to save the lives of human beings. It is they, far more than I, who carry on the daily labors that make Public Sanctuary possible for us. Jokingly, yet seriously, I say to them, and about them, "Wait for me, I'm your leader." I hope they know how grateful I am for them!

    During this period we were able to make a high quality video tape entitled A *Sanctuary Church* in which we tried to explain our reasons for declaring Public Sanctuary and to share our experiences. Many of the Task Force persons appeared in that video, along with the refugees, and the result is a compelling record which other groups can view as an introduction to the Sanctuary issue.[4] Making that video was a complex undertaking and was professionally done under the direction of George, a career public relations person; Martha who, though in the midst of a high risk pregnancy, assumed the responsibilities of publishing a Public Sanctuary Newsletter, Ten Twigs, as well as scheduling the use or purchase of the video by other groups and churches; Roberta, a public high school teacher of enormous dedication; and Joan, a sympathetic teacher, drama director, and writer.

We also arranged for Joel and Gabriela to speak to as many groups as possible, always accompanied by members of the Task Force. Inevitably, whenever people heard the stories told by the refugees, understanding and support grew for what we were doing. That kind of response made it increasingly clear why the government wanted to silence the Public Sanctuary Movement. The information shared by the refugees about their experiences of death threats, torture and persecution challenges the truth of the "official" position of the Administration which contends that they are "economic" refugees. When the refugees explain their deeply religious motivation for opposing the repression and injustice in their countries, it is not stretching the truth to suggest that they are, in fact, *religious* refugees, as well as political ones.

Also, by telling people what had happened to them personally and what was taking place in their country, Joel and Gabriela (along with all the other refugees in Public Sanctuary) are raising serious questions about United States policy in Central America: the giving of military and economic support to repressive governments on the simple grounds that they are "anti-communist." The refugees' reports also bring into question the accuracy, completeness and integrity of the information our government disseminates about what actually is happening in Guatemala and El Salvador and Nicaragua.

[4]For information regarding the rental or purchase of A *Sanctuary Church*, contact Martha Ankeny, c/o LuraMedia, P.O. Box 261668, San Diego, CA 92126.

But always the groups to which the refugees spoke, or that we otherwise were able to reach, involved relatively small numbers. It is hard to remember, in such circumstances, Jesus' word about faith being like leaven in the lump of dough. Especially when the dough in this case is millions of dollars of TV and newspaper reportage of the Administration's views to which a majority of people (even after Watergate) ascribe total credibility. I think again of what Elie Wiesel has said: "The opposite of love, I have learned, is not hate but indifference."[5] Perhaps the first symptom of indifference is our willingness to be deceived: partly, because to find any truth requires effort; and partly, because there is often something demanding and uncomfortable about any truth. I understand that indifference and am often subject to it. Part of the truth of me is that sometimes I'd like to give up this wrestling with, and for, the truth regarding Central America and just sit by the fire, drink tea and tend my soul...that is, if by doing that I'd have much soul left to tend. So, the slog of being leaven ...and hoping the lump rises.

One group to which I went to speak along with Ted Walkenhorst, our Task Force attorney, was the University of Delaware Law School's forum on public events. Perhaps fifty students and guests attended, along with a few professors. The third person speaking that afternoon was Arthur C. Helton, Director of the Political Asylum Project for the Lawyers Committee for International Human Rights in New York City. Helton is soft-spoken, mild-mannered and rapier-sharp. He was very effective, focusing primarily on the legal implications and applications of the Refugee Act of 1980, which is the law of this country and which conforms to the 1967 United Nations Protocol relating to the status of refugees. According to that law, a refugee is defined as:

> "any person who is outside any country of such person's nationality or, in the case of a person having no nationality, is outside any country in which such person last habitually resided, and who is unable or unwilling to return to, and is unable or unwilling to avail

[5]Reported in THE PHILADELPHIA INQUIRER, Saturday, April 20, 1985, page 6-A. Excerpt from Wiesel's remarks on receiving the Congressional Gold Medal from President Reagan. Reprinted by permission.

himself or herself of the protection of, that country *be-cause of persecution or a well-founded fear of persecution on account of race, religion, nationality, membership in a particular social group, or political opinion . . ."* [Italics mine][6]

By that definition, it seems evident that persons fleeing from persecution or fear of persecution in Central America, and seeking asylum in this country, are political refugees. Certainly one of the key issues raised by the Public Sanctuary Movement is precisely who is breaking the law: those who give refuge to these persons or those who deny such refuge?

Nor is there much doubt about the government denying political refugee status to Central American refugees. In his talk to this University of Delaware Law School forum, Arthur Helton quoted a persuasive conclusion based on some compelling figures from an article he'd written:

> "Ideology also continues to dominate asylum decision making, translating into ready asylum grants for applicants who flee from Communist-dominated regimes, and into far less generous grants to those who flee regimes in which the United States has good relations, irrespective of their human rights records. Statistics provided by the INS for fiscal year 1983 support this conclusion. For example, seventy-eight percent of the Russian, sixty-four percent of the Afghan, and forty-percent of the Romanian cases decided received political asylum, all involving persons fleeing Communist-dominated regimes. On the other hand, asylum was granted in less than eleven percent of the Philippine, twelve percent of the Pakistani, two percent of the Haitian, two percent of the Guatemalan and three percent of the Salvadorian cases."[7]

I came away from that session with two disturbing realizations underscored: one, that the law is discriminatively applied and, in this

[6]Immigration and Nationality Act (INA) para. 101 (a)(42)(A) 8 U.S.C. para. 1101 (a)(42)(A) (1982).

[7]From "Political Asylum Under The 1980 Refugee Act: An Unfulfilled Promise" by Arthur C. Helton, JOURNAL OF LAW REFORM (Vol. 17:2 Winter 1984), page 253. Reprinted by permission of University of Michigan Journal of Law Reform.

case, with at least a hint of racism; two, that the law is written and interpreted with as much attention to political considerations as to concerns for justice. Of course I know, as does anyone who thinks about it for ten minutes, that justice — as well as its relationship to the law — is relative and of little matter as an abstraction. The determination of justice is contingent on complex realities, and those "realities" are weighed by persons conditioned by vested perspectives. So, obviously, justice and the law are always defined in large measure by politics. The danger is that I, or we, naively forget that. We uncritically tend to give to the law a pristine and majestic status it does not have — however fundamentally invaluable and indispensable it is.

In my view, part of our human struggle is to press for law — both in adoption and application — to approximate justice more and more closely. That struggle involves an essentially religious component because, in the Judeo-Christian tradition, the call to do justice is one of God's primary summons to us. Therefore, the vision of justice is understood as of transcendent origin and in constant judgment of all more parochial concepts. That is why religion is inevitably, though not infallibly, involved in politics. That is one apologia for the church declaring Public Sanctuary.

On two other occasions, my speaking for Public Sanctuary took me to the nation's capital. The first time was with Joel and Gabriela and Lucy, along with a group from our Public Sanctuary Task Force. The occasion was a briefing, arranged by Congressman Bob Edgar, at which the refugees and I and Ted Walkenhorst were to address a group of congresspersons and staff personnel. We traveled in a borrowed van which I drove, and just outside of Washington I was flagged for speeding. When Joel noticed the flashing lights of the police car, he was very frightened, immediately assuming that the police were after him and Gabriela. While I stood outside talking to the police officer (who had the universal knack for making traffic violators feel like convicted felons), the other members of the Task Force stayed inside the van trying to calm Joel by explaining what was happening.

By the time I'd received my ticket and we had resumed our journey, they had succeeded in getting Joel to join them in laughing at me. As for me, I simply felt embarrassed and, curiously, lonely. If there is a parable in it, it is that part of the power of the law is to make one feel isolated from others simply by being accused of breaking it. That isolation is experienced as others dissociate themselves from you with a certain relief, if not delight, because someone other than them has been caught for a potentially punishable transgression. I remember John Calvin contending in the *Institutes of the Christian Religion* that the joy of the saved in heaven is enhanced by the torments of the damned in hell. Quite apart from arguing the virtue of such a position, I suppose that the relief or delight of not being the accused one helps explain why so many church people shun Public Sanctuary simply because the government accuses us of breaking the law.

The briefing in Washington went well, though only one or two members of congress other than Bob Edgar were present. However, there were several dozen congressional staff members present, along with quite a few local and national media people. The session was held in a hearing room of the Rayburn House Office Building, and the sense of history — as well as the trappings of power — were evident not only in the surroundings, but in the continuous procession of limousines pulling up outside to discharge or pick up various dignitaries. I suspect we were quite an unimpressive and inconsequential little group in that situation to people whose daily fare consists of the wheelers and dealers of power and influence.

Still, after Bob Edgar made a strong and gracious statement of support for the refugees — and for the work of our church in metropolitan Philadelphia — Joel and Gabriela, intense eyes peering over the top of bandannas, made statements that were eloquent in their direct, guileless, deeply personal testimony. It was a very difficult task for them, speaking in the center of the government which had arrested them and wanted them deported. They were courageous and effective. I looked around that paneled, high-ceilinged, chandelier-lighted room with its judicial atmosphere and wondered if, of all the millions of words which had been spoken in that place, any were actually more powerful or potentially consequential to the direction of our country than those spoken by this humble, untitled, unmonied man and woman from Guatemala. Would their words have any effect on the policies of our nation or on the votes of congresspersons whose staffs were there? I suppose there is no way of assessing, except that, as they left that room at the end of the briefing, the persons in attendance did look more thoughtful and less preoccupied than when they'd rushed in. Probably it was only momentary. But who knows when some fragment, some impression, some bit of what they had heard and seen might, at some moment in the night, or in the deliberations around some legislation, tip the scales in a different direction, tip them toward justice. If that happened, it was all we could ask for, and it would be enough.

As we walked back to our van, past those great buildings in which the business of government is carried on by countless finite human beings, I kept wondering what *did* make the difference in their decisions. Indeed, I often wonder as I preach how thin webs of feelings and impressions get woven into our subconsciousness and then suddenly get jiggled into our awareness again when just a sliver of some other perception or experience unsuspectingly wanders into them. I know about theories of perception and association, but of all the *possible* perceptions and associations, why do only *certain* scenes and strands become part of our psychic or spiritual or political webs? How does that happen with me? It is a mystery, finally, a mystery in God's keeping. So, however it happens with others, all I can do — all any of us can do — is to keep telling our bit of the truth by whatever means lies at hand and to keep hoping, trusting it does make some difference, somehow. I guess all I can do, personally, is to keep wrestling with the Stranger and hoping for, even demanding, a blessing. Maybe half the trick is to *recognize* a blessing when it's given. So I slog on, trying to keep half an eye open to perform that half a trick.

The others in the Task Force drove the van back to Philadelphia with Joel and Gabriela and Lucy. I stayed overnight in Washington with friends so I could demonstrate the next day in front of the South African Embassy with Bishop F. Herbert Skeete and members of the Eastern Pennsylvania Conference of the United Methodist Church. The congressional briefing had not been planned to coincide with the demonstration. However, that by chance or providence the two events came on two successive days did emphasize to me that the situations in South Africa and in Central America are connected, and that the knot of the connection is tied in Washington because of this nation's critical involvement — and its potential for remedial action

— in both circumstances of human oppression.

The demonstration went as planned, as we had been briefed it would. As we went through it, I couldn't help recalling the Civil Rights demonstrations of the sixties and how different this one was. This time the police were exceptionally polite, even though they must have been weary. They had been going through this ritual day after day as group after group had demonstrated in front of the embassy, had refused to move on when asked, and so had been arrested and taken to the police station and booked. So it happened with about thirty of us. We were handcuffed with a plastic device, loaded into police vans and taken away. All very civilized!

I kept recalling my fear during the Civil Rights demonstrations and arrests, and I kept thinking that, by comparison, this was boring — except that they ran out of vans and three of us were transported in a squad car which, we were told, was the very one in which Stevie Wonder had been driven to the station during the demonstration the day before. Now that, I thought, must be worth something. Maybe I could charge Stevie Wonder fans at home for the opportunity to touch or kiss me — but where? Well, a chuckle, even a private one, is half a blessing, isn't it?

In any case, by about ten o'clock that night, the police had finished the paper work and fingerprinting on all of us, and we climbed on the bus for Philadelphia. It was about one-thirty Saturday morning when we got back to the conference office parking lot and piled in our cars to head home. And I still had a sermon to write! Slog, slog! But then, out of the shadows along the highway came the realization that in the experiences of the past two days were treasures to talk about from the perspective of faith. Another half a blessing, at least!

The other speaking engagement in Washington came about suddenly and unexpectedly. My good friend, Rev. Craig Biddle III, National Director of IMPACT, called and asked me to speak briefly on Public Sanctuary to a meeting of about six hundred IMPACT delegates from around the country who would be convening less than a week later. IMPACT is an ecumenical legislative information network which monitors congressional legislation around issues of the arms race, economic justice, and human rights. The opening in their agenda came when Congressman Joe Moakley (D., Mass.) was unable to

keep his engagement to address the meeting. He had been scheduled to speak with Senator Dennis DeConcini (D., Ariz.) on the bill
they were jointly sponsoring to give "extended voluntary departure"
status to refugees from El Salvador — which means simply that refugees from El Salvador could stay in the United States until it is determined by an objective study that it would be safe for them to return.

I took an early commuter flight to Washington, a cab to the Rayburn House Office Building (which felt like an old friend this time) and
found my way to the enormous room in which the meetings were
being held. Congressman Les AuCoin (D., Oreg.) was speaking on
arms control when I arrived, but I managed to spot Craig's wife Neil. It
was good to see her again. Finally, after a short intermission and a bit
late, the section of the agenda in which I was participating began.
While I waited, I chatted with Senator DeConcini. I asked him why he
had not included Guatemalans under the provisions of the
DeConcini-Moakley Bill. He said he thought that support for the bill,
which was tenuous, would not sustain inclusion of refugees from Guatemala. I pressed and asked him why, and got the expected answer:
the government of Guatemala is more stable and has long standing
ties with our government, and the civil war there is more under control. I glibly responded, "You mean tyranny entrenched is less dubi-
ous than tyranny embattled?"

He smiled and said, "I have to deal with political realities." Ah,
yes, don't we all? Maybe the senator is right — that it is better to get
extended voluntary departure status for El Salvadorans without Guatemalans than to include Guatemalans and get extended voluntary
departure status for no one. Still, it feels like a Sophie's choice: which
of your children do you choose to have killed in order to save the
other? It must be tough to be a politician for whom the guideline is
morality by winning.

By the time it was my turn to speak, the allotted time had shrunk
from the original thirty minutes — which was to include questions
from delegates — to ten minutes, period. I made my statement, felt
depressed about it, said good-by to Craig and Neil, and made my way
out of the room, answering the questions of a few people as I left. I
was about to go when a familiar face pressed forward and walked
alongside me. He was the brother of a woman in our church, and he

began to tell me of the crisis his sister was facing regarding an im-
pending divorce and the unsettling circumstances involved. I already
knew most of the information, but I was struck with the obvious pain
the brother was experiencing in this family turmoil, and how urgent
was his concern that I do something for his sister and her children. I
promised I'd call his sister as soon as possible.

As I walked from the terminal across the tarmac to the commuter
plane, another friend — a member of our church who was a pilot for
the commuter airline — intercepted me. He'd finished his flight duty,
and we were flying back to Philadelphia on the same plane. I'd officiated at his wedding to a young divorcee several months earlier. His
personal opinions on most issues — including the arms race and how
the Iranian hostage crisis should have been handled — differed
sharply from mine, and though we had talked about those differences, he hadn't come to church for quite a while. However, we liked
each other and talked together on the flight. He listened attentively
to what I said about Public Sanctuary, but was much more concerned
about telling me what was happening in the neighborhood school
where his son was one of the few white children in a predominantly
black public school. His insistence was that the church should be
doing more about the problems of public education rather than dealing with refugees from another country. My response that they are all
connected didn't seem persuasive to him.

Still, we gave each other a hug when we said good-by at the airport. As I walked through the terminal toward the parking garage, I
remembered hearing him talk about his admiration for the "macho"
attitude of his fellow pilots — an admiration which often put him in
conflict with his feminist wife and with what he called the "progres-
sive religion" at the church. One of the things he liked about me was
that I was an old "jock" and at least could understand his struggles. I
was surprised — and glad — that he'd dared to give me a farewell hug
with his captain's uniform on, at the arrival gate of his own airline
company. Slog, slog... half a blessing... maybe more.

Later, Craig Biddle sent me a note expressing gratitude for what
I'd said at the IMPACT meeting and telling me that many delegates
had voiced support. Who knows? I remember seeing a plaque in St.
Paul's Cathedral in London showing a man broadcasting seed. The

inscription read, "Never fear to sow because of the birds." Richard Niebuhr, the professor at Yale Divinity School who most deeply influenced me and was a theological giant for a generation of students, put the issue in another, more theological way:

> "Responsibility affirms: 'God is acting in all actions upon you. So respond to all actions upon you as to respond to his action.' Our action in our lostness, however, is the action of distrust...Yet such distrust is occasionally converted into trust."[8]

I remember going into Dr. Niebuhr's office the first time. He looked at me with those piercing, somehow sad eyes overhung with burning bush eyebrows, and almost forgot my name, let alone why I'd come to see him. "God is acting in all actions upon you..." *All* actions. Who can stand it? It'd be like a permanent drunk.

What would it be like to trust *all* the time? Yea, what would it mean to trust *some* of the time, just once in a while, just to have "distrust...occasionally converted into trust"? Dumb question! It means hugs in airport lobbies, and chuckles in police cars, and jokes about a criminal van driver, and refugees putting thoughtfulness on cynical D.C. faces, and the tending work getting done so people can live. It means, I guess, slog, slog, slog and...lookout there's God in the shadows, in the snap of twigs and handcuffs, in the shift of light in someone's eyes on a late night bus, in the courage of a family struggling with crisis, in kids trusting parents and authorities to take care of them as they should — and parents trying as best they can.

"God is acting in all actions upon you. So respond to all actions upon you as to respond to God." *All*? My God, I can't collect all the stones on the beach! So, gather a few, scatter some seed, and trust once in a while. Once in a while...Slog, half a blessing; slog, half a blessing; slog, half a blessing. It's enough. Thank God, it's enough. More than enough. Enjoy the geese and be glad. You don't have to fly.

[8]From page 126 of THE RESPONSIBLE SELF by H. Richard Niebuhr. Copyright 1963 by Florence M. Niebuhr. Reprinted by permission of Harper & Row, Publishers, Inc.

Anger

"Never ask the sword what the wound feels." Those words became the insistent refrain in my mind, their rhythm accompanying the hum of the tires on the pavement as we rode from the airport into the city of San Salvador on the afternoon of Easter Monday, April 8, 1985. Never had I felt more part of the sword than in those moments and in the days that followed. We were sitting behind bulletproof glass in a United States Embassy van, while in the front seat were two Salvadoran soldiers — one driving, the other discreetly holding an automatic weapon pointed toward the floor. Beyond those windows was the wound: utter, raw, undisguised poverty and human misery. Neither the statistics and analyses I'd studied, nor my own experience during the Depression had inoculated me against the shock of it. I wanted to look away, but could only stare with something of the same kind of fascination as a person gawking at accident victims. I wanted to scream, or cry, or shout obscenities, but could only sit silently, as if somehow silence would blur the ugly reality of the scene.

Certainly part of my shock was of my own naivete. What had I expected? How had I thought it would be? Whatever my expectation, the reality was as if the pictures of bloated-bellied kids and dull-eyed adults crowded around filthy huts had suddenly come to life...or death. Jammed on the sides of ravines, perched perilously on small bluffs, squatting behind scrubby brush were ramshackle, one room, windowless, gapping-doored shacks knocked together from pieces of packing boxes, scrap wood, jagged-edged corrugated metal, whatever the inhabitants had managed to scavenge. Those shacks would make our worst slums seem relatively attractive. I'd read somewhere these urban conglomerates of humanity were known as "mother's hearts," because they, too, have room for everyone. Yet, that many people, in those conditions, surely would break any mother's heart, including God's.

Along the road were people moving slowly, carrying things on their backs and heads. Occasionally, there were emaciated looking cows standing or moving on the shoulders of the highway — sometimes even across it — forcing traffic to wait or swerve. I looked for children. They were frequently gathered in small clumps around the doors of the shacks, but seldom engaged in animated play. Yet El Salvador, according to the media in the United States, was supposed to be improving politically, economically, socially. Okay, it was the first impression of a middle class gringo on his first exposure to the Third World. Okay, the highway from the Philadelphia airport into the city isn't exactly scenic either, and not one on which to reach any significant conclusions. And yet...and yet...

The bulletproof glass between us and what we were seeing was thick. One theory has it that pornography is a matter of distance, which dehumanizes the relationship between the viewer and the viewed. What I was seeing did seem pornographic to me, and it was distance I was sensing between me and those people in those obscene shacks. Of course, there are a thousand kinds of distance other than spatial, and a thousand ways to establish that distance. There can be pornographic distance between husbands and wives, just as there is between customers and images on the screen of X-rated movies. Obviously, it is difficult to be a Good Samaritan if you don't walk the Jericho Road where the beaten person lies abandoned. Yet, the hard truth is you can walk that road and still maintain the distance between you and the beaten person by passing on the other side, one way or another, and all the reasons for that detour are simply definitions of distance.

And passing by was just what I was doing, not only literally, but emotionally because, at that very moment, I felt *thankful* that I did not have to live in that brutal, dehumanizing condition. In some quite terrifying way, I was glad to be part of the sword, grateful for the distance between myself and those victims of poverty and oppression, and not very eager to reduce that distance by much more than could be accomplished by some readily manageable act of charity. That awareness was terrifying, because with it I had to confront my spiritual poverty — part of which is the hypocrisy which permits me to be a comfortable advocate of morally challenging causes, a tongue-clucking tourist of suffering.

Hard upon that awareness came a deep sense of guilt which I do not think was, or is, pathological, but quite realistic. The ultimate fact is that I no more deserved to be born into my privileged condition than these people deserved to be born into their oppressed one. And yet I assumed, if unconsciously, that somehow I *did* deserve my advantage, at least to the extent that I was willing to marshal several arguments to "justify" not giving it up.

Of course, I knew that if I gave everything I had to help relieve this poverty and went to live among these people as a servant, it would not change their condition much, if at all. It would change mine, of course, but how? To act just to assuage guilt, or achieve sanctity, surely would be only a subtle, insidious form of spiritual self-seeking. Even as would deliberately sitting in the lowest place at a banquet, knowing that such assumed deference supposedly would get you the reward of being called up to sit at a higher place (to apply Jesus' parable[1]). Once again I felt the vice of my existential conflict, the most painful part of which was my feeling of terror. I did not know what to

[1]Luke 14:10-11

do about that terror except to acknowledge it, and to sense that somehow it might be the thread of my humanity linking me to these oppressed people. I shuddered and gulped. O Christ, we hadn't been in El Salvador for much more than two hours or even arrived at our hotel yet! The Stranger obviously knows no national boundaries. It was going to be a hard trip, "a hard day's night," as the old Beatles song has it.

"Never ask the sword what the wound feels." Those words were a paraphrase of one of the quotes I'd passed on to Bill Coffin as we had flown into Tucson back in January. Now, three months later, he was my roommate in the hotel in San Salvador as a part of the fact-finding delegation to Central America headed by Congressmen Bob Edgar and Ted Weiss. The delegation was scheduled to visit El Salvador and Nicaragua, and negotiations were underway at the time of our departure for a few of us to visit Guatemala as well. No funds for the trip had been provided by the government, and each participant had paid some or all of their costs (though a few of us were heavily subsidized by money solicited from private sources). However, the leadership and presence of the congressmen in our group resulted in the delegation having contacts with high ranking persons and access to places that would have been unavailable to most visitors. The trip was arranged through the Nicaragua-Honduras Education Project which has offices in Washington, D.C., and very knowledgeable, capable tour guides in the countries of Central America. Our project director was a tough-minded, delightful woman, Jody Williams.

Other people on the trip were my friend and member of our church, Robert Musil, the Director of the Sane Education Fund; Phillip Berryman, author and lecturer who had lived and worked in Guatemala for many years and whose excellent book, *What's Wrong in Central America*, was on our required reading list in preparation for the trip; Ione Vargus, Dean of Temple University — School of Social Administration; Mary Poppit, a nun who had taken a sabbatical from her work to serve as a volunteer on Bob Edgar's staff; Elizabeth Werthan, on the staff at Children's Heart Hospital in Philadelphia and trained in health care delivery systems; Joseph Hoeffel, a law student and a young, former Pennsylvania State Legislator who is still politically active; William DeWeese, former U.S. Marine and present Pennsylvania State Legislator, with a background in military issues; Sandy Grady, Washington correspondent for the Philadelphia Daily News, a fine reporter who several years earlier had shifted assignments from the sports beat to political reporting without losing the lively style and sharp sense of a sports journalist; William Sloane Coffin, Senior Minister of Riverside Church in New York City and one of the foremost Protestant clergypersons in the United States; and I.

At an earlier briefing, Bob Edgar had indicated the three purposes he had in mind for the trip:

1) to examine *the role of the church* in what was happening in Central America, especially to evaluate what portion of that ferment might be traceable to the increasingly activist theology and practice of the Christian church in contrast to the Marxist-Leninist ideology and infiltration usually exclusively "blamed" for it;

2) to look at the *justice issues in relation to the legal systems* of the countries, particularly as they related to political opposition;

3) to determine what, if any, peace processes were being explored in Central America as *options to the military solutions* being espoused and pursued by our government in alliance with, or opposition to, the governments of those countries.

Those purposes seemed accurate to me. Yet, in spite of their scope, they also seemed strangely inadequate, partly because the answers seemed reasonably apparent, if not completely documentable. One, yes, the church is responsible for some, if not much, of the ferment in Central America because, whatever its official and institutional position, wherever the Gospel is preached, heard, lived by even a few, there is ferment. And the easiest way to control and/or dismiss the church is to blame the ferment on Marxist-Leninist influences — even as the ferment caused by Jesus and the early church was labeled political subversion by the established powers.

Two, clearly the legal systems in Central American countries fall short of justice, particularly regarding political opposition. Else why

death squads, "disappeared" people, critical reports from international human rights agencies such as Americas Watch, and the flow of
refugees such as Joel and Gabriela.

Three, obviously, whatever peace processes are proposed (for
example, by the Contadora nations[2] in regard to Nicaragua), they are
rejected in favor of whichever power diplomacy or military solution
has made the area "secure" — i.e., the U.S-backed government de-
feating the rebels in El Salvador, the U.S-backed rebels overthrowing
the government in Nicaragua, and the U.S.-backed government de-
feating the rebels in Guatemala.

The point is that these "answers" are fundamentally interpretations based on information I've read and heard, *just as are opposing interpretations based on information others have read or heard.* Facts, studies, data,
statistics simply do not lead to any indisputable conclusion. It is just
that the official positions espoused by our government seem to carry
more weight of "truth" than any other interpretations, even though
the government usually has a greater vested interest in those "truths"
which serve to support certain political ideologies and justify disproportionate allocations from the national budgets to the military.

In any case, I was not convinced I was in Central America to amass
socio-economic and political facts, important as these are. Indeed,
there was another reason why the stated purposes for this delegation
seemed inadequate to me: people don't go ":on scene" primarily to
get facts and figures, but to attempt to get the kind of *truth which eludes
data* — the kind of truth which most captivates me, and the search for
which most compels me. As I unpacked and reflected on the scenes
I'd experienced on the trip from the airport, I realized that, without
warning, I'd already begun to get a powerful "feel" for the situation.

Only two years earlier, I would have been hard pressed to locate
accurately on a map the several countries of Central America. Then, as
that region pushed its way into the news with its civil wars, the rape
and killing of nuns, the assassination of Archbishop Oscar Romero, I'd
begun to learn a little more about those countries, a learning rapidly

---

[2]Contadora Nations: Colombia, Mexico, Panama, Venezuela

accelerated as our church had begun to consider declaring Public Sanctuary. The learning became more intense and personal as I listened to the stories of Joel and Gabriela, and other refugees, but there still seemed to be something abstract about it — almost like hearing someone tell about a trip they'd taken to some country I knew little about.

But on the way in from the airport, all the statistics and reports had taken on flesh and feeling, become incarnate in my gut. The experience had been like a revelation and a reminder. It is just that kind of "feel" which constitutes the elusive truth which captivates and compels me. That "feel" also unfailingly disturbs me, too, by making me vulnerable to the criticism of those who insist on being "practical" and "realistic." But it also makes me vulnerable to a sense of the wondrously mysterious which runs through and beyond the human scene.

It is the "truth" of the story, of the illuminating metaphor, that shudders us when, rather than quoting unemployment or income figures, the ancient prophet poetically and dramatically states:

> "Thus says the Lord: 'For three transgressions of Israel, and for four, I will not revoke the punishment; because they sell the righteous for silver, and the needy for a pair of shoes...they ...trample the head of the poor into the dust of the earth, and turn aside the way of the afflicted.' "[3]

Or when the modern prophet, with similar poetry and drama says:

> "I have a dream that my four little children will one day live in a nation where they will not be judged by the color of their skin but by the content of their character."[4]

I believe that truth in the story, in the "feel," is why Jesus taught

[3] Amos 2:6-7a, RSV

[4] From I HAVE A DREAM by Martin Luther King, Jr. Copyright © 1963 by Martin Luther King, Jr. Used by permission of Joan Daves.

in parables which are open-ended; why the truth of Jacob is not so much in the carefully inventoried number of domestic animals he sent ahead to placate Esau, but rather is in the undercurrents of betrayal and courage, craftiness and mercy, hauntedness and healing roiling in the story of his wrestling with the Stranger in the fog and moonlight. So, perhaps unknowing at the outset, I was aware now that I'd come to Central America to look for some sort of revelation; to look for some story that would help make sense of all the information and statistics and history I'd accumulated over the last months and that would be rushing in torrents at us in these forthcoming days.

But I was aware, too, that I was searching for something more on this trip — some impression or "feel" that might also make sense of me, of my place in this human struggle, of my place in Public Sanctuary, yes, of my place in the world and in the church, as well. I wanted somehow to wrest a blessing for myself through this, but I wasn't at all sure what it was, what it would be. . .another "name" perhaps?

Yet, clear and convinced as I am about my way of seeing and learning — which is more intuitive than analytic — I am also apologetic about it, which makes it hard for me and for others who resent my shuffling about it. The issue is not just a psychological one, but is also methodological. Though the story, the metaphor, is more enduring and essential to me, it is also more elusive to find, to express, to grasp. Facts, statistics, information are available to research and corroboration, making them more comfortable to deal with. Supposedly, their results are conclusive. . .if properly gathered, weighed, interpreted — an if often and conveniently overlooked. Stories seem to leave you with a question — "What does it mean?" —and a decision — "In what direction will you move in response to it?" I wondered what stories would tell themselves to me on this trip, and whether I would be perceptive enough to hear them. I looked across the room at Bill Coffin, my old friend, and thought of all the battles he'd led, all the prophetic thundering he'd done in his own incomparable way. I was envious, yet I loved the man, and once again felt a surge of gratitude for him. Now, if only I could be all right about my way of "thundering" and realize that no one had, or had to have, all the truth. I smiled to myself and finished unpacking.

El Salvador

...Off to the left, outside our hotel window, was a small mountain shaped exactly like a camel's hump, scarred with brown gullies, sprinkled with sparse foliage. Nestled around the base were sections of San Salvador, but there were no buildings on its slopes. Barely visible on the crest was a fortress-looking building and some antennae. It was a major government communications installation, and we had heard that a few days before our arrival, guerrilla forces had successfully attacked and destroyed a major portion of the installation, though it was down-played in the media.

Official reports in the United States and El Salvador had the guerrilla forces shrinking in numbers, effectiveness and support among the people. The significance of the attack was that, contrary to those official reports, the guerrilla forces had demonstrated that they *did* have sufficient numbers, sophistication of planning, communications and logistics, and support of local inhabitants to execute a major attack.

Response to the attack also highlighted a new dimension in the war. The Duarte government had recently acquired from the United States at least two heavily-armed military planes with body heat sensors and infra-red devices which enabled gunners to spot anything moving in the dark. Those planes have the fire power to spray bullets every square foot over the area of a football field in one minute. They were reported to be a major new weapon in the government's war against the guerrillas, and one was called into action immediately after the attack.

I didn't hear the number of casualties suffered by the guerrillas in that attack, but again and again during our talks in El Salvador, I learned of the extensive use of those planes in areas controlled by the guerrillas — use which inevitably involved civilian populations as a form of intimidation against assisting the guerrillas. Of course, the awful danger — if not ugly reality — is that such violence is visited upon human beings who actually have nothing to do with either the guerrillas or the army, who want only to take care of themselves and their families, but who become caught between opposing forces ...as people have from the beginning of human warfare.

The other, probably grimmer, truth is that the government in power — quite apart from any concerns for human rights or justice — can use this kind of violence against any and all political opposition by identifying that opposition as guerrillas and/or Marxists. I wondered how many "guerrillas" were among those people jammed into the inferno of the urban slums I had seen, slums which might make even Dante stammer. How many of them could be given food, or put to work in technical assistance programs, or helped medically or with housing, with the money *one* of those planes cost? I felt anger at my government for its blindness, for its strangelove assumption that somehow weapons of war can solve problems of hunger, educate kids and give them decent homes, and cure disease. I agree with whoever suggested that tyranny begins with a lack of imagination — begins and is supported by a lack of imagination!

I thought about the mountains of Guatemala in which Joel and Gabriela had hidden and were hunted as subversives as they fled from their country. Their faith as Christians is strong and unswerving. It was their faith, not a political ideology, which had propelled them — especially Joel — to seek justice, a fair, living wage for themselves and others; to turn the oppressive government of Guatemala toward more humane policies. But Joel's activism, generated by his faith, constituted "subversion" and justified killing, silencing them. How did it feel for them — and for these guerrillas in El Salvador — to believe in something so deeply as to risk their lives for it? How did it feel for them to be running, crawling, falling down that mountain while the plane screamed over them like a falcon over rabbits? What did the fire power of those planes, and all the rhetoric about Marxism, have to do with those festering sores of humanity, those urban slums I'd seen? Once again I recalled the terribly dangerous, if not deadly, simplistic, arrogantly rigid ideological stance of the Reagan Administration as expounded by Jeane Kirkpatrick who was the United States Ambassador to the United Nations when she said, "Marxism is the enemy, and any action taken to defeat it is moral."[5] *Any* action? Even the denial of our own identity, our own principles? If so, what difference does it really make who wins what?

I remembered seeing a man in the Miami airport as we walked through to catch our plane for El Salvador. He was wearing a yellow T-shirt with the slogan, "The end of the world is coming soon for all except saved Christians." Who was it said evil is banal? Put that T-shirt slogan alongside Joel's commitment to justice because of his faith, and its banality is obvious. Yet, that same simplistic sloganeering seems to shape our government's policies. Can't we come up with anything more compelling than anti-Marxist-Leninist rhetoric to determine what we are doing in the world? Is that all we have to shout from the mountain top, or keep others from shouting? Surely the old psalmist meant something more profound when he said, "I lift up my eyes to the hills. From whence does my help come? My help comes from the Lord, who made heaven and earth."[6] Whatever the psalmist meant, the struggle is for me to decide what the psalmist' summons means to me. I watched the El Salvadoran mountain outside the hotel window slip into the shadows of night. At a briefing after dinner, Bill Coffin summed it up by saying, "Speaking truth to power isn't easy, because power always replies like the character in a Ring Lardner story: 'Shut up,' he explained."

=====

...By six o'clock the next morning the sky was blue, and life moved in the streets below. I'd been up for an hour, shaved, showered, read, watched, waited. I wanted to go to the chapel where Archbishop Oscar Romero had been killed. I'd been told it was close by, a

[5]See Kirkpatrick reference on page 88.

[6]Psalm 121:1-2, RSV

small chapel on the grounds of a hospital near where he'd lived and into which he'd welcomed the poor. Finally, Bill stirred. I explained my plan, to which he agreed — which was good, since he spoke Spanish and I didn't. Already I'd experienced what a serious handicap my lack of Spanish was. The handicap got worse.

Twenty minutes later we were in a cab. The driver smiled when Bill told him our destination. Archbishop Romero is still a powerful presence in El Salvador. His picture is everywhere. The cab groaned up a hill, through the narrow, winding streets until shortly it ran along the white walls which signaled an institution and pulled through the narrow gate onto the hospital grounds. Just ahead was a small, modern chapel — sharp pitched roof, glass panels in the front all the way to the peak, tropical plants around the low sides of the building. The glass mirrored the rising sun. It was quiet, serene.

Inside...a polished marble floor, contemporary lighting, wooden pews in the main chapel and the small transepts, three steps up to the altar behind which was a huge crucifix. Candles were lit, flowers crowded the altar area. I found it hard to believe that a priest had been murdered in this place —murdered while he was saying Mass; murdered (no one seems to contest) by a right wing death squad still not brought to justice; murdered because he had increasingly identified with the cause of poor people; murdered because he'd had the audacity, on national radio, to implore, beg, command the killing to stop. On his last day he told the El Salvadoran soldiers that they shouldn't obey orders to kill, that there was no human command higher than God's command. I felt a strong urge to touch the place where he'd fallen (though it wasn't marked); to stand where he'd stood; to imagine seeing the gunmen burst in, watching the gun barrels spit fire, and falling into oblivion, into the arms of God. Maybe there is no better place to die than in front of the altar with the bread and wine on your lips — or no worse place. I stood for a long time, staring at the crucifix, the altar.

Then I realized there was a loudspeaker, and a voice was speaking steadily. I asked Bill, and he said it was a news broadcast. There were several nuns in white habits saying the rosary. It seemed altogether fitting for the prayers to be linked to the news of the day. We knelt and said a prayer. As we left, I actually backed down the center aisle, looking at the altar, the dominant statue of Christ on the cross with his almost serene expression — or was it patient? It was as if I were watching for something to move. Why weren't the stones crying out at the terrible offense that had been committed here? Why wasn't the altar tipped over and broken in testimony, the blood still running down the steps? Yea, why weren't voices being lifted around the world — in Rome, in Washington — demanding the killing to stop, espousing the cause of the poor? Why? "Marxism is the enemy, and any action taken to defeat it is moral." Any action? Any action we take *and* any action taken by those we support, fund, and encourage? Is "Marxist" really the label for anyone who is an advocate of the poor, an adversary of killing?

At the door of the chapel I remembered the closing words of Robert Bolt's great historical play, A *Man For All Seasons*, in which another cleric of conscience is killed for opposing the King. The drums roll for the beheading scene and then suddenly stop. The Common Man says to the audience:

> "I'm breathing. . . Are you breathing too? It's nice isn't it? It isn't difficult to keep alive, friends — just don't *make* trouble — or if you must make trouble, make the sort of trouble that's expected. Well, I don't need to tell you that. Good night. If we should bump into one another, recognize me."[7]

Bill and I walked back down the hill to the hotel. It was a lovely morning. I breathed heavily all the way, with tears in my eyes. Yet, strangely enough, I did keep recognizing something in the walk, in the feel of it. We were going through a wealthier section of the city, and the homes were surrounded by high security walls. Sometimes the chins of the red blossoms on flowering trees in the courtyards of the

[7]From page 94 of A MAN FOR ALL SEASONS by Robert Bolt. Copyright © 1960, 1962 by Robert Bolt. Reprinted by permission of Random House, Inc.

homes were cupped in the jagged edges of broken glass cemented atop the walls to make them more secure. My breath kept catching in my throat. Maybe it's harder to stay alive, really alive, than any of us think. What trouble did I have to make in order to be free myself? What trouble has to be made before the people of the world are free? "Never ask the sword..."

———

...Dust was the difference. We stood on the steps of the San Salvador Cathedral on one of the busiest streets of the city. Buses groaned to stops for people to climb off and on, then snarled their way back into the morning rush hour traffic. The traffic was lighter, the vehicles older and more used looking (including many battered trucks carrying people in the back), but still the scene was similar to other cities. Across the street was a park — a fountain, benches such as might be found anywhere. And though the people rushing through it and on down the sidewalks were more plainly dressed, they were like most people in the world on their way to work or market.

At the corner were vendors of foods and handcrafts such as crowded the streets in sections of New York or Philadelphia, though these goods were visibly poorer and flies swarmed around the unprotected food. On the buildings were billboards with Latin counterparts to the U.S. blondes selling the same basic jeans, soft drinks, cigarettes. Squatting on the steps of the cathedral was a beggar, hat over his eyes, wrapped in a blanket, barefoot, skin an eruption of festering sores, his eyes — when he lifted his head to acknowledge the clink of my coin in his cup — blind from the invasion of some disease that made me look away. Still, I was familiar with beggars and street people. I sensed the difference was the dust.

As I thought about the difference inside the cathedral, it slowly began to make sense. The cathedral itself was starkly plain...unfinished, or so it appeared. The pews were simple, uncarved wood as might be found in a village church. The walls were poured, rough concrete, and the wall behind the altar was finished in rectangles of pressed wood of some sort. To the right of the high altar was a large poster of the head of Oscar Romero — a poster, not a portrait. Spotted around the walls were fluorescent lights, their long bulbs casually, almost embarrassingly exposed, a bit like the spindly legs of weary old women with their stockings rolled down around their ankles. In a center front section was a group, apparently catechumens, getting instruction from a young lay teacher. Sound reverberated as it would in an empty warehouse. Along the sides were smaller altars, some of the statues adorned with what appeared to be real hair. But that effort to make them more life-like seemed, instead, to make them more pathetic. In one stubby but wide transept was a chapel dedicated to Romero, and over a flower-laden altar was a more formal picture of him.

I sat quietly watching, listening, smelling the place, wondering about the people who came, quickly knelt, prayed, left. . .and pondering why dust seemed to be the difference between this city, this people, and what I knew of my city and my people. I knew it was the dry season in El Salvador, and the rain was due to begin in two or three weeks. But the dust felt as if it had to do with more than dryness alone. Dust seemed out of place in my experience of a city. Dirt, smoke, grime, exhaust fumes, litter, yes, but somehow not dust, not in the center of the city. I grew up in the Dust Bowl with small town, stunted-crop, foreclosed-farm, Depression-racked poverty. Dust is of dirt streets, brown fields, scrawny chickens, hard times. It is of the black peoples' shanties out at the edge of the city where the pavement and the plumbing stops even now in some Southern cities in the United States. Dust settles on things and feels like gnarled-fingered, squint-eyed, bone-wearied, wispy-haired despair. The prophet Amos is right — where else would the head of the poor be trampled but into dust?[8] There is a kind of dust that rain does not wash away. That was the dust I was aware of on the streets of San Salvador.

[8]Amos 2:6-7a, RSV

Yet, as I sat there, it occurred to me that dust also whispers of something primitive — primitive not just in the sense of unmodern, but also in the sense of elemental. Maybe that was it. There was something unpretentious about the streets, about the cathedral, about a plain poster stuck on the front wall; about the plainly dressed people; about the piety slowly prompting lips of those kneeling here and there around me to visibly form the words of their silent prayers; about the people riding exposed in the early morning down the streets of the city in the back of open trucks — men and women holding each other, nursing babies, cuddling sleepy children; some people laughing, some talking, scratching, yawning, eating, thinking, whatever, all in full view. Partly, the elemental sense of it had to do with survival, but partly with simple, human things — birth, life, love, sex, families, death — all unhidden and, therefore, somehow unashamed, like rough concrete walls, like a life lived well enough that it needed no gilding and, in fact, honored a poster.

I was being sentimental, I supposed, but then maybe dust isn't a bad reminder not just of cultural and national differences, but of common things, the things that unite us — such as mortality and all the wonder and responsibility and sad, hopeful truth of it — as well as of Whose Word it is that stands forever. Dust and a poor cathedral in San Salvador — or a cathedral anywhere, for that matter — do go together. After all, dust really does settle everywhere. It's just more apparent some places. I got up to go, thinking maybe this trip would help me keep an eye out for dust where it isn't so apparent. Actually, that's something of what Public Sanctuary is about, though it hadn't occurred to me just that way before.

━━━━━━━

...The United States Embassy in San Salvador seemed like a military bunker. It was fringed by concrete pillars set closely together to defend against vehicles intent on penetrating its security. Inside the outer concrete ring were chain fences topped with barbed wire and linked by electronic surveillance equipment which also controlled the heavy gate through which we entered in our chauffeured vans. United States military personnel, heavily armed, were all around, along with security people from El Salvador.

Inside the embassy, security was just as stringent. We were issued passes through a small window in a thick glass enclosure and escorted through two doors heavily reinforced with prison-like bars, operated by more electronic devices. We were taken down a flight of stairs, through the corridors of embassy offices and shown into a large, paneled briefing room which was similar to a small theater in which the floor sloped gently down to a small stage. We were told Ambassador Pickering would be with us momentarily. He was.

Thomas Pickering is an impressive professional, tall, well-groomed, articulate, smooth, a career diplomat — which meant, though he would deny it, that he was adept at justifying the foreign policy of whatever administration was in power, however divergent it might be from what preceded or followed. If Thomas Pickering sold used cars, they would be Cadillacs. If you asked me if I would buy a used car from him, I'd say that I couldn't afford a Cadillac — which would make me something of a diplomat and give you something to read between the lines.

Pickering began with a statement informing us that Jose Napoleon Duarte — who had just received a boost from the unexpected election of his own Christian Democrat party — was near completion of a democratic revolution; that Duarte had the support of the military which, in turn, had the guerrillas on the run with the aid of U.S. military hardware such as the AC-47 attack planes; that violence and human rights violations were decreasing; and that most atrocities were perpetrated by the leftist guerrillas. As he spoke, there was little doubt that, in addition to whatever professional discretion he had to exercise, he was entirely comfortable with the Reagan Administration's policies in El Salvador and in Central America. Good news from a bunker...

When he asked for questions, Congressman Bob Edgar inquired whether Pickering thought the war could be won militarily. Pickering said, "No," but stated that the objective was to gain military control over eighty to ninety percent of the country, make it secure, and then develop dialogue. Edgar asked about the counter-insurgency programs of the government, and Pickering spoke of resettlement zones in which civilian populations were either moved or enlisted against the guerrillas, thus depriving guerrillas of the support they needed to operate.

Congressman Weiss reported cases where military action had destroyed entire villages, because it was difficult to distinguish between guerrillas and civilian populations. Pickering simply denied the information. Weiss said he also had information that food and aid were not sent to civilians in areas in which guerrillas operated, so that both resettlement zones and distribution of aid were coordinated to intimidate peasants through pacification programs. Pickering sidestepped the issue by explaining that only the El Salvadoran government aid was cut off, but that international relief agencies did continue to send in aid. Apparently that made the action of the United States supporting the policies of the government of El Salvador seem less inhumane, in Pickering's view. If children starve or people go hungry, because the government of El Salvador withholds food — with United States government approval — *and* because international relief agencies can't give enough food to those people, then the United States is not responsible. *Alice in Wonderland*!

The discussion went on, dealing with the issue of Marxist influences in the country (slight, said the Ambassador, except among the intellectuals) as well as the impact of the church (strong, he said, with a conservative hierarchy in the Roman Catholic Church, a growing Evangelical movement with little political interest, a moderate Archbishop replacing Romero). The answers all seemed very civilized, carefully memorized and slickly marketed. I finally asked how the embassy got its information...a dumb question because I knew the answer they'd give, since the real answer supposedly would raise security issues. Pickering said that embassy people traveled extensively and had contacts in the country. The real issue is that it doesn't matter much *what* information gets sent to Washington by these embassies (at least with an ideologically dogmatic Administration), because information doesn't shape policy, policy shapes information.

The real job of the embassy staff is make the data support the policy. As I listened, I got angrier. From my reading, talking with non-government experts, and listening to refugees, I knew our government was dissembling and distorting to justify its actions. Not only couldn't I afford to buy a Cadillac from Ambassador Pickering, if he sold them, but I didn't believe that our nation — or the Central American nations — could afford to buy our policies there.

Finally, Bill Coffin raised his hand and proceeded to say something like, "Look, we're really sending military weapons, helicopters, advisers, and aid to protect U.S. economic interests in this country, and you try to justify it all with a lot of talk about the danger of Marxism, though we could wipe out any military threat in Central America with a few air raids from Texas. Isn't the real truth that you and the Administration just don't give a fuck about these people, or about justice, or about peaceful dialogue with the guerrillas?" Bill had fired a shot heard round the briefing room.

I'll admit, I was a little shocked. This wasn't a locker room, and I was still naive enough to think you didn't use language like that with "important" people, with dignitaries. Say "damn," maybe, since it's a polite, socially acceptable expletive, but not "the old F word," as one of my squeamish friends calls it. I'd been taught that it was a matter of respect, but I had overlooked, as Bill hadn't, that respect has to be earned, and that a title — especially assumed in disguise of morally questionable actions — does not automatically entitle anyone to respect.

Even so, my early Midwestern piety clutched at that word in those circumstances, and I expected Pickering, or maybe one of the congressmen, to deliver a stern lecture on language and morality. Nothing happened. I think I saw a small smile flicker over Weiss' lips, but I wouldn't swear to it. The only other reaction I noticed was a slight ripple in cool, composed Pickering's jaw muscle, followed by a lengthy denial footnoted with several instances of "caring" — a word the ambassador chose to score a charm point over "giving a fuck."

The point finally twisted its way home to me. I'd been subtly intimidated — as are too many people — by the trappings of power and prestige. I'd been taken off guard but, on reflection, became deeply ashamed of my initial reaction to the incident. It also made me recognize that probably most people are more offended by vulgar language than by vulgar actions, at least in polite, dignified company — even after release of the Watergate tapes. Even then, I wonder if many people weren't more distressed by Nixon's language than by his obstruction of justice. It's the issue of pornography again...and deciding what is pornographic.

What Bill did is what prophets always do: tell the emperor he doesn't have any clothes on. But maybe it turns out, after all, that even oblique references to anything with sexual overtones — even the nudity of the supposedly noble — are objectionable, or perhaps dangerously titillating. And we are embarrassed to have them called to our attention, because they might somehow expose us as well ...or something like that. Charming lies — and liars — seem to be more acceptable to us than rough-edged truths or tough-tongued truth tellers. Charm seduces and finally intimidates most of us, and that seems to be what piety has come to. Maybe we are — I am — among those of whom Isaiah so scathingly spoke:

"They are a rebellious people...who say to the seers, 'See not'; and to the prophets, 'Prophesy not to us what is right; speak to us smooth things, prophesy illusions...' "[9]

And to think that Isaiah, also, was in the diplomatic corp of the king.

I recalled, in *Brideshead Revisited*, when Anthony confronts Charles with the effect of his friend Sebastian's charm:

"Charm is the great English blight...It spots and kills anything it touches. It kills love; it kills art; I greatly fear, my dear Charles, that it has killed you."[10]

---

[9] Isaiah 30:9-10, RSV

[10] From page 273 of BRIDESHEAD REVISITED by Evelyn Waugh. Copyright 1945. Reprinted by permission of Little, Brown and Company.

There is clearly a peculiarly United States variety of charm — salesmanship, personality, congeniality, niceness, humor, cheerfulness — and it is the stock and trade of politicians, diplomats, and (God have mercy) ministers and church people. That charm justifies strange things. And it kills love, honesty, compassion, and most of all, kills people — insidiously kills the charmers as well as the charmed, and obviously kills the nameless, faceless "statistics" who ride in the back of open trucks, hugging each other and their children. For it is these same people who become statistics when the guns go off and the bombs are dropped and the bread is withheld; who are charmingly reported to represent an admirable decrease in human rights violations, totalling up to far fewer victims of violence; who represent a successful "policy" of making the country (in this case El Salvador, though it could be any country) militarily and politically secure. And those reports so charmingly made by our government officials on television are charmingly believed by U.S. citizens, because it is the easiest and most comfortable response.

And there I'd been, sitting more or less attentively and dutifully in the embassy briefing room, following the rules and affecting a certain sense of "importance," because I was an official member of a Congressional Delegation and a guest of a United States ambassador. Well, Pickering and the Administration officials aren't the only ones; I'm one of a lot more of us who need to get our priorities straight and start to "give a fuck."

=========

...President Jose Napoleon Duarte wore white socks and was missing the tips of the fingers on his left hand. The socks drooped between the cuff of his creased gray suit pants and the tops of his black shoes, and the nubs of his fingers punctuated his words. I don't know why, of all the many things going on, those two details snagged my attention in that large, ornate reception room of the Presidential Residence in which Duarte was speaking to our delegation, to U.S.

Embassy personnel, as well as to two other congressmen and their staffs, and to a number of media people, including television crews. Were the white socks just gauche, or a studied indifference, or an intentional statement of identity and roots, or a subtle way of shuffling before North American "massas"? Or, perhaps, were they just a way to deal with some persistent skin irritation? And the missing ends of his fingers . . . had that happened, as rumored, as a result of torture when he was imprisoned as a communist by the military government earlier in his political life? (Later I heard from one of his aides that he'd lost them to a conveyor belt while working in an oil field during his political exile.)

Maybe the reason the drooping white socks and blighted fingers so fascinated me was because there was something inescapably human about them and, precisely for that reason, something mysterious as well. Duarte looks something like Jimmy Hoffa and certainly could pass as a member of a Teamsters' or Longshoremen's Local. Or, to keep culturally consistent, he seemed peasant-smart. He's stocky, swarthy, tough, yet disarmingly gracious. When he entered the room, he personally greeted and shook hands with each member of our delegation.

Of course, Duarte is tough, shrewd, calculating, and self-promoting or he wouldn't be in the position of power he is. But Hoffa-like or not, he wears droopy white socks and has slightly handicapped hands, thus making unmistakably apparent the undeniable human condition that is a quality of the counsels of power — however buried that condition usually is under a sartorially impeccable, well-manicured surface. Foolishly or not, I instinctively liked him for his socks and fingers. So much for scholarly analysis!

Duarte spoke briefly, then answered questions. There wasn't much new information, and the issues were familiar:

- How realistic was it to assume a civilian government could operate independently of the military? (The unvarnished truth was, not very, at this point.)

- Since the economic future depended on the support of the business community for the Duarte gov-

ernment, what would defeated Presidential candidate, Roberto d'Aubuisson, and the rightest Arena
Party do now? (Obviously, Duarte didn't know,
though he speculated they'd support him even
though there were strong rumors of their opposition.)

- What about needed reform of the judicial system
which gives disproportionate power to the Supreme Court? (Duarte would give this priority.)

- What about the renewal of peace talks with the
rebel FMLN,[11] building on the negotiation that had
taken place at La Palma? (Duarte was willing, but he
must prepare carefully for such talks —which
meant he had to check such things out with
Washington.)

- What was the role of the church in the peace process? (The church had gotten away from spiritual
teaching and begun to talk about justice and water
problems and economic issues, which was too bad
. . .an answer that was distressingly familiar.)

While he spoke, Duarte sat in a large wing back chair, and a few
feet behind him off to one side sat Ambassador Pickering and a few
embassy staff people listening carefully, smiling, nodding at Duarte's
answers. The topic about which Duarte was most evidently enthusiastic was the two AC-47 attack planes which he just had received from
the United States. He spent several minutes rehearsing their techno-
logical features, all of which would enable him and the army to wage
the war against the guerrillas more effectively. He seemed like a kid
with a new toy and fantasies of himself as Rambo or John Wayne. I felt
sorry for him, somehow, and frustrated. I couldn't help thinking of *The
King and* I when the King of Siam, pondering on what course to lead his
country, sings a soliloquy in which he asks, "Shall I join with other na-

---

[11] FMLN (Farabundo Marti National Liberation Front): an umbrella term for guerrilla
factions in El Salvador.

tions in alliance?...Might they not protect me out of all I own?"[12] It must be demeaning to have a super power looking over your shoulder all the time, monitoring every move, every word, shaping your values, plotting your course. But then, aren't we all in that position somehow, unless...unless what?

Of the other two congressmen present with their staffs, one was from New Jersey, the other from Indiana. The representative from Indiana finally said, "Mr. President, we admire your stand against communism and know you are joining us in the fight to prevent its spread in the world. What do you think you can help us do about Nicaragua?" It sounded like the script from a movie. Even Duarte held up his hand in mild protest at the rhetoric, and then he said perhaps the most remarkable thing of the morning: even though he disagreed with the politics of Nicaragua's government, he said he would *not* support any outside military action against that government because he respected its legitimacy. Therefore, he would only support other negotiational solutions, such as advocated by the Contadora nations, to resolve the problems between Nicaragua and other Central American countries.

I was so surprised at his answer that I forgot to look at Pickering's reaction. If El Salvador — with all its critical problems and the alleged immediate "threats" from Nicaragua —could take a stand of such integrity vis-a-vis this neighboring country whose government it does not like, on what moral basis does the United States take such a contrary position on the same country and fund military efforts to overthrow its government? Do we really have a Divine right — or any right — to overthrow governments we don't like? Or just small governments? Where does it stop? When do we learn to get along on one blue, beautiful planet?

Later we heard that after we'd left the Presidential Residence, the other two congressmen and their staffs had spent most of the rest

---

[12] From "A Puzzlement," THE KING AND I. Copyright © 1951 by Richard Rodgers and Oscar Hammerstein II. Copyright renewed: Williamson Music Co., owner of publication and allied rights throughout the Western Hemisphere and Japan. International copyright secured. All rights reserved. Used by permission.

of the day inspecting the AC-47's and actually taking a ride in one. I suppose that's one way to see a country. The question is, which country? I thought of Linda and Ernesto — the refugees from El Salvador in Public Sanctuary at Tabernacle Church in Philadelphia — and wondered what they would have wanted us, and those other congresspeople and their delegations, to see in El Salvador. I don't think it would have been the AC-47's. "Never ask the sword. . . ."

⸻

. . . The church in El Salvador is as diverse and elusive of simple description as it is anywhere else, and yet the views expressed by a variety of its church leaders are similar when it comes to identifying the war as the primary problem of the country. They interpret the war as traceable more to untenable conditions of poverty and economic exploitation than to ideological issues. But, the information they reported to us about what was happening in the country — particularly concerning the human rights violations — varied from the official reports of either the United States or El Salvador governments. Their information — gathered from on site observers and/or people who were quickly on the scene to interview people who had been present — was that the *army*, not the rebel forces, was responsible for the great majority of these violations.

Increasingly, I felt anger and frustration about that conflicting information. "Official" reports are repeated in the media with the impression they are "factual," while the views of church personnel or human rights groups are seldom reported. Or, if they are, they are conveyed with the caveat that these views probably are skewed by the naivete or idealistic bias of those groups.

Archbishop Arturo Rivera y Damas struck me as anything but naive. We met with him in a small, plain room late one afternoon after a lengthy briefing by Maria Julia Hernandez, the Director of the Human Rights Division of the Archdiocese. She strongly contradicted the statements made at the United States Embassy that more killing was done by the left than the right. "Absolutely not true," she insisted, which more or less summed up the briefing. "Never ask the sword..."

Archbishop Rivera succeeded Oscar Romero and fundamentally follows a similar policy — which means he is critical of both the government and the opposition. He said the Roman Catholic Church was involved in three ways with the civil war:

1) to try to mediate a settlement and encourage dialogue between the adversaries; (He indicated that earlier that day he had transmitted a letter to President Duarte which he had been given by the rebel leaders to that end.)

2) to try to humanize and contain the war and its results, and to monitor human rights violations committed by either side;

3) to alleviate the results of the war by aiding widows, children, refugees, and to develop international aid for them.

As Archbishop Rivera spoke about the suffering of the people — and the fact that there are a million refugees from El Salvador and Guatemala outside Central America — I thought of the argument of our Immigration and Naturalization Service: since the suffering caused by the wars in these countries involves nearly all its citizens, no particular persons, or groups, can be granted political asylum in our country as special victims of persecution. Rivera was careful in his choice of words, wary in his attitude. He is a relatively large man with a broad face, a gentle manner, but the pain and weariness he felt was evident. Someone asked him why Pope John Paul II is not more actively supportive of the movement for social justice in Central America. He smiled softly, almost sadly, I think, and said, "The Pope is a teacher, not a politician." Another asked him about Oscar Romero and what his death had meant. Again, Rivera smiled, and then spoke quietly, "He was killed by the army and the people of the political right, but he lives in the hearts of the people here and elsewhere." Of course, he was careful with his answers, guarded, but at the same time he seemed quite lonely and vulnerable. He must have wondered, as did I as I listened, whether he, like his predecessor, would be killed for trying to speak, even carefully, for peace and justice in his parish. As we left the room, I looked back at him sitting at a little table, looking very alone. I felt a spasm of my earlier terror as I walked down the steps and out into the melancholy light of the late afternoon. I keep Archbishop Rivera in my prayers. "Never ask the sword..."

...The basement room had the same feel as most basement rooms in church buildings: no frill, functional folding chairs with a list; windows filtering the early morning light through two seasons of grime; coffee urn on a card table in the corner. On the way over in the van, someone had commented that if you're going to burn the candle at both ends, you'd better have plenty of wax. The ten people with whom we were meeting were obviously burning the candle at both ends in terms of the work they were doing, but they seemed, now, to be running out of wax. They were frustrated, tired, borderline angry. They were ministers, social workers, teachers, youth workers of the Evangelical churches in El Salvador, including Lutherans, Mennonites, Baptists. A few were missionaries from the United States, the others Salvadorans. (I wondered where the United Methodists were, but didn't ask.)

Each of the ten spoke in turn, describing the work they were doing, while sometimes subtly, sometimes not, lamenting the limitations to what they could do in the face of such enormous need. One mentioned that when he tried to organize indigenous people or incoming refugees, they became frightened because the army (which really runs the country) punishes people who organize. The others nodded in agreement and discouragement. I thought of Joel who was picked up and tortured in Guatemala for his work in organizing students and workers. The result of such officially sanctioned intimidation by the army is that these church workers are restricted to dealing only with the victims, not the causes of the war. The war, said one, was the long standing conflict between wealth and poverty which left over five million of the five and two-tenths million Salvadorans in poverty. However, in the clear opinion of all of these Evangelical church workers, though the war is caused by this inequity, the war will not solve the problem but only make it worse. Indeed, in the judgment of several of them, the army is a major factor in keeping the war going, because it creates pressure in the United States for more military aid.

One of the Baptist youth workers said that young people in El Salvador have four options: enlist with the guerrillas, enlist in the army, leave the country, or steal. Since the first two options are not attractive, and since Salvadoran refugees in Mexico and the United States are mistreated and often deported — commonly leading to disappearance or death — delinquency in the country is radically increasing with no solution at hand.

A Lutheran minister who worked in the refugee camps suddenly stopped telling us of what he was doing and, as if distracted by some compelling memory, said simply, in urgent testimony, "History reminds us that God's work is always misunderstood. We all get paranoid here, you know? A Lutheran minister was killed last year, but the strange thing is, people seem to be getting more courageous, not more afraid. I think the church is stronger, not numerically, but in its inner life. God's love strengthens us. Your visit is part of that strengthening." His voice was a blend of insistence and something like hope, and he looked at us as if wanting verification. I looked down at my feet and noticed how familiar asphalt tile on the floor was. I thought to myself that, however common the feel of this church basement room, the courage and commitment of the Evangelical Christian workers gathered in this one was all too uncommon. I could only hope that, in fact, our visit *would* strengthen them, would give them a bit more wax to burn...though I confess I didn't see how. Maybe it was just that we cared, that we listened, that we would remember and tell others when we got back to the United States. That seemed too little to be of much strengthening. I kept staring at the floor, thinking...

Maybe part of the mystery of grace is that others do get more from you than you actually give. Come to think of it, why should that mystery be surprising to a minister? It happens for me all the time.

Come to think of it even more, isn't that something of what has happened since the refugee family entered Public Sanctuary with us in Philadelphia, only compounded in that not only they, but *we* get back more than we give? Curious that I should be reminded of that while sitting in this basement room several thousand miles from home.

So, come to think of it one more time, maybe there was more in common here than the appearance of a room, after all. The word is grace. Maybe, almost by definition, a blessing is a gracious gift that sandbags you when you're looking in a different direction, and it happens by a river, in a strange land, even in a basement, with Evangelicals (who usually make you edgy, because even as they're out to love you, in Christ's name, they make you feel hunted). Yet, these men and women seemed a winsome blend of discouragement and determination. Even their talk about being strengthened by God's love and our visit revealed the underlying sense of impotence they were feeling in these circumstances, in their frustrations about the war, and in the limitations they felt in doing anything about it. But, as I experienced them that morning, describing their work, they were not really powerless at all. In fact, one of them spoke powerfully for them all when asked how they managed to keep going in the face of the odds. He replied, "Theologically, the explanation is that our work is a sign of God's kingdom." I hope, past theological propriety, they feel that explanation personally. I did.

When we left, I thanked them for their coffee and their courage, for once again I sensed that courage may be more than half of what faith is — though I suppose some Evangelicals would deny it. But then, that only suggests that the Stranger is sneakier than we know, and that, indeed, people do get more than we give, and we get more than they give, and we all get more than we give ourselves. I was smiling when I climbed into the van, maybe because I was feeling a little braver than I had been.

...Three small children were standing immobile, staring through the wire fence as we walked up to the gate of the refugee camp. Then they were everywhere — children watching us with their huge, dark eyes; some watching shyly, clinging to mothers' skirts or tucked in the little hiding places children seem always able to find; some watching boldly, pressing close to see us better. The camp itself was clinging to the outskirts of San Salvador and was run by the church. (We'd been told that the difference between a church refugee camp and a government refugee camp was that the aid in a church camp was dependable.)

According the the camp director, there were 549 people crowded into this small area about half the size of a football field, with perhaps half a dozen small buildings on it, the largest serving as a crowded, open dormitory. Of that population, 228 were younger than ten years old, and an additional 152 were between ten and fourteen. The only place for these children to play was in the cramped walkways across which fluttered clotheslines full of wash done in open tubs in a common area for washing everything — from children, to clothes, to food, to the huge pots in which the common meals were cooked over wood fires in sheds.

The poverty and pain of these people was palpable, even though this was a very decent camp, as refugee camps are measured. A few old men sat smoking under one of the few trees in the camp, their eyes dulled by the mixture of rage and resignation with which they very briefly told their stories. The women worked slowly and silently, scrubbing, cooking, picking up, watching children. Only the children smiled, and not all of them. This was not the home of these people, yet they lived there now because they had no other place to go. How long would they have to remain in this camp? Would this be what shaped these children's lives? What would they remember as their childhood?

Once again I had the impulse to avert my eyes even as I tried to take in what I was seeing, hearing, smelling. Once again I realized the distance between these refugees and me —a distance that wouldn't be shrunk by the few hours we'd share; a distance I was glad existed because I didn't have to live here, homeless, possibly futureless. And with that realization, there came again the terror at my own spiritual poverty.

We gathered in a corner of the dormitory building to listen to the stories of these refugees. We sat on boxes, on cots which were jammed about a foot apart. Scrawny chickens wandered in and out through the open doors, scratching the dirt floor, hopping up on cots until someone shooed them away. Almost reluctantly, with an affect that conveyed the numbness of deep grief, the refugees spoke, one after another. I tried hard to listen and record in my notebook what they were saying, but before long their stories began to run together — a blur of violence, brutality, fear. I kept thinking of Joel and Gabriela and little Lucy, and hearing echoes.

A woman told us her twenty-two year old daughter had a leg amputated from injuries suffered in prison, where she had been taken by the army as a suspected subversive and raped during her interrogation.

Another woman told of helping her friend give birth while bombs dropped around them, leaving the mother and new baby covered with dust and rubble.

Repeatedly, the refugees spoke of "the slow one" (their name for the AC-47 planes). They told of trying to hide while "the slow one" dropped flares and machine-gunned their villages, spraying bullets at anything that moved in the surrounding fields.

One toothless woman told of the army invading her village, which was in a guerrilla controlled zone, and killing everyone except those who, like her daughter and herself, managed to run into the woods and hide. She reported hearing the screams and crying of children being killed, seeing two old men shot in the back because they couldn't run fast enough to make it into hiding. When they went back into the village after the army had gone, everything was burned, including the bodies of all the children and others who had been killed.

Another told of being transported with some other men in an army truck which was taking them to prison in San Salvador and, when the truck stopped on a bridge, watching as the soldiers threw two of the prisoners off the bridge. When he had protested, he had been hit on the head with a rifle.

Another told of being held in underground cells for days and tortured. One technique used was to shine bright lights on skeletons and threaten him with the same fate. He heard screams played over loud speakers to mask the real screams of the prisoners.

Many spoke of army sweeps into their villages, being forced to leave, going for two or three weeks without food, fearing for their lives — especially when planes and helicopters flew over shooting at any moving target.

On and on the reports went, in quite matter-of-fact tones, almost as if what had happened to them was commonplace. And while the adults spoke, the eyes of children punctuated the stories — children sitting, standing among us, some leaning on mothers or on whatever was handy, some chewing on oranges, but always watching; watching as if waiting for something; watching as if somehow expecting us to change it all for them, and almost nonchalantly believing we would. I felt sick at heart, heavy with anger, with discouragement, with my own kind of poverty.

The suggestion had been made at one of our early briefings to bring small gifts for the children — a desired gift being ball point pens, because children loved to draw with them. Finally, the children's eyes prevailed over the stories, and I and one or two others of the delegation began quietly to distribute pens to the children. I took out a box of pens and motioned for one little boy to come and get one. As it turned out, I could hardly have done anything more inappropriate. As if by some signal, children began to appear, mobbing us, screaming for pens, fighting over them. Our supply was much too inadequate. The camp director was furious and singled me out for rebuke because I was closest to him and, probably, most indiscreet in giving out the pens. Bob Edgar interceded for me and the others, telling the director we'd been told to bring pens for the children. The director calmed, but my shame persisted. I felt what I had done was a parable of patronizing, of inaccurate response to terrible need, of gross insensitivity, of perhaps good but thoughtless intentions — a gesture of ugly Americanism, Rockefeller scattering dimes to urchins. Maybe, in part, it was my wrestling with a sense of my own spiritual poverty — and the terror it generated — which accentuated the situation emotionally for me. I felt distressed and was relieved when another refugee began to speak, diverting attention from the episode.

On one side of the room was an almost life-size statue of the Virgin Mary holding the Infant Jesus. It was tucked against the stone wall and surrounded by stacks of cardboard boxes and plastic bags stuffed with the meager possessions of the refugees. The statue was in starkest contrast to its environment — Mary and Jesus looking idealized, beautific and antiseptic.

Then, out of the corner of my eye, I noticed a young man slowly, quietly move into and across the room until he stood in front of the statue. Almost timidly he began to touch it and then himself, again and again, touching first the statue and then himself. Each time he completed the cycle, he would look around at the children nearest to him, nodding and smiling. He was obviously retarded.

He repeated his ritual several times, rubbing Mary's face and hands and carefully draped breasts, as well as the face and hands and feet of Jesus, and then rubbing his own forehead, his own chest, arms, groin, legs. He must have believed there was something magical about the statue, that through touching those holy figures and then himself, there would be a direct transference of power and healing — perhaps even of love — from that mother and little brother to himself until he would become part of that family. After the first few times, he turned and touched one or two of the children who were closest to him, and possibly because they wanted to humor him (or possibly because they simply liked and trusted him), they allowed him to do that. They even smiled as if they liked it and believed in the magic, too.

Slowly it occurred to me that maybe this simple-minded, simple-faithed young man was revealing something important to me. However gilded this statue of Jesus — or however gilded we make our image of him — the fact is that Jesus was born and lived and died in circumstances very like those in this camp, very like those on the way in from the airport. And whatever else it means, the incarnation surely means that God is present and at work in even these hellish places and times. So there is a power to be touched, a love to be claimed somehow — even in what seems to be forsaken circumstances, for no circumstances are ever God forsaken.

I thought of Paul's familiar words: "God was in Christ reconciling the world to himself . . . and entrusting to us the message of reconciliation."[13] If reconciliation means anything, it must mean that we are members of one family, and that by touching something — something like trust, or love, or maybe just touching children — we are powerfully reminded that we're all included in God's family. Even me with my spiritual poverty. Somehow there was some peace for me in that thought. If God is at work, then I don't have to feel so desperate about my own duplicities, my own limitations in the face of enormous need. And yet, if God, in Her mysterious foolishness, puts us in each other's hands — which is what it must mean to be entrusted with "the message of reconciliation" —then we have to do everything we can for each other, everything we can to make that family a real, living, just, peaceful entity. But the point is to do everything you *can* — not attempting or expecting more, which is self-righteous and self-defeating; nor attempting and accepting less, which is self-satisfaction and also self-defeating. Somehow prayer is part of the moral life, the moral act, because by it we acknowledge dependence on God and affirm that God's power is at work in and beyond us.

I began to feel slightly light-hearted. Maybe that is what forgiveness involves: a light-heartedness, a release to do what you can. What you can! I guess doing what we can is what Public Sanctuary is. God, in His foolishness, has put three refugees and a ministry of reconciliation in our hands, and so far we haven't dropped them.

When we left the camp, those dark-eyed, pot-bellied children followed us to the gate. They sang a song for us. I put my hands on as many of their heads and cheeks as I could and felt choked up. I realized I, too, was touching something very like the infant Jesus and wanting to claim the power of . . . of mercy, maybe; of the irrepressible hope that yet burned in these children's eyes; of their need which

[13] II Corinthians 5:19, RSV

would strengthen my own resolve not to forget them, not to betray them, but to speak for them, pray for them, write for them, fight for them any way I could...and maybe, thus, to face my terror, my spiritual poverty which is more damning than their physical poverty.

As we drove away, the children hung on the wire fence and watched us go with a kind of longing and trust that haunts, and yet empowers me, still. What is at stake in Central America is not territory or ideology or power politics, really. It is children! "Mothers' hearts," indeed. O God, make room in your heart for those children. Make room in our hearts for them, in the hearts of the people of the United States who can help stop the wars in Central America, and turn planes into plows, bombs into schools. I looked back at those children until I could see them no more, and I promised myself — and them and God — that I would do whatever I could for them. Among the things I can do is to "Never ask the sword..." or be intimidated by it. O God, make room in your heart for us all!

Nicaragua

We landed in the late afternoon at the Augusto Cesar Sandino Airport in Managua, in what the United States government calls an "enemy country." Nothing I saw, heard or felt in any way confirmed my government's judgment.

Perhaps the strongest symbol of Nicaragua is Managua. It was destroyed by an earthquake in 1972 and has not been rebuilt. Over 10,000 people were killed in that quake, 15,000 injured. The greatest portion of international aid for relief was diverted by President Anastasio Somoza Debayle to his own personal bank accounts. The Somozas' father had taken power in 1936 with the aid of the United States, and he and his two sons ruled Nicaragua like a private estate. At the time of the earthquake, United States Marines, once again, went into the country to protect the alleged interests of our country, and thus, the interests of Somoza.

What was once the center of Managua is now essentially barren, leveled earth with the shells of a few destroyed buildings standing here and there as testimony to a nation too poor to rebuild its own capital city. In fact, the gross national product of Nicaragua in 1984 was approximately 2.5 billion dollars. (For perspective, the fiftieth largest industrial *corporation* in the United States, Monsanto Chemicals, had a gross revenue of 6.5 billion dollars in 1983 — a revenue nearly three times the GNP of Nicaragua. It is also interesting to note that Mc-Donald's hamburger chain reported sales of 2.9 million dollars that same year — a figure almost equal to Nicaragua's GNP.[14]) In addition, the foreign debt of Nicaragua — as of most Central and South American nations — is oppressively high, a constant drain on national resources. I do not profess to understand the complexities of international finance, but we had a brief discussion with a British economist at the airport who said that the crushing debt problems of Central American countries are the major threat to stability, making it nearly impossible to address the real economic and social problems of their countries. This view is gaining increasing credibility among many analysts.

Nicaragua is a poor country. Ox carts are still a common mode of transportation. Farming is still not highly mechanized. It is hard to conceive that Nicaragua is a military threat to the United States or to its neighbors. In spite of all the accusations, there is no evidence that arms are being sent from Nicaragua to El Salvador, certainly not since 1981. If the United States is trying to combat a philosophy — a Marxist-Leninist ideology — in Nicaragua, how is that idea to be defeated militarily, by guns and planes? Why isn't our government sending in technical assistance and advisers to out-compete such assistance and advisers from the Soviet Union, eastern bloc countries and Cuba? Every Nicaraguan official with whom we talked said that technicians and aid from the United States would be welcomed on the same basis as those from other nations. Nicaragua does not keep out

---

[14] INFORMATION PLEASE ALMANAC 1983. New York: A & W Publishers, Inc., 1982., p. 60.

such persons from the United States; we refuse to send them in, apparently because there are advisers in Nicaragua from countries we disapprove of.

What are we *really* afraid of? What are we really trying to protect? If it is our business interests in the agriculture and industry of Nicaragua, then my anger escalates at our national hypocrisy. Only twenty percent of agriculture in Nicaragua is government controlled. Is land reform so threatening to us? About forty percent of the business and industry of Nicaragua is nationalized, which means sixty percent is still privately owned. What is so threatening about that? I remember Bill Coffin saying, "If you feed the poor, you're called a saint. If you ask *why* they are poor, and try to change the things that make them so, you're called a Marxist." I never wanted to believe that, but my growing anger makes it easier.

═══════════

. . . The night we arrived in Managua we went to a dinner at the home of United States Ambassador and Mrs. Harry E. Bergold. Most of the United States Embassy people were there, along with several other foreign diplomats. The dinner tables were set on a large outdoor patio at one end of which was a bar. We had drinks and chatted in a lovely setting, watching the sky turn slowly purple and the stars take up their vigil. Hanging in a large cage was a brightly plumed tropical bird, a variety of macaw. The scene was reminiscent of a 1940 movie set in the tropics, and I kept waiting for Sydney Greenstreet to make an entrance.

The embassy staff seemed to take delight in enumerating the problems facing the government and people of Nicaragua, particularly the sparsity of consumer goods and the poor quality of those that were available. One woman laughed about the problems the country was experiencing with light bulbs and toilet paper, concluding they probably came from Cuba. Her final word was that the government and people were "getting what they deserved" — which is an interesting comment when you think about it. I suppose, in the first place, the problems of Nicaragua "prove" that a "Marxist-Leninist" government can't work, just as a bank red-lining a section of a city "proves," ten years later, that that section was not viable; just as, to Job's friends, his troubles "proved" he had sinned. God save us from such comforters!

In the second place, the litmus test the United States uses for giving aid is whether or not a government "deserves" it —which means whether or not that country behaves and believes according to our liking. It is just that kind of paternalism which feeds the anti-United States sentiment in the Third World and creates conditions on which Marxism feeds. Our country's response to Nicaragua is like police clubbing a bag lady for sitting on a steam vent at a busy intersection.

Why can't we see that the problems of Third World countries such as Nicaragua are symptoms of poverty and suffering of a people, and offer us a chance to befriend those people? Of course, we can dominate those small countries, but as Mexican novelist and diplomat Carlos Fuentes pointed out to a Harvard commencement audience, domination creates satellites, and "the great weakness of the Soviet Union is that it is surrounded by satellites, not by friends. Sooner or later, the rebellion of the outlying nations in the Soviet sphere will eat, more and more deeply, into [the Soviet's] innards...The United States has the great strength of having friends, not satellites, on its borders."[15] Obviously, the question is, "How long will we keep those friends and that strength, unless we alter our present policy?" And that question is also at the heart of the Public Sanctuary Movement.

It was nearing midnight when we gathered in Ambassador Bergold's spacious living room for a private conversation following dinner. It had been a long day, and everyone was tired. Bill Coffin sat at the piano and began to play an old Yale song. Bob Musil joined in

[15] From "High Noon in Latin America" by Carlos Fuentes. Copyright © 1983 by Carlos Fuentes. Reprinted by permission of Brandt & Brandt Literary Agents, Inc.

immediately, as did the ambassador when he came in. Suddenly it felt like a gathering of old alums. The aura didn't last.

Bergold hadn't been in Nicaragua long, coming there from a post in Hungary. Even in this informal setting, he gave the impression of some unease as he reported to us his observations of Nicaragua, making one comment which was particularly offensive: "These people will never starve, however desperate the economic situation, because they can always pick fruit off the trees." He went on to lament especially the increasing size of the Nicaraguan army and the importing of weapons. Someone asked if the reasons for that increase might be that the United States, through both government and private funds, heavily supported the contras; that our CIA had illegally and covertly mined the harbor of Managua; that our military forces were a sizable presence in neighboring Honduras, holding major maneuvers close to the Nicaraguan border (which could be seen as provocative in light of our government making threats about military action against Nicaragua). Bergold contended that our policy, rather than being provocative, was in response to provocations by Nicaragua.

Bill Coffin blew up: "What provocations? That this little country had the temerity to set up a government which refused to be dependent on the United States and to choose to have relations with the Soviet Union — a choice which is the perogative of all our allies? Everyone knows we could wipe out this country's military capability with a sortie of planes from Texas any day we wanted to. It is our support of the contras that is killing people in this country and draining its economy. The truth is, you guys just don't give a fuck about these people!" There it was again. This time I smiled. However, Bergold bristled, officially and diplomatically, assuring us that the way to care for these people was to insure that Marxism didn't take over. "And be sure that someone like Somoza is put back in power?" someone countered.

Maybe it was the lateness of the hour, but Bergold slumped a little in his chair, sipped his bourbon and sighed wearily. Then, in what must have been an uncharacteristically revealing statement, he said, "I don't make policy, you know. Washington does. I carry it out." Shortly, the meeting broke up.

But his statement was like lighting a candle around which my thoughts kept flying. It wasn't that it gave new information, but it was the first time I'd ever heard someone caught personally and directly in such a bind say so. Truth is what the boss says it is, no matter any evidence to the contrary, or any other views of the matter. "I don't make policy...I carry it out." My first inclination was to feel sorry for this career diplomat. I suppose he had three options: fight with Washington, or try to moderate the effects of its policy, or resign. I'm not sure if Bergold was choosing any of these options, but from the conversation that night, it didn't seem that he was. And that is the tragedy...a person dead in his job.

What was most chilling about his statement was that I could really see how Nazi Germany could have happened. I don't believe that the United States is like Nazi Germany, but the danger is always there; and not to recognize and acknowledge that danger is to compound it. Later I read something written by psychiatrist Robert Jay Lifton about the Nazi doctor, Josef Mengele, which put the issue starkly:

> "Hannah Arendt gave currency to a concept of the banality of evil in her portrayal of Adolf Eichmann as a rather unremarkable bureaucrat who was killed by meeting schedules and quotas. She is surely correct in her claim that an ordinary person is capable of extreme evil. But over the course of committing evil acts, an ordinary person becomes something different. In a process I call 'doubling,' a new self takes shape that adapts to the evil environment, and the evil acts become part of that self. At this point, the person and his behavior are anything but banal."[16]

The temptation is to sidestep the point Lifton makes by discussing the nature of evil and denying that we do anything like it. But to

---

[16] As appeared in THE NEW YORK TIMES MAGAZINE, July 21, 1985, "What Made This Man Mengele" by Robert Jay Lifton. Adapted from the Nazi doctors by Robert Jay Lifton. Copyright © 1986 by Robert Jay Lifton. Reprinted by permission of Basic Books, Inc.

sidestep the point is to miss it, and missing it makes us more vulnerable to doubling. Who was it defined evil as not loving life? It's a simple but substantive definition, and it's relevant. Not loving life leads
to killing it — perhaps figuratively your own first, in order to get along
or get ahead. Then, figuratively and literally killing others in order to
get along more easily, or to have fewer to get ahead of. Killing them
just because they don't do what you want, or have the same beliefs, or
the same skin color; or because they have something you want; or just
because it's convenient to have someone to blame things on in order
to divert attention from yourself . . . as political practitioners and pul-
piteers have done for generations. I know what doubling is since I
have experienced it a little in myself. Evil is not only the acts you *do*,
but the acts you *don't* do: risks you don't take, things you don't stand
for, words you don't speak. And all those omissions, as well as acts
you do commit, help to create an evil atmosphere to which others
adapt — perhaps especially political leaders, but others as well —
and often it's all done under the guise of patriotism.

I haven't done anything — or *not* done anything — to put me in
the category of world class evildoers. Nothing close! But I do know
what it is to be tired, to cover my behind, to go with the crowd or the
board or the bishop in order to get along or get ahead. Most of us do,
which is why we constantly need our consciousness raised about the
danger of doubling, of Nazism. And that is why, at that midnight hour
in the living room of the United States Embassy in Managua, it became clear to me that Public Sanctuary is the risk of loving life — pre-
eminently, for us, the lives of three refugees, Joel, Gabriela and Lucy,
but the lives of other refugees as well; and the lives of people in Central America who are oppressed and exploited and threatened by
war. Public Sanctuary is choosing *not* to go along with a policy that ex-
presses no love of life, but actually a distain for life; a policy which
creates an atmosphere of death, of evil, to which it expects others to
readily adapt. Public Sanctuary is a small way to help create another
atmosphere — an atmosphere of justice, of love, of life. It is a way
open to us, to me. Of course, there are other ways to love life, other
unavoidable choices to make. But I knew, as I walked later that night
under the star-laden sky in the ghost city of Managua, that singing old

Yale songs together — or whatever anthems we sing — doesn't make the choices any easier, or less necessary, for anyone.

=========

...Three priests we talked with powerfully demonstrate the yeast of the church in the ferment of Central America. That Rome officially disavows them as priests because of their secular activities does not alter their view of themselves as doing priestly work, nor does it brake the movement of the Spirit among the people. Indeed, Nicaraguan people expressed deep hurt and anger at Pope John Paul II who refused to pray for sons of Nicaraguans killed by the contras and who, as he deplaned during his 1984 trip to Central America, publicly shook his finger at Father Ernesto Cardenal as Cardenal knelt to kiss the Pope's ring. Cardenal serves the Sandinista government as Minister of Culture and is an outspoken advocate for the poor in Nicaragua. "Feed the poor and you're called a saint; ask why they're poor, and you're called a Marxist."

One of the priests we met was Dr. Xabier Gorostiaga, a Jesuit and Director of the Nicaraguan Institute for Social and Economic Research, and major shaper of economic policy in Nicaragua. He is a high energy person, bright and determined, who exudes a kind of confidence which generates from some layer deeper than knowledge of facts. His education at Cambridge, England, was one significant source of his thinking on economic policy. Another source was his theological training as a Jesuit. When he spoke to us, he carefully outlined the principles of the revolution, all of which followed from "the logic of the majority." Prior to the revolution, he said, five percent of the Nicaraguans controlled sixty percent of the nation's wealth; another forty percent controlled an additional fifteen percent. Also, over seventy percent of the nation's resources went out of the country annually, and only thirty percent remained within the country. The intent of the revolution was to change the inequity.

Ergo, the four principles as Gorostiaga presented them:

1) political pluralism, which was evident in the fact that forty percent of the representatives chosen in the election of 1984 were not members of the Sandinista party;

2) a mixed economy, with a large portion being private ownership;

3) a non-aligned foreign policy, which meant working out a new relationship with the United States, though pressure from the United States was forcing Nicaragua to turn to the Soviet Union more than it desired;

4) participatory democracy, the goal of which was to open the political process to every Nicaraguan and to initiate an intensive literacy program.

Of course, it was a bit too neat, and who knows how realistic it was to propose the effective implementation of this program. In fact, Gorostiaga said the prolonged war with the contras was seriously diverting the national economy to military purposes and away from the intended program. He also thought that a long term, low intensity war to drain the Nicaraguan economy was the most likely scenario the United States would follow, rather than either direct military intervention or helping to enable a negotiated settlement.

Still, as he talked I thought of Thomas Aquinas and the neatness, the carefully reasoned quality of the *Summa Theologica* — partly, I suppose, because Jesuits are so well trained in Aquinas; and partly because social/economic phenomena seems so amenable to that kind of analytic approach; and partly because it was so obvious that Gorostiaga's values and motivations were thoroughly dominated by his Christian theology, his view of his mission as a priest and teacher.

I wonder if the leaders of the Reagan Administration, and all the pundits great and small in the State Department, have ever read any Aquinas — or for that matter, any theology, patristic, liberation or otherwise, or one of the gospels, or the Acts of The Apostles. They might be surprised — even shocked — at how revolutionary Christianity is, how radical a thing it is to pledge allegiance to the Kingdom of God. In any case, if they read those documents, they might find at least one alternative way to Marxist-Leninist ideology for understanding the origins of the turbulence in Central America — and for understanding a few other potboilers in the United States, one of which is the Public Sanctuary Movement.

But what I liked best about Gorostiaga was his passion. Finally, there is nothing very carefully reasoned about passion. Yet history may well follow more the jagged course of passion than the measured curves of reason. It was Kenneth Clark who suggested that the crucial battle of any age is not between ideologies so much as between fatigue — which can make even an affluent society such as Rome fearful and defensive — and vitality — which is the outgrowth of a peoples' confidence and daring.[17] Gorostiaga is a vital man, an enthusiastic man, and the Greek root of the word enthusiasm is "to be possessed by gods." His lecture was laced with passion, vitality, enthusiasm — which smell more to me of grace than of law or reason — and sitting there, in "enemy" territory, I felt light-hearted again. I don't know if the Nicaraguan revolution will work, or if the principles outlined by Gorostiaga will prevail. But grace? Ah, that's quite another matter . . . quite. If I had to bet, it's grace I would bet on. Actually, it is grace I *am* betting on. How else can I face my own terror and poverty and anger? How else can anyone, even the carefully reasoning Jesuits? Whatever else faith is, surely it has to do with turning feelings into choices, insights into actions, however imperfect. And then, "Lord have mercy on us. Christ have mercy on us. Lord have mercy on us." On *all* of us!

---

[17] Kenneth Clark, CIVILISATION: A PERSONAL VIEW. New York: Harper & Row, Publishers, Inc., 1970, pp. 3-4.

. . . The second priest was Fernando Cardenal, Minister of Education, another Jesuit and the brother of Ernesto Cardenal. We met him for lunch in a crowded little room off the main dining room of a Managua restaurant. He came alone, driving his own car — no chauffeur, no security people. This helped confirm something I'd observed about Nicaragua: it felt safter to walk the streets alone, the people appeared to be less wary, there were fewer military and police personnel around carrying guns and/or automatic weapons than in El Salvador, where armed guards had been assigned to watch the corridors outside our hotel rooms twenty-four hours a day.

Fernando Cardenal has steel-colored hair and a personality to match. He's tough, testy, absolutely serious about what he is trying to do, yet conveys the strong sense that what is important is not himself, but the mission in which he is engaged — the revolution against oppression and poverty. In fact, he lives with four or five other priests in a home in which they follow, as best they can, the austere routines of the order.

Cardenal is the man who headed the enormously successful literacy campaign in Nicaragua, and he talked readily about it. The campaign began two weeks after the conclusion of the revolution and raised the country's literacy rate from fifty to ninety percent within a period of nine months. The techniques of the campaign have been studied by other nations, and won Cardenal a nomination for the Nobel Prize.

The purpose of the campaign, according to Cardenal, was to begin the process of democratization of Nicaragua, which could not be accomplished with fifty percent of the population illiterate. I reflected that such an intensive literacy campaign surely had to moderate any notion that this government was strictly totalitarian. Teaching people to read would be a high risk venture for such a government: people who can read are equipped to think more broadly and critically, and a literate population makes it much more difficult for a government to control the flow of information to its citizens. It is an illiterate, superstitious people who are most subject to exploitation by authoritarian systems.

The fact that Nicaragua's literacy campaign was headed by a Jesuit priest began to alter my prejudice that the Roman Catholic Church itself was an institution which built its power in Central and South America on the ignorance of the people from whom it demanded blind obedience. If that were true in the past, it is changing now — though conceivably this literacy effort could be a divisive issue between people such as Cardenal and the more conservative hierarchy of the Roman Catholic Church. If nothing else, priests such as Cardenal make clear that the Roman Catholic Church is only "officially" a monolithic institution, and that efforts, however frantic, to preserve that official monolithic position may be increasingly impossible.

When asked about President Reagan's peace proposals which advocate direct negotiations with the contras, with the Roman Catholic Church serving as the neutral mediator, Cardenal fumed. In his view — and that of the Sandinista government, if not the Nicaraguan people — the negotiations have to be directly between Washington and the Sandinista government, because without the financial and military support of Washington, the contras would not last long. In addition, Cardenal insisted that the Roman Catholic Church was not any more neutral than he was — a rather refreshingly candid statement about both himself and the church.

Cardenal also insisted that the Sandinista government (which received nearly seventy percent of the popular vote in the 1984 election declared valid by international observers) was the legitimate government of the country and should not be subjected to interference by the United States simply because the United States did not like the Sandinistas. And, Cardenal asked, what right did the United States have to insist on *inclusion* of the contras in the government of Nicaragua while, at the same time, arming El Salvador to fight to *eliminate* the guerrillas there?

His response to questions about government censorship of the press (which had recently been instituted) was to justify it as a temporary measure on the grounds of national security — a familiar sounding reason to citizens of the United States. He said the censorship would be lifted the day the Reagan Administration stopped its aggressive military policies toward Nicaragua. He insisted that, in light of the historical precedents of numerous invasions by the United States, the present threat of invasion from U.S. troops (or other armies funded by the U.S.) was taken very seriously by the Nicaraguan government.

Obviously, Cardenal is a priest who is a strong advocate of the Nicaraguan revolution, a man who espouses the values of his government and the love of his country with the same intensity as we do ours. Then, toward the end of our conversation, he said, softly, "Don't believe everything you hear during your visit, even from me. Talk to as many people as you can. See for yourselves. Make up your own minds. Where is the truth? You find it only by going deep."

It might have been the comment of a consummate politician. It may have expressed his weariness of having to defend his country to us, even though there were two congressmen present whose votes against aid to the contras he may have been courting. But beyond that, there was about his words and the way he said them, a kind of confidence, a sense of trust in his country and what it was trying to do. And, finally, maybe a trust in us: that we would see and somehow honor not only the truth about his country as we encountered it, but more, we would see and honor the vision to which he was attempting to be faithful in his work.

I sensed, in a compelling way, that he was speaking as a priest to a congregation. And I realized, as a preacher, how much easier — and safer — it is to speak only about that larger vision and to remain silent, as most preachers do, about how to make it incarnate in the nitty-gritty of the common life, the political/social/economic life of a people. When you try to do that, you run the risk of tarnishing the larger vision with the muck and grime of the nitty-gritty — which surely is why popes and congregations try to insist on keeping politics out of the pulpit. The only problem with that policy is that you also keep the gospel out of the pulpit, as well as Christians like Cardenal, and thus turn the larger vision into a lovely irrelevancy.

I didn't ask, but I knew Cardenal would understand a church declaring Public Sanctuary. I left the meeting feeling grateful that he continued to consider himself a priest and his work a priestly vocation, no matter what the church hierarchy said. Somehow it made me feel better about my own vocation. Such an unexpected confirmation of my vocation was a curious and easily misunderstood gift for me to claim to have received from this leader of an "enemy" government. But there it was!

———

. . . The third priest was Miguel D'Escoto, Foreign Minister of Nicaragua — a post comparable to our Secretary of State. We met with D'Escoto late in the afternoon in a conference room outside his office. The meeting went on into early evening, lasting more than two hours. I was surprised that a busy, high government official would give that much time to a relatively unimportant delegation, but we found D'Escoto in a reflective mood, willing to talk not only about his pragmatic world view, but his religious view as well. In fact, he impressively braided those two views together.

D'Escoto is the son of a Nicaraguan diplomat, and a Maryknoll priest. As did Cardenal and Gorostiaga, he chose to devote his priesthood to government service, which prompted Pope John Paul II to suspend him from the priesthood, although Maryknoll still considers him a member. He is a short, powerfully built man who speaks in a soft, gentle manner. In spite of the fact that he smoked constantly, he had about him an aura of a peace that the turbulence and pressures of his work and its related issues seemed not to disturb.

Bob Edgar put the first question to D'Escoto: "We hear a great deal about Marxism being the source of the unrest in Central America, but as a United Methodist minister, as well as a congressman, I have a sense that the church is a primary factor in what is happening. What is your view on the role of the church in your country and in Central America?" I recall smiling to myself, thinking how totally improbable it would be to begin a conversation with Secretary of State Schultz with a question about the role of the church in the United States, and expect a substantive answer — except that the church should stay out of politics, away from controversial issues, and shun actions such as Public Sanctuary, because those things are not religious, or, by implication, the concern of God. In effect, that is what our government says about the role of the church.

D'Escoto spoke for a long time, sounding as much like a theologian as a Foreign Minister. He said that the army and the church were the two pillars of the old, oppressive order in which the church preached resignation. However since Vatican II, the church was being "Christianized" — a provocative description which stirred my imagination. I suppose that's been the essential struggle from the beginning of the church: how to Christianize it. For D'Escoto, Christianizing the church meant for it to be involved, as Christ was, in being a servant, in caring for the least of our brothers and sisters — which meant being involved in shaping a revolutionary approach to the systemic problems of poverty and exploitation in his country. He spoke of Jesus telling his followers they were salt, which D'Escoto took to mean a preservative against corruption, as well as a seasoning to add savor to life — savor for the poor clearly involving at least the simple necessities: food, housing, education, medical attention.

As we sat talking together, I realized it was one of the few moments I had felt a sense of tranquility during the trip. We were touching on a view of life that ran deeper than national interests or cultural differences. Maybe it was the long shadows that began to stretch across the room at day's end, or the quiet tone of this man, or the sturdiness of a faith unembarrassed in expression.

But strangely, I felt a strong kinship with this man that was embarrassing to me, partly because I knew that if I told people about it, I would be labeled by some of them as an "enemy sympathizer," a dupe. I thought of Peter, standing by the fire on the night Jesus was arrested and denying that he knew him. Of course, this wasn't the same, but I realized again how easy it is to deny your beliefs, to go against your deepest intuitions because . . . because why? You don't trust your own gut, your own experience, your own thoughts? You want to be safe, to belong, so you sell out and end up not belonging to anyone, even yourself — which is perhaps the least safe you can be? You give to others the power and authority to decide what's right for you? But if that kind of arrhythmia of the soul prevails, you're already dead in all that matters. And if it had prevailed for others, neither history nor the kingdom would have Moses, or Deborah, or Jeremiah, or Jesus, or Luther, or Mary Daly, or *any* witnesses to the presence of another Power operative in human affairs other than just the power of mammon.

I remembered hearing a priest who heard the confessions of nuns say it was like being stoned to death with popcorn. I suppose that is what the life of the Christian and of the church is reduced to if it be lived in the cloister of spirituality unrelated to the dirt and blood of market place or political arena; if morality is confined to the trimmed lawns of personal behavior untrampled by the grunt-and-grime challenge of complicated social issues. Christianizing the church? Yea, Christianizing Christians, Christianizing me. I knew it would be an ongoing sweat to discern what that means in my case, in my ministry, but in that moment, at least, I felt an ease about it. It was as if, at just that stage of the wrestling match, I caught a glimpse of the Stranger's eyes and knew that he/she was not an enemy at all; indeed, that there were no final enemies except those I created for myself through fear. Of course, the moment didn't last long.

D'Escoto expanded on his view of the church's role by saying that it was one of a leavening, transforming agent insisting society into becoming more and more fraternal; that it was to develop an inner disposition to life and, thus, to the demand for generosity we all are called to manifest. Based on his belief that human beings are made in the likeness of God, D'Escoto stated his conviction that we are co-creators — which means we are to be active in making a better society, not spectators who allow ourselves or others to be marginalized. So D'Escoto participates in the social revolution in Nicaragua because its purpose is to replace the old order of injustice and oppression with a new order of justice and fraternity. In the attempt to affect justice, he said quietly, the greatest sacrifice will have to be made by those who have most. But, he added, with a note of longing and of challenge, "To have less money would give you something more valuable: peace."

I felt we had gotten close to the nub of the conflict and tumult in Central America. Most of us in the United States — and certainly the businesses with interests in Central America — are those of the earth who have the most, and who, in any movement toward justice, would be called upon to make the greatest sacrifice. None of us — including me — hear that challenge without squirming, without casting about for loopholes in that summons to do justly. For Christians, for any avowedly religious people, the squirming is particularly painful, and so the temptation is great to relieve the pain by accusing anyone who initiates movement toward justice as espousing some heretical doctrine — Marxism, godless communism, treason. So the landscape gets sprinkled with crosses and bomb craters.

Once again the pornography of affluence and the aggrandizement of it — as well as my complicity in it and my spiritual poverty — hit me like a sudden fever. I quivered. I began to see very clearly that, until we begin to learn that having less money (or less of what money buys) might really give us the greater value of peace, probably there would be no peace in the world or peace in our own lives. But the call to have less — when the dream, the American Dream, is to have more, to have it all — is unwelcome. No wonder the word of government and business leaders drowns out the word of the church — not only because the word of government is so loud, but because the word of the church is so soft. No wonder people are readier to believe the unrest in Central America is inspired by Marxists rather than the church, for if it were the church, that would make the gospel something radical. (And most of us don't want to believe that it is.) But in that dimly lighted room, I realized two things: one, I didn't have that valuable peace and didn't believe anyone could as long as *everyone* didn't; two, I had a more focused vision of where peace is than I did before, and in that, I felt the outermost ripples of peace wash up on the shore of my soul. I saw, in a simple but persuasive way, how fundamentally spiritual the conflicts of the world are, and in particular, the conflict between the United States and Nicaragua. I felt confirmed, as well, in the religious accuracy of the Public Sanctuary Movement and our church's participation in it.

We went on to talk about some international issues. D'Escoto reminded us — as he said he is often reminded, and not too subtly, by our government — that the United States is a hundred times larger than Nicaragua and thousands of times more powerful. To have such an awesome neighbor peering over your shoulder and rumbling on your borders is a difficult thing when you are trying to be independent, he said. The power of the United States to pressure the international community is also a very complicating factor.

D'Escoto gave some examples of how the Reagan Administration intimidates other nations by viewing any support for Nicaragua — or any disagreement with United States policy vis-a-vis Nicaragua — as an open act of hostility against the United States. The Administration has even been caught distorting the facts to create the illusion of support from others when such support is lacking. In one instance President Reagan claimed Vatican support for the United States peace proposals until the Papal Secretary of State was forced to issue a public disavowal. D'Escoto also mentioned another occasion when Colombia was embarrassed by Washington's claims that the President of Colombia favored Washington's positions when, in fact, Colombia had taken care (as a Contadora nation) to remain non-aligned.

What most struck me through D'Escoto's recital of problems caused by the domination of the United States in Central America — and the implications of that for his country — was D'Escoto's lack of bitterness or recrimination in his words or attitude. He believes in what he says, in what he is doing, in his mission as a priest, in his view of the world as the arena of God's work. I genuinely felt something like love radiating from this man — love for his people, love for us who represented a country intent on eliminating his government, love of God. It was a powerful experience. When we left, several of us hugged him and were hugged back. I was one of them, and it is a hug I will not soon forget. It is much better, much more human, than the diplomatic handshake.

So, I carry with me the glimmer of a peace more valuable than money, and the memory of that moment in D'Escoto's conference room when I had the unshakable sense that, in truth, I have no enemies, really, except those I create out of my own fear. Nor, I suspect, do any of us — even this beloved nation we live in. But, oh, the strength of those enemies . . . As I battle them, I remember with gratitude and love Brother Miguel. I am not embarrassed to admit that.

=====

. . . The road to Esteli climbs gently into the mountains north of Managua. The rainy season was still a few weeks off, and the brown, dry country emphasized the poverty of the farm buildings and the scrawny cattle. The driver of our small bus was good, but he must have been a frustrated Formula One car racer, because he darted in and out of the traffic as if he were negotiating the Managua Grand Prix. For the most part, the traffic was ox carts, ancient-looking farm equipment, lumbering old buses loaded with commuters to wherever, and various beat-up trucks usually toting several people in back. At the outskirts of Managua, the road becomes two lanes and is the route the revolutionary army followed into Managua.

The further we traveled from Managua, the sparser was the traffic, and the quieter became the early morning conversations. I thought of Daniel Ortega Saavedra, the President of Nicaragua, with whom we'd met the night before in a home in Managua. We sat in high back wicker chairs and listened to this not-yet-forty year old head of state speak carefully of the negotiations he was seeking with the United States to bring about an end to the war, insisting that it was U.S. military aid to the contras that was the single most decisive factor in the prolongation of the conflict.

Two things impressed me most about Ortega: one, his youthfulness, which confirmed the fact that most of the ranks of older Sandinista leaders had been decimated during the revolution; two, his absolute, unmitigated seriousness as he spoke, as he listened to the interpreter translate the questions of our congressional leaders and made his diplomatic responses. We were told earlier that it was his gifts as a mediator and peacemaker that had led to his ascent in the FSLN,[18] first as coordinator of the Junta in 1981, then as the successful FSLN candidate for President in 1984. That he was dressed in olive military garb suggested that Fidel Castro might well be one of his

---

[18] FSLN (Frente Sandinista de Liberacion Nacional): Sandinista National Liberation Front

models, though he had none of the swagger and loquaciousness of Castro.

After our meeting, Sandy Grady (who had begun his newspaper career as a sports writer) observed that Ortega somehow reminded him of a Pittsburg Pirate third baseman: "Danny Ortega — good field, no hit." We laughed, though there was poignancy in the description. Here was a head of state in the major leagues of power politics but with limited resources to play the game, and certainly without much power with which to hit the hard ball pitchers (Reagan and/or Gorbachev) of the major powers. I found myself hoping he could pull it off without striking out or getting beaned by either of the two curveballers in the international league. Now, looking out the window of the bus, I tried to imagine how Daniel Ortego had felt moving down this road into Managua as the revolution had come to an end. I wondered if it was anything like Jefferson and Adams had felt moving into Philadelphia at the conclusion of our revolution.

As we moved higher into the rough mountainous country, I thought of Dora Maria Tellez. She is one of three women who hold the title of Commandante Guerrillera (out of fifty-two who hold that rank in Nicaragua). We'd met with her as the head Commandante of Managua and listened to her speak, with hard-headed toughness and winsome charm, of the military, economic and political situation in Nicaragua. Probably it was the unusual combination of her attractiveness, and her military uniform (she was a veteran of much military action), and the big revolver on her hip that caused several men in our delegation to scramble to get their picture taken with her.

Dora Maria Tellez is twenty-nine years old. In response to a question about how she had gotten involved in revolutionary activity, she told us she was the daughter of middle class parents — a devout Roman Catholic mother and a Liberal father who was anti-Somoza (in large part because he was a descendent of the general who had submitted to the United States Marines in 1929-1933 when the United States had been instrumental in paving the way for the Somoza family to assume power). She had attended religious schools, lived in a rural district, entered medical school intent on becoming a doctor. As a student she became aware of the exploitation and repression of the country by Somoza, with the support of the United States. She became frustrated as a medical student when she found herself repeatedly treating the same children for malnutrition, which she began to see more as a political problem than a medical one.

So, she joined in demonstrations which were violently repressed by the Somoza government. Finally, she became involved in FSLN activity as the only course open to deal with the issues. At last, circumstances and her own choices forced her underground, which was very frightening because, as she put it, "I was sure I'd end up in a tomb. We were taught that we would probably not live to see the victory of the FSLN, and that was hard because I wanted to see that victory."

She decided to join the guerrilla forces in the mountains and described the night she and a guerrilla soldier, who was her guide, climbed to a guerrilla base on a steep mountain while she carried a seventy-five pound pack on her back. The climb began at seven o'clock at night and at three o'clock in the morning "we were still crawling up the mountain," she said. Once they arrived at the base, however, she said, "I was never again shown disrespect by a man offering to help me with my pack." She went on to tell us that her life as a public administrator in Nicaragua now is like climbing that mountain again, trying to deal with the problems that her country faces. Looking at her, listening to her, knowing she was quite ready to die for her cause, I wouldn't bet against her making it. As we got nearer and nearer to Esteli, I wondered if any of the mountains around us was the one she'd climbed. I thought about the mountain we are climbing in Public Sanctuary. Whatever the odds, in the long run I wouldn't bet against us either.

Our first stop in Esteli was a building across from the town square. The square is like a park, and although the grass was brown, two or three trees bore bright red blossoms. On the sidewalks around the square, vendors displayed their goods. War seemed far away until we heard a distant, familiar "whop-whop" which grew louder until we could see the helicopter circling the town, perhaps as part of the security arrangements for us and for Manuel Salvatierra, another Commandante Guerrillero and the Military Commander for Esteli and five surrounding departments. We were escorted into the building for a briefing with Commandante Salvatierra.

Manuel Salvatierra is also twenty-nine years old and could be the twin of Dora Maria Tellez in appearance, demeanor and motivation. He'd come out of one of the barrios in Managua, had been part of the student demonstrations brutally repressed by Somoza, had gone south into rural areas in 1974, and since had been involved in both political organizing and directing military action.

According to his report, there are 4,800 contras in four bases in Honduras, with another 1,800 in logistical support. The leaders of the contras are primarily former Somoza National Guard soldiers, and the contras' main target is the civilian population, which they hope to intimidate into withdrawing support for the Sandinista government. To counteract the contra action, Salvatierra said that the FSLN has recruited 3,200 young men to strengthen the regular army of 5,800, and has set up local militia in the villages to protect them against contra raids. Additionally, the FSLN has a few helicopters, a few air transports of World War II vintage. What is striking about those numbers is their smallness — especially in view of the Reagan Administration's presentation of Nicaragua as a threat to the United States and to Central American stability. (For perspective, 7,000 persons have been killed in Nicaragua in the last five years, which proportionately would compare with 35,000 being killed in New York City, most of them in an age group that would nearly wipe out a generation.) In spite of the fact that the contras are well equipped and well-advised by United States military and technical personnel, Salvatierra was quietly confident that the FSLN could prevail against the contras unless the United States intervened militarily. Then? He shrugged and smiled. I gritted my teeth and prayed.

We went directly to a Christian base camp on the edge of Esteli. The camp was laid out in a large open area, on one side of which was the main road and on the other, a wide ravine lined with scrub trees and underbrush. The streets between the small, painfully poor houses were gravel, and at the edge of the streets were trenches with pools of stagnant water. Children played in the streets and around the houses, and occasionally a pig wandered along snuffling for food or wallowing in the muck around the puddles of water. Overhead some electric wires drooped from pole to pole, but only rarely was there a feeder line into a building. In the near distance rose blue-green mountains.

The chapel, where we congregated immediately upon our arrival, was a neatly painted adobe building with a large portrait of a man and a woman on the outside wall facing what served as the town square. In front of the chapel was the yellow Toyota pickup truck of the priest who served a large area. Further in front was a small grave marker monument on which was written a Spanish inscription. We entered the chapel through a small door, and at first the inside seemed quite dim. The room was plain, perhaps forty by sixty feet with unfinished brick interior walls and a dirt floor. One or two naked light bulbs (which were not turned on) dangled from the ceiling. The room's light and circulation of air came from the open space between the roof and the walls. Up in front was a wooden table serving as an altar, and on it were a small arrangement of flowers and the chalice and platen for the communion elements. On the wall behind the altar was a portrait of the same man and woman as on the outside wall. Slowly the pieces of the story came together.

The man and woman whose faces were painted on the chapel walls were Mary and Felipe Berreda. Mary and Felipe had been local land owners and business people who had put aside their wealth and privilege to identify with the poor and the revolution. They had become lay Catholic activists, going off to pick coffee with the poor, even though they were in their fifties. One day the contras had kidnapped and then tortured them, insisting that their lives would be spared only if they gave up their work at the mission. The interrogation had taken place at some distance but in full view of the village people who had heard the screams of Mary and Felipe as the contras killed them. The words on the grave marker are translated: "Mary and Felipe. They didn't take your life. You gave it day by day building the new Nicaragua. For the kingdom of God and His justice, we will follow your example."

What took place in the chapel on the day we visited confirmed that sentiment. These people were poor, many of them displaced, but they were committed to justice and the kingdom of God. The room was full of people of all ages and many children. The adults sat on benches and chairs around the sides of the room, and the children wandered freely about. In one corner was a small band with guitars and drums and flutes, and as we took our places, they began a song. Everyone who knew the words joined in. Translated, they sang:

> "You are a God of the poor;
> a humble and simple God;
> a God who sweats in the street;
> a God with a ruddy face.
> Because of this we address you
> as One very close to us;
> we speak as your people,
> Jesus the worker among us."

The song was lively, and I watched the faces of the people as they sang. They reflected some of the expressions I'd seen twenty years earlier during the Civil Rights demonstrations, especially the March to Montgomery in 1965. On the faces of these people were surprise and delight at what was happening in their lives — they were actually experiencing the heady wine of freedom. And there was on their faces a fierce determination to stay free as well; and in their hearts, a faith that this was what God called them to be, and that God was with them in it. They were poor, but not shuffle-footed or timid. They were claiming their birthright. One of them even spoke of it as a "new exodus."

A member of the community read the prophetic scripture from Isaiah:

> " 'I will rejoice in Jerusalem, and be glad in my people...no more shall there be in it an infant that lives but a few days, or an old man who does not fill out his days, for the child shall die a hundred years old ...They shall build houses and inhabit them; they shall plant vineyards and eat their fruit. They shall not build and another inhabit; they shall not plant and another eat...They shall not labor in vain, or bear children for calamity...They shall not hurt or destroy in all my holy mountain,' says the Lord."[19]

[19] Isaiah 65:19-23,25, RSV

I had never paid such close attention to Isaiah's words before. No matter what the political analysts say, those words are a clear, unequivocal, operative creed and vision for the people in this Christian base camp in Esteli. I can only guess for how many others those same words would be true — and would far outweigh any Marxist-Leninist ideology — but I believe it is thousands, yea, tens of thousands. Why can't we — and our nation's leaders — hear those words? Maybe because if we did, we'd either have to disavow Isaiah and other prophets as part of our own religious heritage, or start living by that vision ourselves.

A Delegate of the Word — a lay Christian leader of the community named Rudolfo Rodriquez — conducted the service until it was time for the Eucharist. He began by calling different members of the community forward to tell their stories, in order to give a context for communion. The stories echoed those we'd heard in the refugee camp in El Salvador, only this time the atrocities were reported as having been committed by the contras. Once again, the stories stunned our sensitivities: young people killed or wounded as they were ambushed while returning home from a wedding; youngsters killed when their truck blew up while carrying them to the fields to pick coffee; a twelve year old son dragged to death; repetition of rape, kidnapping, indiscriminate violence by the contras. The people spoke of having to carry rifles in the fields as they picked coffee.

Finally, a lovely older nun who'd spent her life in Nicaragua got up to speak, and when she had finished, Congressman Bob Edgar asked her what she needed to help her with her work. Her answer was one word: "Peace." Then she went on, pleading with us, "Please, tell President Reagan about us. Tell the American people about us. Ask them to help us and to make peace by not sending arms to the contras to use to kill us." The heads of the people in that small chapel nodded in urgent agreement.

Then an older man, obviously highly respected in the community, stood up and spoke quietly, but with fire in his voice: "We have a right to be respected. Children need and want an education, and are getting it here. You see, the church is a people committed to liberation, and we have this chance to put faith into action. The hierarchy of the church, well, they see power slipping from their hands, so they preach against us. But it is *their* interests they are defending, not the church's. What we are doing is God's work." I heard later that his wife and two sons had been killed by the contras.

All the while, the children would come and stand close to us, staring wide-eyed, full of wonder, with that terrible trust that silences argument and puts your life in simple relief. Finally, one little girl of perhaps four or five years of age, dressed in a red pullover, climbed up onto my lap and snuggled against me. "As you did it to one of the least of these . . . you did it to me."[20] This little girl had done something to me, a gift of love. I held her close and rocked her, with tears in my eyes. This is what it comes down to, over and over: children, children to teach us, children to claim from us our best, children to be true to, to protect with justice, to give peace. I took communion with the little girl in my arms and believed that somehow both were the body of Christ. I would never forget her eyes looking up at me, the warmth of her body curled on my lap, the courage and the faith which was palpable in that chapel.

At the end of the service we filed out of the chapel into the bright sun, timidly reaching to touch each other, not knowing how to say much but *gracias*. We walked to different homes where we were guests for lunch, knowing that everything we ate put a pinch in the family food supply. Some of the homes were not much more than shacks of wood planking, others were rudimentary brick and mortar. The home where I had lunch consisted of one large room in which we ate; a small kitchen area in which cooking was done over a wood fire and which opened out into a small, cluttered back yard; and a bedroom which was closed off behind pulled drapes. In one corner of the living room was an old fashioned model of sewing machine powered by a foot pedal. The young wife used it to sew together school uniforms which were cut elsewhere and assembled in homes such as hers. It was a form of cottage industry and helped feed the family. The husband worked on a farm. They had three children who lived in the house with

---

[20] Matthew 25:40b, RSV

them, along with an elderly grandmother. They told us, as best we could understand, the plans the village had to build more homes and to bring in electricity and sanitation facilities as soon as the war could be stopped. These were poor people, but they had discovered their power and pride in themselves and in what they could do, and an aggressive faith in God. They indeed deserved respect. They had mine. I hoped they would get my country's respect.

Then it was time for five of us to reboard the bus for Managua where we'd catch the plane for Guatemala and the human rights demonstration the next day. The others of the delegation would go on to the El Regadio Agricultural Cooperative. Somehow, it was hard for me to leave. When I'd come out of my hosts' home after lunch and begun to walk down the street, the little girl in the red pullover came up to me, and I'd carried her as we walked around the village. Now I had to put her down. She was so somber, her eyes so full of questions she didn't know how to ask and I didn't know how to answer. I thought of my own daughter, Karen, and my sons, Mark and David and Tom, and all the hundreds of children I had held at the baptismal fount over the years — all of them with questions they didn't know how to ask and I didn't know how to answer. I knelt down beside this little girl and kissed her and said, in English, "I love you. Do you understand?" She nodded her head solemnly and kept looking unblinkingly at me. I think, past the language barrier, she did understand what I'd said to her. I also think she was asking me if I understood. I remember her eyes. And I know it will take all of my life — time, energy, spirit — to really understand what it means for me to love that little girl, to love my own children, to love the children of the earth. Yea, to be a child of the earth, a child of God, "a God who sweats in the street. . .as One very close to us." So the Stranger snuck up on me again in Esteli as a little dark-eyed girl.

On the trip back to Managua, I felt overwhelmed, yet curiously grateful. I felt close to the people I was traveling with — to Bob Edgar and Ted Weiss, to Bill Coffin and Phil Berryman. They, and the others of the delegation, were brave and good human beings, faithful to a larger vision, daring to drag the vision into the dust and scuffle of the arena. I felt I had asked the wound what it felt — a hundred wounds, a thousand wounds; wounds of these people of Central America, but my own wounds as well; and the wounds of my traveling colleagues and my country, too. With insistent clarity I'd heard a word to speak back to the sword: "Beat yourself into plowshares." With the support and challenge of these companions, I felt that maybe I could say those words a bit louder and clearer wherever I was. With their help I could say those words for the sake of the wounds and the children of the earth. More than ever I understood what Public Sanctuary is about.

Awe

"How afraid are you?" I felt awkward in asking. I didn't recall ever putting that question to anyone before, the assumption being that either you're afraid or you're not; and if you are, you try not to show it or say so (especially if you're a "man," or pretending to be one). You just buckle on your helmet, or pull up your jock or your socks, or grit your teeth and spit (if your mouth isn't too dry), suck in your gut and have at it. Yet somehow, for all my awkwardness in asking, the question seemed accurate to the circumstances. We were on a plane plowing through the darkness toward Guatemala, and we were on a mission we'd been advised not to undertake because it was potentially dangerous. So, I knew we were all afraid. But, for reasons I couldn't have articulated at that moment, it seemed important to me to find out how afraid my companions were — and how afraid I was — so I could synchronize the pounding of my heart with the scurrying of my brain and try to match emotion to some semblance of reality.

Fear is a curious emotion. It can instruct, and it can intimidate. It can warn of danger, and it can fabricate or inflate danger. I knew that the fear I and the·others felt was grounded in reality. Death threats had been made against the two Congressmen Bob Edgar and Ted Weiss at the last minute, forcing them to withdraw from the planned trip to observe the human rights demonstration in Guatemala on April 13, 1985. Despite the fact that the death threats included the other three of us as members of the delegation — Bill Coffin, Phil Berryman, and myself — we had decided to go anyway. We did not carry the same political and diplomatic responsibilities that rightfully concerned Edgar and Weiss. Still, because of the volatility and uncertainty of the the situation in Guatemala, not to have been afraid to go would have been a symptom of pathological bravado.

But once the decision had focused the blur a bit, I knew that bravado hadn't been the issue. During the first moments of the flight, I came to realize that the choice we'd had to make as we wrestled with the options in the Managua airport was not whether we *should* go into Guatemala for the demonstration, but whether we *would* go in. Maybe, more often than not, that's the choice we actually have as human beings, as people of faith, as the church of Christ. And as we face that recurring choice, fear plays its hand, usually intimidating us by inflating any possible danger. Too often my fear has argued me out of doing things I should have — or into doing things I shouldn't have — frequently in the guise of morality, so I don't even have to admit that fear was my real motivation.

I suspect most people are like that, which is probably why more congregations haven't followed the example of the Good Samaritan by declaring Public Sanctuary. I really don't think it's because they necessarily believe in the morality of the law, or the government, though that is their defense — a defense based on the strange contention that the legality of an act is the prerequisite of its morality rather than vice versa. But rather, it's because they are afraid of the potential consequences of anything that has even a whiff of civil disobedience about it. I'd guess the real problem is that they are frightened of the penalties if they are accused or convicted of breaking the law. For me, the issue of whether or not to participate in Public Sanctuary has been a continuation of my life-long learning that the essential struggle of life is the multi-dimensional struggle between fear and faithfulness, of which the wrestling in the Managua airport had been an extension course.

"How afraid are you?" I looked over at Bill Coffin sitting in the middle of the row of three seats, and at Phil Berryman next to the window. The question had surprised them, startled them out of their private thoughts. As soon as I'd broken the silence, something Nikos Kazantzakis wrote unaccountably flashed through my mind:

> "There are three kinds of souls, three kinds of prayers.
> One: I am a bow in your hands, Lord. Draw me lest I rot.
> Two: Do not overdraw me, Lord. I shall break. Three:
> Overdraw me, and who cares if I break!"[1]

I was bemused that my remembrance of Kazantzakis coincided with the fact that there were three of us together on this venture. I really don't think I was trying to determine which category each of us fit into, so much as which prayer each of us might be uttering or getting ready to utter.

"How afraid am I?" Bill echoed. "I suppose on a scale of one to ten, about seven and a half."

Phil nodded, "Yeah, I guess about that."

I felt relieved. Allowing for macho adjustments, we were all in the same ball park. I was glad I'd asked; it helped. It dawned on me that maybe courage is half corporate and begins in confession. It's only a partial truth that fear alerts us to danger. Maybe the rest of it is that the danger — announced by the snap of twigs, the shift of shadows, the rustle of wind — isn't necessarily demonic and destructive. It can be — maybe usually is — some form of a confrontation with something, or someone, holy and awesome. Maybe whatever the lurking danger, and the fear it provokes, it is an invitation to wrestle with ul-

---

[1]From page 494 of REPORT TO GRECO by Nikos Kazantzakis. Copyright 1965 by Simon and Schuster, Inc. Reprinted by permission of Simon and Schuster, Inc.

timate things such as the meaning of your life, your loves, your loyal-
ties, your mortality, and your gods. Maybe danger, crisis, simply gath-
ers up your life and squeezes it so close and tight you can't squirm out
of dealing with it and deciding about it — and not just once, but again
and again, since danger is an inevitable condition of mortality. And
there is old Jacob thrashing by the Jabbok . . . and old Loder thrashing
toward Guatemala with my friends, whom I sensed were part of the
blessing the Stranger bestows. If a major portion of Jacob's blessing
was to become Israel, a nation, surely a major portion of my blessing
was to be graced with some friends.

So we began to talk, at first as if we were part of a Woody Allen
movie. At one point, Bill and I assured Phil, who is physically much
smaller than either of us, that if there was trouble and any shooting
started, we would protect him. Phil, who had lived in Guatemala for
several years, speaks fluent Spanish and looks quite Latin, smiled
knowingly at us and replied, "If there's trouble and they start shooting, I'll see you big gringos later." But increasingly the talk moved to
more serious levels. We talked about why we were going, about what
was happening in Central America, about the ferment and struggles
of the Third World countries, and about the seemingly intentional
drift of the two great world powers toward increasing armaments, he-
gemony and the possibility of war. Despair always chews at the edges
of such talk.

So, we were prompted to circle back to ask again *why* were we
going — three little people off to Guatemala on such a relatively inconsequential mission when weighed on the large scale of international events and world history. We fumbled with it for a moment before Phil said something I'll never forget: "You know, what impresses
me now is not the enormity of the darkness, but the courage and faith
and commitment of a few people in spite of it. I've come increasingly
to trust the community of the resurrection, because I have seen it and
experienced it in these people again and again. I've had friends
killed in the struggle, but something unpredictable and powerful always happens because of that, and beyond that. I believe that's what
resurrection is about."

I don't remember what we said in response to his words, and it doesn't matter. What I do remember is that if someone had asked me if I belonged to that community of resurrection, at that moment I would have said, "Yes!" I was with two other members of it. Oh, I limped, of course, on feet pierced by my timidities and fears, heart skewered by my duplicities and betrayals, hands crimped by frailties and doubts. Still I was there, winging in the darkness toward the darkness, but with light enough as one of three — a member of the community of resurrection. There was a quiet kind of joy in it. If someone asks me now if I belong to that resurrection community, I say, "Yes," still, however I may stammer it. "Yes, if only a probationary member. Short of forever, maybe that's all any of us can be, but we can be that."

The "No Smoking, Fasten Seat Belts" sign winked on, and the descent began. Almost shyly I suggested we say the Lord's Prayer, and almost reluctantly, Bill and Phil agreed. We joined hands and repeated the prayer, but even as my lips formed the words, I knew that the moment of our most exposed vulnerability had passed, and we were girding up for whatever battle we were about to engage in. The lights of Guatemala City glowed brighter outside the window, attaching to identifiable buildings as we roared in over them. I thought again of David rejecting Saul's armor, choosing instead his sling and five smooth stones. I wondered what our stones were . . . and hoped we'd chosen the right one. The tires hit, squealed on the runway, the engines roared to slow us, the cabin lights came on. We'd arrived in the land of beauty and terror which Joel and Gabriela loved, feared and had told me so much about.

Bill swore he smelled the smoke even before we entered the reception area. In any case, Roger Gamble — the Deputy Chief of Mission of the United States Embassy in Guatemala — had a long, black cigar in his teeth as he and three other embassy staff people met us as we deplaned. Whether or not the smoke was from the cigar, under the veneer of their congeniality unmistakably glowed the smoldering coals of irritation. To them, we were potential trouble-makers who had come to Guatemala in total disregard of their warnings and, to top it off, had pulled them away from who-knows-what Friday night frolics. The only thing that checked their irritation was their knowledge of Bill Coffin's reputation — a reputation which, however useful,

I'd come to see as being a trap which isolated Bill from people, to the loss of everyone. The thing I couldn't figure was why, sensing that isolation and its sad consequences, I still envied his instant recognition factor whenever I was with him, and somehow felt belittled by it. Was it Augustine who said, "The motions of a man's heart are more numerous than the hairs on his head?" If not, whoever said it is right, at least in my case. Maybe the secret to purity of heart is baldness. Well, my hair *is* getting thinner...

The embassy people convened us in a corner of the reception room and began to explain to us the dangers of the situation and to inform us that they could not be responsible in any way for our safety. They told us there was talk of a coup; the situation was extremely fluid; there had been more death threats against CoDel (this time I chuckled at that code name for the Congressional Delegation which made the three of us seem much more important than we were), so we would be well advised to take the next plane out. We countered by telling them we understood the dangers but were intent on staying. If that was the case, they suggested we stay at a hotel out near the embassy so we'd be safer. We asked where the other observers of the demonstration were staying, particularly those from Americas Watch, the international human rights organization. They told us those people were probably at the Pan American Hotel in a bad section at the center of the city where a student from the United States had been killed recently. Nevertheless, we said we preferred to stay there. Mr. Gamble curtly informed us that he would supply a car to take us in, but that would be all the embassy could do for us. I asked if they would also supply a car to take us to the airport on Sunday morning. Mr. Gamble said he would try to arrange that, but it would depend on the availability of a vehicle at the time. With that, the conversation ended. I thought to myself that if we were a pain in the ass to these people, they'd have to stand in line for treatment behind a lot of other folk to whom we'd already transmitted that affliction. But then, sometimes being a carrier isn't all bad.

The embassy delegation escorted us through customs, providing us diplomatic immunity, and took us to a car where Mr. Gamble bid us good-by and turned us over to his assistants — most particularly to

Lynn Schiveley, a political officer at the embassy. As it turned out, Lynn Schiveley was our primary contact person with the embassy during our two days in Guatemala. On the drive to the hotel, he told us he had been a successful dentist in Orange County, California, and had made a mid-life career change to the diplomatic service. None of us pressed him for details or asked what qualified him, as a dentist, to be a political officer in the United States foreign service. He was certainly congenial, and maybe that's all it really takes. There are many noteworthy examples of how far a little shrewdness and a lot of congeniality can get a person in the world of politics.

Guatemala City could easily pass for a southern California city, at least at night. There are modern neon signs, prosperous looking showrooms, expensive and recent vintage automobiles on the streets — payoffs of a repressive, totalitarian government to those who don't make trouble for it. When we arrived at the Pan American Hotel, Schiveley went in with us to help see that we got registered, a process Phil Berryman undertook since he knew the language and carried the funds for the trip. After several minutes, I realized Schiveley had disappeared, and I assumed he'd gone back to the embassy. But he reappeared as we were talking with some priests from Canada who had heard we were coming. They had been waiting in the lobby for us because they felt completely underbriefed about what was happening. Schiveley (whom we kept calling "Shiverly" because it seemed to fit him) motioned us to one side and told us that a car would pick us up at ten o'clock the next morning for a briefing at the embassy. Some Roman Catholic priests — from a section of the country where the guerrilla action was heavy — and Aryeh Neier of Americas Watch would be there as well. For whatever reasons, the invitation clearly signaled a change in the embassy's attitude. We agreed to the briefing, said good-by to Schiveley, and told the Canadians we'd meet with them in an hour in our hotel room. We went up and started unpacking while we shared impressions and tentative plans. Phil got on the phone to contact some people he knew in Guatemala. It had begun.

Within an hour there were eight people in our room: Beatriz Manz, a Chilean-born anthropologist and PhD fellow at Radcliffe Col-

lege, who herself had the terrifying experience of having been arrested, detained and gruelingly interrogated by the Guatemalan military
in 1983 during a field trip to study the Maya-Quiche Indians; Gloria
Kinder, who had also lived in Guatemala as a missionary of the Presbyterian Church, U.S.A.; the three Canadians — Reverend Pierre
Goldberger, Principal of United Theological College of Montreal; Father Ernie Schibli of the Social Justice Commission of Montreal, and
The Peace and Justice Office of the Archdiocese of Montreal; Reverend Chris Ferguson, Presbyterian-United Church of Canada Chaplain
at Magil University; and the three of us. One of the Canadians took his
tension out on a pipe wafting off clouds of smoke which gave the
dimly lighted room a rather eerie character, as though we'd moved
from a Woody Allen to an Ingmar Bergman movie.

None of us had much updated information about the situation,
except that the human rights demonstration was going to be held
despite the intimidating actions of the government. So, the discussion centered on devising a strategy for the few of us to follow. Some
of us — notably Bill Coffin and Beatrice Manz — wanted to initiate
bold, provocative action of some kind which would confront the brutality of the Guatemalan government. Others — notably Phil Berryman and I — held that we were there as observers, not leaders of the
demonstration, and that our presence was a clear, strong statement
of support and concern beyond which we had no right to go . . . especially since three of us, at least, might be seen as representing the
congressmen in a way which could compromise them. Also, any action
of ours that led to trouble could discredit the indigenous leadership
of the demonstration.

It was the start of a conflict that continued and intensified during
our stay, and about which I felt increasing inner turmoil. Motivation is
always murky territory, and I wasn't certain whether the position I advocated was based on timidity or responsibility. Even though Phil
with his experience in Guatemala agreed with me, I felt vulnerable to
the charges of moral waffling to which Bill kept alluding during the
discussion. I wish I wasn't always caught in the complexities of issues
which make me stammer instead of toss off effective one-liners. But
then, how do you maintain integrity? How do you resist being cor-

nered into simplistic stands and statements by the simplistic stands and statements of the opposition, however tyrannous? Bill has his way of resisting, I struggle with mine. I knew from experience that there are times when angry advocacy becomes oppressively arrogant; even as there are times when quivery caution becomes the cowardice of complicity. The trick is to sense when and how either begins to happen in you or to you. Was this such a time? There certainly was tension among us as we tried to determine how to respond to the situation, but there was nothing to do but argue it out, however uncomfortable it made any of us. My gut was in a knot.

Finally, someone made the suggestion that we hold a news conference before the demonstration which was scheduled to begin at three o'clock the next afternoon. We could issue a joint statement, then answer questions individually. The recent news about the threats to CoDel, plus the fact that Bill Coffin was with us, made it reasonably certain that both TV crews and newspaper personnel would cover the news conference. In El Salvador we'd already talked to reporters from *Time* magazine and *The New York Times* and knew that they were scheduled to come in for the demonstration. We'd contact them and get the word out. Bill agreed to write the joint statement which we'd edit before issuing. The meeting broke up.

Phil immediately got on the phone, Bill went into the adjoining room to begin drafting the statement, and I laid on my back watching the residue of smoke move in curious patterns around the room, depending on the way the air currents took it. So moves the Spirit as well, I mused dreamily. I thought of Phil's reference to the resurrection community. There's nothing in scripture or history to suggest the resurrection community can't — even shouldn't — fight among itself. The problem isn't the fighting, painful as it might be, but the self-righteous way it's usually done . . . or not done. Too often Christians' avoidance of fighting openly and directly tends to reduce love to a superficial niceness which doesn't enable honest dialogue, nurture personal growth or confront controversial issues. As a result, local congregations are immobilized into gatherings of cosmetic congeniality, layered over boils of gossip and the scars of rejection of brothers and sisters with different views and life styles.

I became aware in those moments that part of what I was thinking about was my own longing for personal sanctuary in a community of care and faith; and how closely related my longing was — and, no doubt, that of many others — to the commitment to Public Sanctuary. For me, Public Sanctuary — as was this demonstration for human rights in Guatemala — is based partially on the theological insight of Reinhold Niebuhr's "Christian Realism": in a sinful world any power, however seemingly good, must be countered by another power, because in its human exercise, all power becomes corrupting and idolatrous. But personal sanctuary seems to push the issue even deeper. The question becomes, "Within the community of faith and love, how does the necessary confrontation between your power and my power — i.e. the views and ideas, convictions and needs of each of us — become *our* power?" That has been the struggle and the longing of my professional life, and here it was again. I wondered if I'd ever find a way to unsnarl the knot of it. Maybe it begins in some mutual realization that, this side of the grave, none of us are ever finished getting resurrected. Perhaps the peace of it resides in realizing that if the part that's up to us is to "sin on boldly" (which is how Luther described trust), the resurrecting part is up to God. So it occurred to me, as I lay there, to start praying as best I could. At least when you're praying, stammering must be acceptable.

At last we fell into bed, exhausted. Early that morning we'd left Managua, Nicaragua, for Esteli; and now, well past midnight, we bedded down in Guatemala City on the fringe of a political hurricane. I don't know how many minutes it was after we turned out the lights that the telephone rang. Our designated answerer was Phil, and through the muffle of near sleep, I managed to track his initial conversation with the operator and learned the call was from Edgar and Weiss in Managua. Then his voice shouted, incredulously, "Collect? What do you mean they're calling collect?" I started to laugh and could hear Bill laughing in the next bed. "Refuse to pay," I mumbled. Shortly someone was on the other end of the line and Phil kept asking, "Why did you call collect? My God, a collect call! I know you gave me money to pay for our expenses, but what if we run short? Why a collect call?" Finally, some satisfactory explanation must have been forthcoming, because the conversation droned off in more subdued tones, and Bill and I laughed ourselves off to sleep.

But somewhere just before I teetered off the edge of conscious-ness, I remember thinking that in some way every call we get is a col-lect call — wanting something, asking for something, forcing some sort of answer — especially if the call is from God . . . which it always is, one way or another. H. Richard Niebuhr's assertion keeps getting con-firmed for me, even though I never quite enact it: "God is acting in all actions upon you. So respond to all actions upon you as to respond to his action." Imagine: life is a collect call! Now that's a thought to fall asleep on. Even so, the springs of laughter run deep and the Stranger never lets you alone, even if occasionally the hold She gets you in tickles.

Early the next morning, the eight of us met for nearly two hours with the three women leaders of the Grupo de Apoyo Mutuo (G.A.M.) — the Mutual Support Group — which had organized the demonstra-tion for that afternoon. We met in a small conference room off the hotel's main dining room. Few meetings have left me more deeply marked. The three women were accompanied by Joe McIntire, a member of Peace Brigade International which had offered them a "safe house" to live in prior to the demonstration and provided them with constant companionship in an attempt to a protect them.

Two weeks earlier, there had been six leaders of the Grupo. But as the announced day for the demonstration drew nearer, the gov-ernment of General Mejia Victores intensified the pressure on the leaders, trying to intimidate them into canceling their plans and at-tempting to discredit the demonstration by announcing that it was managed and directed by subversive elements. On March 30, 1985, Hector Gomez, one of the leaders, was apprehended by four armed men as he left a meeting of the Grupo, and the next day his body was found. He'd been tortured, tongue cut out, and shot to death. In the following week, another Grupo leader — Maria Rosario Godoy de Cuevas, a young mother of twenty-four — was found dead in her car, along with her twenty-one year old brother and her three year old son. The "official story" was that they had died in an accident when their car fell into a ravine. However, the car was undamaged, and independent sources — including Guatemala's Archbishop Prospero Penados de Barrio — said the three had been murdered by asphyxiation. A third Grupo leader had gone underground and reportedly left the country to save his life.

Now the three remaining leaders sat drinking coffee and talking quietly with us on the morning of what was surely one of the most crucial days of their lives. One of the first things they said was that they knew it could be their last day on earth, or close to the last, because of the risk they were taking in leading the demonstration. Their names were Nineth de Garcia, Blanca de Rosal and Isabil de Castanan. They were physically small, almost fragile-looking, and each of them wore a visor-type cap which gave them a childlike appearance. But once again, the most memorable, powerful feature about them was their eyes — large and unblinking, dark and deep set, sad but fiery. I'd seen those eyes in Joel and Gabriela, and years before had seen them in the young marshals of Martin Luther King, Jr.'s March to Montgomery. They were the eyes of people who had faced death — their own death — and not flinched. Yet, the presence of these women was profoundly one of life, of the holiness that life radiates when rendered to its essentials. The power of it eludes ideological or religious labeling. These women might never have heard of W.H. Auden, but they exemplified his insight: " . . . life is the testing you are bound to refuse until you have consented to die."[2] They were alive, witnessing for life. Chris Ferguson, the Chaplain at Magil, rightly observed that they were reminiscent of the women who first visited the tomb on Easter morning and came back with an awesome spirit and vision.

Nineth was the spokesperson, and the story she told was simple, urgent, compelling. Once again, I heard echoes of what Joel and Gabriela had told us. The kidnapping or unexplained disappearances of people in Guatemala had been going on for decades — between fifty and seventy-five thousand people in the last ten years. In 1983 when

[2]From "For The Time Being: A Christmas Oratorio" from W. H. AUDEN: COLLECTED LONGER POEMS, edited by Edward Mendelson. Copyright © 1944, renewed 1972 by W. H. Auden. Reprinted by permission of Random House, Inc.

General Oscar Mejia Victores came to power, the kidnappings intensified against students and labor leaders, and spread to urban areas,
in addition to the villages where the disappearances had been con-
centrated before. Since 1983, there had been over three thousand
disappearances.[3] I thought of Gabriela whose brother had disappeared two years before and was never heard from again. As people
went from morgues to cemeteries to government offices to church
leaders looking for members of their families who had disappeared,
they repeatedly met and recognized each other. Four women, each
looking for a son, or husband, or father, decided to get together and
form a group for mutual emotional and spiritual support, which is how
the name Grupo de Apoyo Mutuo was chosen. Nineth explained that
the rationale for the group could be found in the peasant saying,
"One swallow doesn't make a spring." It is a poignant, poetic sum-
mary of the hope and faith of the group. The members of the Mutual
Support Group simply wanted their loved ones returned to them
alive, and they believed it could happen.

Early on, they went to Archbishop Barrio and asked him to add
his name and influence to their group and to the statements they
wanted to make to the Guatemalan government as families of the
kidnapped people. The Archbishop refused, citing what had happened in El Salvador when Archbishop Oscar Romero had spoken out
for the people: Romero had been called a communist and killed. The
Archbishop was sympathetic but unwilling to be involved. (A testimony to how cruel and oppressive the situation has become is that in
June, 1985, Archbishop Barrio, in contrast to his earlier silence, issued
a statement demanding that the government give definite responses
on cases of disappeared Guatemalans.)

So the women went to the media, for two reasons: one, they
thought that if their names and faces were made public, as well as
their insistence on the non-political orientation of the Mutual Sup-

---

[3]It is extremely difficult to document the numbers of "disappeared" persons in Guatemala. The figures given here are those quoted by the families of "disappeared"
persons.

port Group, the government might not be violent against them; two, they wanted to advertise an invitation to other families of disappeared persons to meet with them the following Saturday morning. (Apparently that kind of advertising in the print media is common in Central America.) On the following Saturday, twenty-nine additional families were represented. At first, the meetings consisted of each family telling their individual story, sharing information and hope. It became clear that government security forces were behind the disappearances and that the number of disappeared included many children from six to sixteen years of age, as well as a number of pregnant women. Within a few months, the Mutual Support Group grew to representatives of six hundred and thirty families from twenty-two departments of the country. It was no longer possible for each family to tell their story, and the group divided into sub-committees with various tasks: Organization, Publicity, Executive.

There have been only three or four cases of disappeared people reappearing, and Nineth named them and the circumstances. The most telling story was of Alvaro Rene Sosa Ramos. He had been picked up by army personnel less than a month earlier, had been accused of being a guerrilla, and was tortured with ax handles and electric prods. Finally, he had agreed to take the soldiers to an address in Zone Nine (which he knew was close to a foreign embassy) where he said he might identify some other collaborators. On the way the soldiers had seen two women they thought they wanted to arrest, stopped the car and run after them. Though Sosa Ramos was handcuffed, he managed to jump out of the car and run to the Belgian Embassy. The soldiers shot and wounded him. They also tried to storm the embassy, but the Belgian Ambassador told them to stop. Shortly, some embassy staff managed to slip Sosa Ramos, who was badly wounded, out the back and to a hospital where he had to be guarded from further attack. Fortunately, the soldiers did not massacre people and burn the embassy building, as they had the Spanish Embassy and personnel in 1980 in a similar incident. Later, the Guatemalan government apologized to the Belgian Ambassador for what had happened. Sosa Ramos is now a refugee in Canada, which he reached under the protection of the Belgian Embassy.

Nineth also told us of some incidents when kidnappings had been witnessed, especially the kidnapping of children from the villages after the army had machine-gunned people and destroyed their homes. Beatriz Manz indicated she had visited some of the scenes of those massacres. As the time grew short, Nineth told us that in the past several weeks the government had intensified its pressure on the Mutual Support Group — especially on the leadership — labeling them revolutionaries and subversives in an attempt to discredit them and undermine popular support for their efforts. Since the murders of Hector Gomez and Maria Rosario Godoy, conditions had become very uncertain. The only certainty was that the government seemed intent on carrying out its threat to exterminate the leadership of the group.

Nevertheless, the women were determined to carry through on the demonstration no matter what the personal consequences. "This may be our last effort," Nineth said, snuffing out the last of a chain of cigarettes she had been smoking. Then she looked at each of us and thanked us for being there, for being willing to walk beside them, because by our presence we gave them strength to do what they must do. None of us could answer at first, and then Bill Coffin said, for us all, "It is we who thank you." The women got up and left. I stood and watched them in awe. They were so small, so few, so vulnerable, so outrageously courageous. I would not forget their eyes, deepened by the struggle, until they were bottomless, hinting at the true source of their strength and validating Jesus' words: "The eye is the lamp of the body. So, if your eye is sound, your whole body will be full of light."[4]

Lynn Schiveley was waiting for us with a car. Manz, Kinder, Coffin, Berryman and I were driven to Roger Gamble's home for the briefing with the three Roman Catholic priests who were in Guatemala City from a combat area of the country. The priests were all originally from the United States, and two of them had lived in Guatemala for over ten years. Their names must remain anonymous to protect their identities. The danger in which they work is extreme and, indeed, one of

[4]Matthew 6:22, RSV

them was a fairly recent replacement for a priest who had been killed in their area. (No one made any accusations about which side killed their colleague.) Aryeh Neier, the Executive Director of Americas Watch, and Jemera Rone, a young woman attorney with a New York firm who had recently joined Americas Watch as counsel, sat in on the briefing.

The priests were warm, friendly, but understandably wary. My memories of the briefing are somewhat fragmentary. We sat on a large, airy, glass enclosed porch, and the day stretched lazily in the sun. The intensity of the time with the women of the Mutual Support Group had left me drained, and I had difficulty keeping my attention focused. I kept wondering what these priests knew about the disappeared out in the villages, and what the embassy staff persons present knew — that staff including, in addition to Mr. Gamble and Mr. Schiveley, the political counselor, the counsel general and the press officer.

It was obvious from the outset that the priests would not be able to answer any of the sensitive questions we might want to ask them, which made the meeting a bit stiff and tedious. At times I caught myself watching the Guatemalan gardener working on the Gamble's lawn right outside the window. The family dog, which had been ushered out shortly after our arrival, kept nipping at the gardener's heels and generally pestering him. I could tell that the gardener was getting frustrated with the dog but could do nothing about it. I suppose you could see that as some sort of parable about the relationship of the United States with the people of Guatemala, if you wanted to press it. I didn't.

In essence the priests told us that their work was increasingly confined to "pastoral activity" because of government constraints on the one hand, and guerrilla activity on the other. The villages where they carried on their ministries were harassed by both sides, and combat action swept back and forth through and around the villages. They had to be careful not to take sides which would compromise them with the people, with the guerrilla forces, or with the army, since to alienate any of the three factions would endanger their work, if not their lives.

As they spoke, it was evident they were being careful not to of-
fend — even by inference — the official policy of the United States in
Central America. So, even if we had desired them to speak more
plainly — as we did — we understood the difficulty of their circumstances. We expressed our appreciation for the information they
shared, and the meeting adjourned. The priests had to leave, and we
were scheduled to have further discussion with the embassy staff and
with U.S. Ambassador Alberto Piedra, who had just arrived.

As we got up and moved into the living room, Bill and I hung back
and managed to ask one of the priests, who had been longest in Guatemala, what would happen to Guatemalan refugees such as Joel and
Gabriela should they be deported by the United States back to Guatemala. Without hesitation, the priest replied, "Almost without doubt
they would be killed within days, a few weeks at most." It was the
most revealing moment of the briefing. A knowledgeable on-the-
scene observer had confirmed our basic contention with the Immigration and Naturalization Service that the refugees were not economic
but political refugees, and if returned to their country would be in extreme jeopardy. But, sadly, we could not use the information to make
our case for our refugees, since without specific names, dates and testimony — which we could not get without endangering the priest —
what he had just told us would be considered hearsay evidence in
court. It was a poignant moment, one of those times in which a bit of
truth lodges in your heart as what must remain a private pain. But, it
was also a powerful propellant to carry on with the Public Sanctuary
effort.

In the living room the conflict of the night before broke out again.
Gamble, Piedra and the embassy staff had learned of our planned
press conference and were intent on dissuading us from holding it at
all, or at least postponing it until after the demonstration. They insisted that having a press conference could be personally dangerous
for us, as well as unnecessarily inflaming to the situation.

Almost immediately, the primary adversaries were Gamble ver-
sus Coffin, Coffin finally arguing that if we were arrested and detained,
it would help the cause. As the discussion progressed, it became evident that Coffin, Berryman and I were adamant about *having* the press

conference, but that there was some disagreement among us about *how* to handle it. Exposing our disagreement in that setting made us very uneasy and actually fueled Coffin's "full speed ahead and damn the torpedoes" attitude.

Finally, Aryeh Neier mediated a resolution. He pointed out, more effectively than either I or Berryman had been able, that the danger was not only to ourselves — about which we had a right to decide — but more particularly to the members and leaders of the Mutual Support Group, who would be most subject to retaliation by the government should we be unnecessarily provocative in what we said. Pressed by the shortness of time, and with some residual fuming, we agreed on a compromise: we'd issue a statement in support of the Mutual Support Group and only mildly, indirectly critical of the Guatemalan government. But, we would issue the statement as scheduled, an hour before the demonstration began (when the press would be available) — not after it, as Piedra, Gamble and the embassy people wanted (when the press would be less apt to attend). With that, we went to lunch, prime candidates for heartburn.

Conversation at lunch was strained. The embassy staff seemed intent on persuading us that the situation in Guatemala was not nearly as bad as we might think. The political counselor, Richard Graham, argued that the Guatemalan elections in 1982 had moved the country toward democratic rule and that the elections were "non-fraudulent." After some relatively gentle ebb of conversation about just how democratic the system actually was — since, no matter the appearance, the government has been and is run completely by the military — followed by Graham's flow that the "non-fraudulent" elections gave validated civilian power rather than military leadership, Neier plunged into the discussion with an angry splash. "It depends entirely on what you mean by 'non-fraudulent,'" he asserted. "If you mean no ballots were tampered with, probably that is true of the 1982 elections and will be true in the 1985 elections here, as well. But if you mean that the elections freely and openly express the will of the majority of people, it is obviously not true. Probably no ballots are tampered with in Russia either, but surely we wouldn't call their elections 'non-fraudulent,' would we?"

It was a decisive point deftly made, and the debate was over, though Mr. Graham continued to sputter for a time, and the other staff, half-heartedly and ineffectively, tried to plug the leak in their dam. Aryeh Neier, who looks Darrowsque, unimposing, and rumpled every time I see him, had diplomatically leveled the third "You-guys-don't-give-a-fuck-about-these-people" I'd heard on this trip. In essence, that made it three for three: Coffin, to the U.S. Embassies in El Salvador and Nicaragua; Neier, to the U.S. Embassy in Guatemala.

On the way back to the hotel for the press conference, we tried to sort out how to proceed. Phil, who we'd agreed would make the statement to the media, expressed some minor reservations, one being that he was still *persona non grata* in Guatemala. I said if he was uncomfortable doing it, I'd make the statement, which, after all, we'd shaped together. Immediately, Bill objected. "You'll waffle, Loder," he said. The words hit like acid on my spirit, burning, eating at me all out of proportion, because Bill had tossed them . . . and probably because something in them might be true. Angrily, defensively, I spat back, "And you'd be arrogantly provocative." He was riding behind me in the third seat of the car, and I quickly turned away toward the front, clamping my jaw, trying to breathe and focus my eyes. My God, here we both were in dangerous circumstances, against the wishes of a lot of powerful people, and yet we had to drop our plumb lines to expose the other's list. Why? The ego which most needs resurrecting dies hardest.

After a few more minutes of talk about some necessary details, Bill put his hand on my arm and said, "I'm sorry. I didn't mean that." I nodded and replied, "That's okay. I didn't mean it either." That was the end of it, except I think we both dodged the truth. I think the truth was that we *did* mean what we'd said, but much more deeply, we meant something infinitely more important about each other that we *didn't* say: maybe something we couldn't say at that moment — being men, and competitive, and ego driven, and a little scared under it all — but something we wanted to say; something about mutual weakness and dependence, trust and love — real things we so desperately need to say, and hear, yet somehow lose track of, as though relationships and issues between two or three people aren't as critical as those seemingly more decisive relationships and issues involving great numbers of people. Maybe someday we'll learn. After all, Jesus began with only twelve and the integrity of their relationships. Ah, the resurrection community! If nothing else, it's about hope.

An unexpectedly large number of television crews, newspaper and magazine reporters had assembled in one of the hotel's larger conference rooms by the time we arrived. We joined the Canadians in the lobby for a brief, hurried consultation about procedure. Then we entered the room and took seats at a large table. Phil read our statement, followed by Reverend Goldberger making a statement for the Canadians. The restlessness among the press from the United States was noticeable.

After one or two questions about the congressmen and the CoDel death threats, a young reporter from *The New York Times* asked, "You mean you called this press conference just to tell us you think human life is valuable?" Clearly he was baiting us. Everyone, including the press, knew how inflammable the situation was, which was why there was such extensive international media coverage. But the most saleable "news" is about fire, not tinder, so many of the press people were looking for a match and a headline. I was sitting next to Bill, who had been chaffing and whispering asides to me throughout the conference. Now he rose to the bait, though shrewdly, insisting that we were there to stand with the Grupo and to support their demands to the government of Guatemala for the release of the disappeared people. It was a strong response, made with some well polished Coffinisms, and avoided being overly provocative.

After a few more cursory questions, the conference ended. It had accomplished its purpose: calling attention to the reasons the congressmen were unable to be present (which accurately reflected the repressive quality of the Guatemalan government); alerting the Guatemalan government and other governments of the international community that some CoDel people were there to observe the human rights demonstration; and stating that we strongly, though unofficially, supported the Mutual Support Group, its accusations and demands.

Yet, as we left for the demonstration, I thought that in a basic sense, yes, we *had* called the press conference to say that human life is valuable. The danger in the situation, if not in the world, is that such a witness is not very newsworthy these days. I thought of a Talmud saying on an artist's rendering which hangs in a friend's office: "Whoever preserves a single soul, scripture ascribes to them merit as though they saved an entire world." Something of that truth is why we'd come to Guatemala to watch and support the Mutual Support Group, and why we'd declared Public Sanctuary. Even if governments could not — or did not — believe in the basic value of life (or operate on that level), it is still the moral, faithful response of an individual to neighbor, and ultimately to self. Either human life is *that* valuable or the world is that damnable. Like a lot of things you wish you'd said after the fact, I wished we'd said something like that at the press conference. I hoped our presence might have, even if our words hadn't.

At three o'clock on Saturday afternoon, April 13, 1985, the Mutual Support Group demonstration began. We walked through the streets to the staging area in front of a modern looking office building about three miles from the hotel. When we arrived, perhaps five hundred people had gathered to begin the march through the streets to the National Palace which housed the government of Mejia Victores. One of the marchers was Jack Malinowski from Philadelphia who is the Director of Human Rights/Global Justice for the American Friends Service Committee. Jack had attended some of our services for Public Sanctuary and had been in Guatemala for several weeks perfecting his Spanish. It was good to see him, a living reminder of all those who shared in and led the fight for justice and human rights in the United States and around the world. And, of course, the press was there, TV cameras and microphones thrust at us from all sides, asking questions. The presence of the press in such number, as well as TV crews with equipment mounted on the tops and backs of station wagons moving out in front of the procession, gave a sense of some security to the demonstration.

But very noticeably absent were any uniformed police or army personnel, such as might have been expected and which were always around during any demonstrations in the United States. This absence heightened our sense of danger and made us wary. We did see some of the U.S Embassy staff people milling around, keeping an eye on us. This made us smile, since their original plan had been to have only undercover people in the demonstration. And here we were, forcing the regular staff out on the street and continuing to ruin their weekend. Actually, they were doing their duty: we had been introduced to one of the undercover people when we arrived at the staging area so we could recognize someone who could help in case of trouble.

In a quick strategy conference with Aryeh Neier, who was much more experienced than we in this sort of situation, it was decided that we would spread out and walk at intervals on either side of the procession, keeping an eye on each other as well as the demonstrators, and being sure not to straggle behind where we could get in trouble. Neier, Rone, Manz, and Kinder were to walk on one side; Coffin, Berryman and I on the other; the Canadians together on either side they chose.

The demonstration began to move out. In front was a large pennant stretching across the entire street, bearing the words (in Spanish): "For respect of human dignity, life and liberty! The Mutual Support Group." Walking behind the pennant were Nineth, Blanca and Isabil; and the widow of Hector Gomez, carrying a placard with his picture, and a tiny baby who was his orphan; and the family of Maria Rosario Godoy, also carrying a placard with her picture. Behind them were twenty-three other unintimidated families of disappeared persons, followed by indigenous Indian women from Quiche, Chimaltenango and Quetzaltenango, each dressed in colorful native garb and walking barefoot. (These women were there at great risk, because they came from rural areas and had to account to the authorities for their absence when they returned home.) At the end of the line were law students and other students wearing bandannas in an attempt to disguise their identities, because so many students are among the disappeared and killed persons in Guatemala. There totaled approximately one thousand people in the procession, many joining along the way, resulting in a final number in excess of what had been expected. I thought of Joel and Gabriela as I walked and tried to notice every detail. This was their country, their capital city, their people; finally, their danger which, having fought and resisted as long and well

---

as they could, they'd had to flee.

As the procession moved through the narrow streets in the downtown shopping area, the three women, using a bull horn, led the marchers in rhythmically shouting the rallying cry of the Grupo: "A united people cannot be defeated." Because of the absence of police help, traffic snarled at intersections as we crossed, the cars and marchers dodging each other artfully, sometimes irritably. At about the midway point, someone in a side street threw what turned out to be a smoke bomb at the procession, and people scattered for safety in a moment of near panic. No one knew if it was a real bomb, if others would follow, if it signaled the arrival of the army to disperse the march, or worse. It turned out to be a harmless interruption. The march went on, the street sometimes widening out into a boulevards, sometimes narrowing into a span as of an ancient city. Along the route, people leaned out of windows or stood on the rooftops, watching. Many had cameras or video equipment. There was the ominous sense that the army and secret police, perhaps the CIA, were watching and recording everything.

The earlier word was that there wouldn't be many people on the streets watching the parade. There were, but it wasn't clear whether they were primarily shoppers and only coincidently observers or vice versa. I suspect they didn't want to be clear. Almost without exception, they watched quietly, giving no visible sign of support. I could see fear in their eyes, which may have explained why the only approval for the march they could muster was simply *being* on the walks as the procession passed, and making even that look unintended. Still, they were there and that was a small victory.

As we walked along the street, shopkeepers on either side pulled down heavy metal screens to protect their stores. The sound of those screens clanging into place punctuated the march — the sound of doors slamming, like heavy prison doors. The sound emphasized the pervasive oppression of the country by the government — an oppression which, like an insidious virus, infects people, robbing them even of their will, their identity as human beings. I recalled marching through the black sections of Montgomery, past old black men and women sitting on porches, shaking their heads, tears rolling down their checks as Martin Luther King, Jr., lead that procession from Selma to the capital of Alabama. Those black people couldn't believe what was happening, couldn't claim it as their exodus, either. They'd been intimidated too long, made to stay so long in a place of segregation — not only of body, but of mind and spirit — that they couldn't move beyond it. That happens to people, sometimes without their realizing it. I hope that doesn't happen to me about my perspectives. I thought about some women I know who share that bondage of spirit about their femaleness, in spite of women's liberation. I understood anew, there on the streets of Guatemala City, thinking just how inextricably connected things are, how insidious oppression is, how constant and inclusive the exodus is, and must be. For as long as *any* are in bondage, no one is really free. As long as doors clang shut between people, those on both sides are imprisoned, one way or another. As we marched, the metal screens rumbled into place, the padlocks clicked shut.

When we arrived at the National Palace, the procession stopped. There was a high wooden fence around the plaza in front of the Palace, behind which was construction for a parking building. Just outside the fence was a big mound of earth, and many marchers climbed up for a better view. On the balconies of the Palace, behind pillars, soldiers were in place, though the ground level entrances where shut. Finally, the three women read their demands over the bull horn. There were four: one, the immediate release of all kidnapped or disappeared people and their return alive to their families; two, a meeting with General Mejia Victores at which he would report the results of the Tripartite Commission on Human Rights; three, the apprehension and punishment of the people responsible for the death of Hector Orlando Gomez and Maria Rosario Godoy de Cuevas; four, respect for the right of persons to demand that the disappeared be accounted for (which meant the guarantee of the physical safety of the members of the Mutual Support Group). One of the women took the demands, rolled them up, and placed them on the gate barring the entrance to the Palace.

Then each of the three women threw a long-stemmed white carnation onto the sidewalk in front of the Palace. On signal, one after another — groups of three, four, a dozen, fifty — the marchers threw the white carnations they'd carried on the march high in the air, over the heads of those in front of them, onto the sidewalk. Then the marchers moved around the corner of the plaza and dispersed silently, quickly. I looked at the nearly one thousand carnations lying there forlornly. Those flowers were a symbol of the Mutual Support Group, of their non-violent struggle for justice, of their simple human compassion for freedom. I thought of the students at Kent State who, during their protest against the Vietnam war, had put daisies in the gun barrels of the National Guard Troops. . .just before several students had been shot by those edgy soldiers.

Flowers are supposed to be tokens of peace, of love, of good will. But the white carnations on that sidewalk looked wilted, almost pathetic, as though they had been measured by the strength of the guns of the soldiers who peered from perches in the Palace. The carnations symbolized only weakness, irrelevancy. Maybe. . .maybe. But, as I thought about it, it occurred to me that the marchers who had thrown those carnations were much less afraid, really, than were the soldiers and the wielders of the apparatus of power in government who squinted out at them from behind locked doors and pulled drapes. I kept seeing the eyes of those three women, and I understood that not to be afraid is already to have triumphed in the only battle that matters, finally. As for the rest, let the witness be made. However dark is midnight, the dawn would break. The truth, muted, would be sung in chorus one day. Love trampled would rise to embrace and uphold tomorrow. The kingdom prayed for in rasped voice would come with wonder. That, really, must be what those carnations whispered as they lay on the dusty sidewalk. That really is what the wrestling match with the Stranger is. The resurrection community *is* more impressive than the darkness, and in that moment, once again, I felt awed by the mystery of it. Perhaps that day we had marched the Emmaus Street.[5]

[5]Luke 24:13 ff.

I remembered those in the church in Philadelphia to whom I would be returning shortly who, in their faithful work in Public Sanctuary — and in other equally important ways of witness for justice and compassion — were making their own demonstration, engaging in their own march. I felt profoundly related to them, standing there thousands of miles distant. We'd celebrated Easter together only six days before, standing and singing, with trumpet and tympani, "Christ the Lord is risen today, Alleluia!" And then the last verse:

> "Soar we now where Christ has led. . .
> Following our exalted Head. . .
> Made like Him, like Him we rise. . .
> Ours the cross, the grave, the skies, Alleluia!"

I wonder how many of us knew whereof we sang. I knew at least a little more now.

On one side of the plaza was the great cathedral of Guatemala City. I left the group and went in by myself. It was cool and very peaceful inside, people here and there praying, others walking about looking at the side chapels and the art work. There was also the bustle of preparation for the several masses which would be offered the next day. I sat and tried to pray, and maybe that's what I did, though not in words but in all the images and feelings that spun around in my mind and gut. I thought about the refusal of the Archbishop to join in any advocacy of the Mutual Support Group — and, indeed, neither he nor any of his priests were part of the demonstration. Was that because, as far as the government was concerned, the Archbishop and his superiors had chosen accommodation over opposition? Was that wisdom or just prudence, faithfulness or pragmatism? What is the guiding spirit of the resurrection community? And is a resurrection community what the church usually, or often, is? How is Christ's blood transubstantiated, not just in bread and wine, but in the actual blood and tortured bodies of the oppressed? If the peace in the cathedral is one the world gives — via the tyrannous government of Guatemala — then surely it is a peace the world can take away. And yet. . .what about my peace, or lack of it? What about the peace of the church in my beloved country? I prayed for the Archbishop and me. And for the Mutual Support Group. Lord have mercy, Christ have mercy, Lord have mercy.

I got up and walked around the cathedral, thinking, wondering, trying to assimilate some of what I had seen and felt that day. As I walked, Bill Coffin came up beside me. I was glad to see him. We walked around in silence for a few moments, and then sat in one of the side pews and prayed together briefly. I think it was some sort of offering, our kind of mass, our little act of penitence and petition for healing. As we walked out, I felt there was some ease between us, and I was grateful. Maybe it was just the acceptance of some accurate distance that we needed for the integrity of the relationship. We didn't talk about it. Instead, we walked back toward the hotel, looking for a place to shop.

We found a small store open late which carried a variety of Guatemalan clothes and small art objects. We looked at everything, talking to the woman owner, asking Phil Berryman (who had been waiting for us outside the cathedral) to translate. It was a kind of unwinding, a shift of emphasis. I bought a dress for Jan, and Bill bought gifts for his wife Randy and for people in his church office. Late Saturday afternoon shoppers in Guatemala! I was losing track of myself.

Finally, we walked back to the hotel and pulled up some chairs in a corner of the lobby and ordered beer. People kept coming over to chat, many of whom knew Bill. Some were newspaper people asking for our impressions of the demonstration. After an hour or so, Nineth, Isabil and Blanca came in, accompanied by Joe McIntire of the Peace Brigade. They looked exhausted but exhilarated. A fire of relief and triumph burned in their eyes. They thought the demonstration had been a success, though they knew that even now the government was looking for them. They were going to shower, eat and then go underground for a while. They thanked us again for being there, and then they left. It was the last time we saw them. Just before he left, Joe asked me what I thought they should do. At the moment, we were standing in a small corridor near the telephones, and there was pain and confusion in Joe's eyes. I said I didn't know, but I'd guess they should get out of the country before the government found them and they joined the disappeared. He nodded, and said, softly, "Their work may be over here." I answered, "But what a work it was." He smiled, shook my hand and asked me to stay in touch. Then he left. I haven't heard from him since that night.

At dinner, Aryeh Neier came in and told us he was trying to find a way to get Hector Gomez' family out of Guatemala quickly and asked if we had any ideas. What was really needed was an embassy that would give them asylum status and get them out. The Canadians offered to contact their embassy. I asked Neier if one of the Public Sanctuary cities in the United States would take the family. That would give maximum visibility to them and to the situation in Guatemala. Neier said that any of those cities would be great, but the immediate problem was how to get the family out of the country before they were killed. As we talked, I thought of Joel and Gabriela, and the irony of the situation. Several people were in real and present danger of being killed in Guatemala for political reasons, and yet we could not go to our own United States Embassy and ask them to help by giving asylum to people who were obviously political refugees. Not being able to help get the Gomez family out, I felt like an accomplice to tyranny and brutality. Thank God, Neier had a few other possible alternatives, and the Canadians might come through. I love my country, but right then I felt apologetic for being part of it.

Early the next morning we flew out, back to Nicaragua to join the rest of the delegation and then back to the United States the next day. But for me, in some critical way the Central American trip was over. One week earlier, I had had no idea that I would even be in Guatemala during the trip. It was a vague, long shot. Now I'd never forget it — all I had seen and experienced and felt. I knew it would take a long time to begin to sort it out, to integrate it. And I knew there was a permanent limp in it. Yet, I was unspeakably grateful to have been there, to have shared in that demonstration, to have observed with my heart even a small portion of what makes Joel and Gabriela who they are. The trip was a gift of grace. I put my head back against the seat. I kept seeing the eyes of Nineth and Isabil and Blanca. Those bottomless eyes seemed to hold the secret of what had happened, and I was haunted by them, inspired by them. I wondered what they had seen in my eyes as they looked at me and thanked us for being there. I hope they saw something of courage and compassion and faith. I hope they saw hope, and maybe something of what the resurrection community is about, maybe even joy. I hope they saw love, for I had learned a bit more of it, felt it a bit deeper on this trip — love for them, for my brothers and sisters in the world, for my colleagues on the plane, for my church family back home, for Jan whom I carried in my heart, for my children, for God. Yes, for God. I hope they saw love, at least a little of the love which casts out fear. Yes, I hope they saw that love in my eyes, as I had seen it in theirs.

An old Yankee friend used to say routinely, shaking his head in wonderment, "God love us." He was right, profoundly right in that word and gesture. So I prayed, urgently, shaking my head in wonderment: "God love us. God love Nineth and Blanca and Isabil, and the people of Guatemala. God love all the people of this broken, beautiful, damn world. 'Ours the cross, the grave, the skies, Alleluia.'"

Hope

Things, events, seasons blur. They blur as they sweep toward you, inevitably only vaguely defined and inaccurately anticipated. They blur even as they engulf you, details and patterns often eluding the reach of your attention. They blur, certainly, as they plunge into the dark tumble of remembrance, pleading, as surely did the chaos of those first Genesis deeps, for an ordering Spirit to separate the light of them from the darkness. Perhaps the blur is simply the mortal mix of wonderment, weariness and the whirling waltz of time. Days tumble — yesterdays swept over by tomorrows, the last encounter by the next, that urgent demand by this crucial one, a breathtakingly beautiful scene on the left by another on the right — until the whisper of finitude becomes the clamor of incompleted plans, unfinished work, uninterpreted acts, unacknowledged gifts, unuttered praise. Then, like the end kid in "crack the whip," you stumble, dizzy, half laughing, half crying, fearful that you're somewhere past fun on the way to sick.

So you pause, grasping for a foothold, a vantage point, a place to dig in — or at least dig down — searching for meaning. Call it primal grunt, or prayer, or Sabbath, or simply the perked-ear sense of a footfall in the shadows and the approach of a Stranger you must somehow make ready for. Call it whatever it is makes you human. And, being human, what you get is just a toe hold, an almost-in-focus glimpse of a shank of the blur, and then the digging must stop, for the mystery moves on. The sift of one more memoryful will not yield conclusions, nor will another analytic scoop secure the view. But the toe hold is enough to launch you out into uncharted space and time, swinging after what you glimpsed, trusting there will be, as there always has been, another toe hold, another glimpse. Call that prayer, too. . .and passion, and faith, and hope. Maybe call it the beginning of peace. . .and whatever joy is about.

So the whirl went on and on. I returned from Central America more convinced than ever of the rightness of Public Sanctuary. There were interviews, television talk shows, speeches here and there, along with an appearance with Bob Edgar and others in the delegation to report to some of his constituents about the trip. I wrote an editorial piece against military aid for Guatemala which was carried in *The Philadelphia Inquirer*. It provoked an invitation from Congressman Lawrence Coughlin (R., Penn.) who had an opposing editorial in the same edition. He invited me to "discuss" the issue with a State Department official in a public forum which he was moderating. The date conflicted with an out-of-town commitment, and I was somewhat relieved; I was not ready to assume the mantle of "expert" on Central America, and this promised to be a set-up audience anyway.

But the advocacy for Public Sanctuary accelerated. In early June, 1985, Joel and Anne Ewing (Co-Chair of our Public Sanctuary Task Force) and I spoke to the nearly one thousand delegates at the Annual Conference of the United Methodist Church, Eastern Pennsylvania Conference. At the time of the arrest of refugees and indictment of Public Sanctuary workers in January, 1985, our resident Bishop, F. Herbert Skeete, had requested that the National Division of the Board of Global Ministries of the United Methodist Church call a consultation of the ten United Methodist Churches which had declared Public Sanctuary for the purpose of sharing information and planning strategies. It had taken the Board six months to respond, but that consultation was held at our church in Philadelphia in late June.

In the meantime, Ted Walkenhorst and the Legal Committee of the Public Sanctuary Task Force were working on the preparation of Joel's and Gabriela's petition for asylum, as well as gearing up for the trial in Tucson of Public Sanctuary workers in which Joel had been subpoenaed to testify. Rallies and public gatherings of various sorts for various causes invited someone from Public Sanctuary churches to be present or speak, especially Joel and/or Gabriela if they were available. Joel began to suffer emotional fatigue and decided to withdraw for a time from any public appearances. The Public Sanctuary Task Force people were frayed and a bit testy. Public Sanctuary still seemed to lack a personal corollary for many of us.

At the same time, other aspects of my life went on. Our church was in the midst of a search for a new Director of Music. We were putting together a non-profit community economic development corporation. We were planning and raising a budget for fiscal 1986. We were in rehearsals for the production of *Equus*, in which, in a fit of ego and total miscalculation of talent, I'd agreed to play Dysart. I was finishing my Christmas book, *Tracks in the Straw*. My wife Jan was making a career change that involved some significant family and financial adjustments. My daughter Karen announced her engagement and forthcoming marriage. People were dying, being born, hurting, celebrating all around me, accurately claiming my attention and care.

In May, 1985, not long after the Central American trip, my publisher and emerging friend, Lura Jane Geiger, sat in my office and asked if I would write a book about my involvement in Public Sanctuary: how it had changed me; what I had learned, given up, received because of it; what the struggle was meaning to me as a person — spiritually, morally, professionally. My first, strong instinct was to resist. I was afraid to try to put that struggle in writing with integrity and honesty. In fact, I wasn't sure I could sort it out, or that anyone would be interested in such a book if I did. I am not a leader in the Public

Sanctuary Movement and have no right to claim the issue as mine in any significant way, or to speak for it. Lura countered every objection, assured me of her commitment to the project as a publisher.

After much agonizing over many days, I agreed. I hoped — and seduced myself into assuming — that I could dash off such a book in a month. On all counts, my decision and assumption have proven to be yet another instance of a spasm of ego complicated by an over-exaggerated assessment of talent. The book has taken months of sustained effort squeezed into assorted cracks in my schedule. I have wakened in the night, sweating on wrinkled sheets, knowing I would never finish the book, or anything else.

Then suddenly winter was upon us again. One cold January midnight as I walked our dog around the block, I met Ned, my neighbor across the alley, coming home from a Philadelphia Flyers hockey game. Ned is a young executive in the insurance business, a Yale graduate. Donna, his wife in an interracial marriage, is a lawyer, and their first child Andrew is nearly two years old. We stopped to talk under the stars. Ned had read something in the paper about the trial of Sanctuary workers in Tucson and was curious, because he knew I was the minister of a Sanctuary church. I told him how the government had sent paid covert agents, without warrants, into churches to tape record services, prayer meetings, bible study groups, regular meetings. I explained that the judge presiding at the trial had ruled that those tapes were admissible as evidence, even though the probability is high that critical First and Fourth Amendment rights were violated in their acquisition. The judge had also ruled against almost all grounds for defense of the accused: not allowing matters of religious conviction and motivation, or U.S. policy in Central America, or questions of the interpretation of the 1980 Refugee Act to be introduced.

In addition, I explained that the primary government witness, Jesus Cruz, is a paid informer with a serious criminal record. The government case is slowly coming unraveled as Cruz is caught in contradictions and misinformation in his testimony. I told Ned how the refugee family in Public Sanctuary with us had been betrayed by Cruz. He had befriended them when they passed through Tucson after crossing the border. He had professed to be a Christian, proclaimed his love for the refugees' children, and prayed with the Sanctuary workers. They had all affectionately referred to him as "Uncle." Yet, Cruz had betrayed them by taping church meetings at his discretion, with a court order. It was partly as a result of his betrayal that the Immigration and Naturalization Service had arrested Joel and Gabriela and subpoenaed Joel to testify at the trial against the Sanctuary workers who had helped him.

I spoke to Ned of my anger at government tactics, as well as at the falsehoods the government is orchestrating against what is happening in Central America and in the Public Sanctuary Movement. "All that," I said, "coupled with the orgy of Rambo-esque patriotism in our country these days, deeply disturbs me, because it issues from the lowest, not the highest, in our national psyche and history."

Ned smiled and looked bemused. "Why are you doing this?" he asked. "I mean you, personally. I suppose I ought to get more involved in issues, but by the time I get home from work, and spend time with the family, and take care of the house, that's about it."

The quickness of my response, as well as the spark of anger in it, surprised me. But it felt true: "I do it for the same reason that I'd be there for you, if you and Donna ever needed help." He looked sheepish. Not long before our conversation, a black family had moved into a neighborhood in Philadelphia and received a violent reception which had forced them out. Ned knew what I meant.

But then, just as quickly, I went on to say that often I *did* wonder why I was involved in many things. I am not a prophet in any sense. I am not politically shrewd. Usually, after I get in the middle of something, I'm not at all sure how I got there. It's just that once something becomes possible — because someone lays it on your desk, or your conscience, or your heart — the question is, "How can you *not* do it?" That's what I meant about him and Donna: if they were in need, if their lives were threatened some way, either physically or spiritually or psychologically, how could I *not* do whatever I could for them? Once it became clear that it was possible to try to save refugees' lives, how could we *not* do it? That isn't a rhetorical question. It is the gut question of life, of faith, and it is never easily dismissed or conclusively answered.

Was it Thomas Paine, or Aristotle, who said, "Democracy is a daily plebiscite"? Well, faith is a daily plebiscite, too, and so is love, and morality, and life itself. It all comes down to a vote taken daily among the legion who argue inside you. Decision by decision, step by step, you shape your life in the midst of the blur, perhaps, mysteriously, with the help and insistence of the blur. I thought of W. H. Auden's line: "The distresses of choice are our chance to be blessed."[1] And choices do involve distresses — deep distresses, for the most part. I tried to convey that to Ned, even quoting the Auden line. I told him I often feel overwhelmed; that the long haul of the daily is frequently draining; that I can't ever keep up with all the information that pours out from a hundred sources about Central America, let alone all the other worthy causes and claims. But I know of no way to avoid the choices. I see choices as our chance to be blessed — or damned, too, I suppose, though not making choices as responsibly and intentionally as we can seems more likely to result in damnation.

Ned and I stood there shivering, chipping away with our toes at the ice crust in the alley, trying to chip away with our conversation at the ice crust that forms between neighbors who don't know each other very well. But the ice crust seemed thicker than the pick of our words, and I sensed that both of us felt uncomfortable: Ned, because the issues we touched on disturbed him in ways he couldn't identify precisely; I, because the issues disturbed me in ways I couldn't explain persuasively, even to myself.

I thought of this book, which I was trying to finish, and the title I'd chosen for it, and the reasons for the choice. Annie Dillard has stirred and stretched me through her writing, and I have underlined and re-read this passage many times to help me get through hard days and nights:

[1]From "For The Time Being: A Christmas Oratorio" from W. H. AUDEN: COLLECTED POEMS, edited by Edward Mendelson. Copyright © 1944, renewed 1972 by W. H. Auden. Reprinted by permission of Random House, Inc.

"Who shall ascend into the hill of the Lord? or who shall stand for us in his holy place? There is no one but us. There is no one to send, nor a clean hand, nor a pure heart on the face of the earth, nor in the earth, but only us, a generation comforting ourselves with the notion that we have come at an awkward time, that our innocent fathers are all dead — as if innocence had ever been — and our children busy and troubled, and we ourselves unfit, not yet ready, having each of us chosen wrongly, made a false start, failed, yielded to impulse and the tangled comfort of pleasures, and grown exhausted, unable to seek the thread, weak, and involved. But there is *no one but us*. There never has been."[2]

As accurately as any words, these express why I am engaged in Public Sanctuary. How could I explain that to Ned, to people like Ned for whom the religious struggles have long since become unfamiliar, if not irrelevant, except on some inchoate level which might be tapped by some crisis or by a chance confrontation such as this? Was I suddenly to play an emissary of the Stranger to Ned's Jacob?

Before I could find words for any of it, Ned put the question I ask myself a dozen times a day, sighing, slamming the desk, praying, stomping around, complaining to Jan. "Does it do any good?" he asked. "I mean, why spend all that time and energy on what isn't going to change anything, as far as I can see? After all, you can't beat city hall." That question unfailingly trips me up and leaves me limping, and immediately I was Jacob again, grappling for a hold.

" 'Pessimism is a form of vanity,' " I countered, quoting a line I'd read somewhere (and have never been successful in tracing to its source). "Do you only make sales calls on guaranteed buyers?"

---

[2]From pages 56-57 of HOLY THE FIRM, by Annie Dillard. Copyright © 1977 by Annie Dillard. Reprinted by permission of Harper & Row, Publishers, Inc.

"That isn't the same," he replied, "but as a matter of fact, I don't spend much time on long shot prospects either. Besides, no matter how hard-headed they are, prospects aren't going to throw me in jail or make me pay huge fines. You aren't being realistic. I mean, if pessimism is a form of vanity, realism is a form of . . . survival, I guess."

Suddenly I felt very tired. How could I answer him, this perfectly decent man who lived across the alley. In that moment I felt as if he were talking to me across a great glacier, and the cold was snapping the key words into indecipherable pieces so we were unable to understand each other. No, that isn't quite right . . . I could understand him, because sometimes the kind of survival to which he was referring powerfully appealed to me. Maybe just resisting the appeal was what surfaced my weariness. But, I felt as if I couldn't make him understand me — maybe because I am always less certain of the values of risk than people such as Ned are certain of the values of survival.

Reflexively, probably defensively, I said the first thing that came to mind, with an edge of frustration to the words: "I saw a bumper sticker the other day, Ned, and it said, 'What if there is no bottom line?' Your kind of realism always assumes a bottom line and all that the bottom line mentality and jargon business operate by. You think if you can't total it up somehow, and make a profit on it, or verify the result to justify the effort, there's no point to it. Was there some bottom line when you and Donna decided to get married?" I hadn't meant to get personal, but there it was.

I'm not sure what the look was on Ned's face — hurt, shock, anger. He shrugged and said, "Well, interracial marriages aren't illegal anymore, and we were pretty sure we could make it. After all, we had a lot going for us. But maybe you've got a point. I'll have to think about it." I felt like asking him why interracial marriages aren't illegal any more — how much blood got spilled and jail time spent to win that fight — but right then I thought that would be too pushy. So I said, "Well, I guess we think we can make it, too." It was a sign-off exchange. We patted each other on the shoulder and said good night.

I whistled for my dog and went in. For a long time I sat at my desk, and then, I think in a reach toward hope, I wrote these lines:

Night wind moans and asks:
  How *does* God possess the soul, and when?
Sighing, like the wind,
  we make a choice almost unaware,
unleashing, by that choosing,
  longing like a leak of air,
which, nearly unnoticed,
  changes our course but little then,
yet each mile more,
  until come we to this strange rendezvous,
we nigh recall from long tracking after
  shreds of what might be true.
Then, assuming we are hosts,
  we are stunned to find we're guests,
and so, when Silence asks our name,
  what answer dare we gasp?
  With whom do we belong
  save with Whom we've made this quest?

Does it do any good? Jan's response is always, "According to whom?" That's the issue, I suppose, but still I consistently snag on the question. I tilted back in my chair and tried to sort it out. I have a friend who says, "God does *something* everywhere, but God doesn't do *everything* anywhere." I suspect if my theology could be put in one line, that might come close to being it. Surely it is an act of grace to do something everywhere, but not to do everything anywhere, for love does enable — perhaps insists on — freedom.

What does it mean to be human but to be free — to have options, choices, possibilities? *Something* is up to us. If the secret of freedom is love, the thrust of it is courage, not certainty. It is courage which struggles with the fear I (and probably all of us) have. Perhaps it is most profoundly the fear of death — one dimension of which is the fear that what I do has no meaning, no value. So, my struggle to claim my freedom always involves a struggle against fear because, for me, goodness is never a certainty, never an absolute; always only a possibility toward which I struggle to move.

And yet, whenever I have experienced or seen what I call "goodness," the achieving of it has been, at best, only partly my doing (or that of anyone else) and mostly the alchemy of a surprisingly gracious mystery. Of course, something is up to us, to me: it is the *doing*, the risking according to my best lights and boldest faith, always tainted with ambiguities and timidities. But the "goodness" is not up to me, at least not all of it, or maybe even much of it. I'm not sure I understand that. In fact, I'm *sure* I don't understand that, especially since so much of my ego and energy goes into trying to achieve good results.

But then, I'm sure the reason I remember the bumper sticker "What if there is no bottom line?" is that it addresses me. Well, *if* there isn't a bottom line — or better, *since* there isn't (at least none that our finite accounting systems can use to audit the universe or even the world) — we're left either to line up at society's pay window for whatever rewards it offers, or "to step out on the promises," if only with one foot, though the other usually follows. There's just no way to tote it up, finally. So, the venture isn't about toting but trusting, and that is hard. "Does it do any good?" I always want to measure it, see it, maybe especially get credit for it, have it both ways. Then I hear Jan asking, with a smile, "Good according to whom?" So all right, God's doing something everywhere...which means wherever I am. And faith is nothing if it doesn't involve my giving God something to "do" with. I believe that's half of what Public Sanctuary is about for me.

But I don't want to be cavalier about some of the good of it, either. Most obviously, Joel, Gabriela and Lucy are alive, when one, or all, of them most probably would be dead or "disappeared" had they been deported to Guatemala. There is little doubt expressed, even in the public media, that the brutal repression, the killing and kidnapping, the systematic violation of human rights continues in Guatemala. As recently as July, 1985, another leader of the Mutual Support Group, Professor Carlos Leonel Caxaj Rodriguez, was assassinated. He was eliminated, surely, in retribution for the Mutual Support Group (still led by Nineth de Garcia) pursuing its public campaign to press the government for information about the fate of the disappeared persons in Guatemala, the number of which mounts monthly. Even since the December, 1985, elections, there have been several deaths of other notables and leaders of the G.A.M. Having been on the death list before he escaped, Joel lives, if not because of

Public Sanctuary, then certainly in it.

Joel's and Gabriela's story is being told and heard, and increasing numbers of people are paying attention. Part of that story is to make clear the low likelihood that recent elections in Guatemala will change the basic structures and practices of oppression there, or improve the economic lot of the poor. The issue isn't really whether the newly elected civilian president, Marco Vinicio Cerezo Arevalo, is a decent man of a relatively moderate political party. The issue is that the new constitution is rigged so that the minister of defense is named by the military, not the president, virtually insuring that there will be no reform within the military. And it is the military that runs the country. The military is, also, by that constitution excluded from the jurisdiction of the judicial branch of the government. The dissolution of the DIT[3] — the Guatemalan Secret Police — only serves to consolidate power in the army.

United States military aid to Guatemala is largely responsible for establishing and supporting the uncompromised power of the military in that country. The justification for our aid is the continuation of the civil war in which the opposition forces are labeled Marxists. So the revolting conditions which generate revolutions go unaddressed, and political labels justify atrocities. As Joel and Gabriela tell their story, those conditions get powerfully personalized. No wonder our government wants to stop the Public Sanctuary Movement. But the contrary is happening. More churches and religious bodies are declaring Public Sanctuary. And, to me, that's good!

It's good, because essentially the same conditions pertain in El Salvador as in Guatemala. President Duarte is also involved in an escalation of seeking military solutions to the social and political problems of his country, again with heavy financing by United States military aid which totalled 174 million dollars five years ago; and President Reagan's budget for 1986 calls for 486 million. Yet, as the war goes on, chances for a negotiated peace fade, and the unjust

[3]DIT: Department of Technical Investigation

conditions which cause revolutions are not addressed. The refugees in Public Sanctuary are slowly but effectively telling that story from their personal experience. Some people are beginning to question the rightness of this nation's policies in Central America — policies with a history which predates this administration (and many previous ones) but which this administration has accentuated.

So, my involvement in the Public Sanctuary Movement stems from a love of my country. Maybe that's why I identify with Joel's and Gabriela's love of their country which moves them to fight to liberate it from its tyrannies. During our Central American trip, Bill Coffin said his favorite definition of patriotism was given by the ancient Roman, Tacitus: Patriotism is "praiseworthy competition with our ancestors." I find that compelling, for my love of country is such that I want to push my country to truly live by and extend our ancestors precepts of liberty and justice which we have come to easily mouth and quickly restrict. Perhaps it is grandiose to view Public Sanctuary as a way of fighting for the soul of my country, but that is something of how I view it.

Maybe that is less grandiose than simply naive, but I keep thinking of Thomas Merton's suggestion that the genius of non-violence is that it promotes dialogue and is based on the faith that injustice is not irreversible, that people can change. Violence, on the other hand, is based on the notion that anything which stands in opposition to our "good" — or even in opposition to what is familiar and comfortable — is a form of evil that must not be allowed to exist. Tyranny, then, results from the belief that there must be no evil or "sin" in the world. So we deny our own evil, project it all onto the "enemy," and strike to eliminate them — usually with some religious sanction. I shudder to think what an accurate description that is of how many of us, myself included, deal with what we consider our own personal sins and frailties. We masochistically lash at the "enemy" within, or self-righteously (and sadistically) lash at the nearest "enemies" outside in a thousand kind of attacks: words, withdrawals, judgments, gossip, ridicule.

I do have hope that Public Sanctuary — as one instance of non-violent action against injustice — is a way of working change in our nation, as well as nurturing change in myself and my relationships. I don't really believe that hope is naive or grandiose (though I confess at times it seems to be a marriage of both which produces the off-spring of discouragement).

What gives Public Sanctuary integrity for me is its relationship to issues in the community — the city where the church resides. People who are not directly involved in the actions around Public Sanctuary, but who are dealing with social issues — racial justice, the homeless, unemployment, the arms race, sexual discrimination, one of the many forms of child abuse, or any of a thousand other aspects of a "lover's quarrel" with our society — are still doing the work of Public Sanctuary. Not only are all these issues fundamentally related through the ways by which the attitudes, the actions and budgets of a nation — or a church — get shaped, but primarily because, in a larger sense, Sanctuary is such a powerful and helpful symbol of what God offers to us and calls us to offer one another — the near neighbor as well as the distant one.

I think that's why the saga of Jacob is so significant for me. When Jacob came his wandering way to the Jabbok that night, leaving in his wake the debris of deceits, betrayals, broken relationships, and various forms of corruption, he was seeking sanctuary — not merely safety, but an ease for his soul, a new beginning, perhaps in the form of a new name or identity, a blessing, a future, a hope, something like rec-onciliation. He was looking for the fulfillment of a promise etched into his bones. He was looking for God. The sanctuary he found was in wrestling with the Stranger and in re-engagement with Esau, the brother he'd alienated. Only so did he become Israel, the forebearer of a people, a community, a nation.

Even so, I repeatedly come to some form of the Jabbok in my life, leaving in my wake at least as much debris as Jacob, and seeking the same kind of sanctuary. I find it, for rare moments, in wrestling with the brother or sister who mysteriously becomes God, and wrestling the God who mysteriously becomes the brother or sister. The obvious symbol of God's people gathering in a sanctuary to become a sanctuary — which is to say, to become a church — ought never be over-looked or taken for granted in all its implications: honesty, risk, mutual accountability and commitment; the difficult but joyful process of working out lives of freedom, responsibility, justice and love.

For me, in some profound way, that process defines my view of my ministry, and also is the process by which I can work out my own life of freedom, justice and love. It is my way of struggling to integrate my personal life and my professional life — or even more deeply, my person and my persona. To integrate means to attempt to have integrity and be faithful, rather than simply having faith.

In the struggle to provide Public Sanctuary, I have become more intensely aware of my search for personal sanctuary. I have become increasingly willing to take the risks of providing, and in some sense being, sanctuary for others, which surely is a large measure of what commitment is. We are all refugees. Maybe the symbol of sanctuary touches on the mystery of how God works, or what it means to try to "Love God . . . and love your neighbor as yourself."

More than any other person, Jan — the woman in whose sanctuary I live as husband — helps me to keep learning this by loving me enough to be who she is with me; by insisting on the integrity of our relationship; and by persisting in providing sanctuary for refugees in families (yes, ours, too) and in the community who are easily overlooked because their distress may be less visible.

But, I also have experienced that inseparable alternation between public and personal sanctuary in some of the more private moments we've shared in the Task Force, and with the refugees. I think of gathering in the lovely, jewel-windowed chapel of the church to hold a memorial service for Joel's brother and cousin who were abducted in Guatemala in February, 1985. It happened about one month after Joel and Gabriela had been arrested by the Immigration and Naturalization Service agents and had had to divulge their real names to the INS authorities. Sometime in March, Joel had gotten the news, confirmed by stories in the Guatemalan newspaper El Grafico. On an early February morning Joel's brother had been waiting for a bus when he was abducted by armed men and has not been heard from again. Two days later, in nearly identical circumstances, Joel's cousin was abducted. He has not been heard from since, either.

One of our reactions was that these abductions undeniably validated Joel's and Gabriela's petition for political asylum by demonstrating the Guatemalan government's persecution of Joel's family. But our deeper reaction was grief and the sobering realization that Joel's participation in Public Sanctuary (and of course, ours) may well have precipitated the kidnapping of these two young men. Our suspicion was that the identification checks on Joel and Gabriela made by the United States Justice Department provoked reprisals against Joel's family by the Guatemalan government. (Since then, we have learned that Joel's family is involved in union activities and human rights efforts in Guatemala, and so the kidnapping of these young men may have been consistent with Guatemala's repressive actions against such activists and not directly linked to the arrest of Joel and Gabriela in this country or the Public Sanctuary Movement. The method of abduction in both cases is chillingly familiar to thousands of families of disappeared persons in Guatemala.)

Still, we had to presume that Joel's brother and cousin were dead. As we gathered for the memorial service, we were dealing with our own sense of regret, our painful awareness of the price we may have exacted by what we were doing, our renewed realization that complexity of moral choices precludes either avoidance or arrogance, our need for forgiveness and renewal, as well as our grief with Joel for his brother and cousin whom we felt were brother and cousin, too. We were re-introduced to the human heart that beats — and often breaks — beneath the political, moral and policy issues of Public Sanctuary. Although the information about the kidnappings is included in the petition of Joel and Gabriela for political asylum, for several months Joel asked that the news be kept confidential. Any further public statement could be picked up by the Guatemalan government and provoke further reprisals against his family. So, with a hiss of prayer and song followed by a meal together, public and personal sanctuary were welded together for a time, and all us refugees were included.

I think also of Gabriela's and Joel's wedding which we celebrated a few months ago in that same chapel. In Guatemala, as in many countries of the world, there are two different marriage services: the civil and the religious. Joel and Gabriela had been married in a civil service, but because of the pressures on them, they had never been able to have the religious service. In addition, Gabriela's family is Roman Catholic, Joel's Protestant Evangelical. But now they wanted to have the religious service. Several factors contributed to their desire. First, our church family slowly had become theirs. Second, Gabriela was pregnant. Shortly after her arrival, she had suffered a miscarriage which had been emotionally traumatic, but now she had reached her second trimester and all was well. And finally, Joel was on notice that at any moment he would have to appear as a prosecution witness in the trial of Public Sanctuary workers in Tucson. Joel had agonized for a long period over the decision to comply with the subpoena, and now he and Gabriela were fearful and simply wanted to reaffirm and ask God's blessing on the strength and fidelity of their bonds — and the bonds which united them with us, us with each other, all with God.

So we had a wedding! People in the church were Joel's and Gabriela's adopted family, standing up with them, being parents who walked down the aisle with Gabriela, as Lucy scattered flower petals. A young woman attorney on the Legal Committee of the Sanctuary Task Force, Karen Andrews, headed the effort to arrange for flowers, candles and a wedding banquet. It was an occasion of great joy and thanksgiving — an expression that the human heart which beats and sometimes breaks at the core of Public Sanctuary is also resilient; that it does experience healing, hope and resurrection.

I think of Gabriela's and Joel's baby who will arrive any moment.[4] Of course, that is an intensely personal matter within their family. But for us who are the adopted extended family, the baby is wonderfully life-affirming, a symbol of the irrepressibility of life — and of the love that generates it — in the midst of life-denying and inhibiting forces. Mary Daly defines evil as "sadospiritual asceticism," a term she uses to refer to people who do not love life — subtly not loving their own life, then more obviously not loving the lives of those defined as "enemies," and, finally, not loving anyone's. I like the notion that evil

---

[4]Joelito, their baby boy, was born on February 17, 1986, healthy and delightful!

is not loving life. So the arrival of the baby is, indeed, "good."

I think of the impressive petition for asylum that our Public Sanctuary Task Force, and particularly the Legal Committee headed by Ted Walkenhorst, has submitted on behalf of Joel and Gabriela. (One of the INS attorneys even admitted it was very strong document.) The legal process instituted by Public Sanctuary — including the progress of the trial in Tucson from which Joel recently returned from testifying in a very effective manner — is a sign of hope as well. Although Joel's testimony, forced by threat of jail and a grant of immunity, was meant to be *against* the Sanctuary workers, Joel's evidence was a powerful proclamation of the conditions in Guatemala which are creating the *need* for the Sanctuary Movement. In our system the courts are established as a check on the unbridled, and sometimes unprincipled, machinations in the political arena.

And more, the courts are the place where there is leverage to hold the system accountable for its profession of justice. Clearly, law and justice are not synonymous. In practice, the law is often the expression of the will of special interest groups, but in avowed intent the law is to approximate the claims of justice as closely as possible. So, however and wherever the effort is made to hold the legal system accountable to its own standards and purposes, it is a good and worthy fight. Public Sanctuary is trying to do just that. The Sanctuary Movement is also trying to inform public opinion about the situation of refugees from Central America so that existing laws will be fairly enforced, and new laws enacted where necessary.

I think, too, of the growth of persons working hardest in the Public Sanctuary Task Force. We have not yet learned to be sanctuary for each other, to care for and resource each other in honest, healing, deeply personal ways. But we are learning the rudiments. We have had a few meetings in which we have tried to "speak the truth in love." But still we get easily frayed, quickly intimidated, quietly sulky, snappishly accusatory. Even within the larger Public Sanctuary Movement, there are unresolved conflicts between those who want to make Public Sanctuary an organization with more clearly defined political goals and spokespersons, and those who want to remain a movement of autonomous local congregations.

So, we are confronted on every hand with our humanity, our frailty and need, and with the inescapable truth that we cannot disguise our personal issues under the cosmetic of a cause without doing some real damage to ourselves and the cause. Sometimes in the process of that learning, I begin to think we are all retarded. But part of the wonder is that we want to learn and are still together, working at our lessons, trying to pass to the next level of trust and love. Maybe the rest of the wonder is that God keeps doing things in spite of and quite beyond our limitations and corruptions, or our intentions and accomplishments. I keep believing that "God writes straight with crooked lines". . . and for me that is what grace means, and at least something of what salvation is. At least I hang on to that belief, and hanging on, I wrestle.

Is it God I wrestle with? That is the question. Is it God whose constant sneaking up on me makes the twigs of the daily snap, shifts the wind, shivers the shadows and scatters the slivers of light that sometimes dazzle me, always lure me on? Is it God who grabs and grapples with me, challenging me to break the hold of despair and doubt; who strengthens my grasp of meaning here, there, while never allowing me to settle in with it? Is God the wrestler whom I curse, and yet fall in love with; whose absence torments, but whose announced approach — as the twigs snap and the light glimmers — terrifies and yet delights me? Or am I dealing only with illusions, psychological projections, childish fantasies, vestiges of a less enlightened, more superstitious age? Is all the effort around Sanctuary just the expression of a wish somehow to return to a less complicated time of childhood when mother kissed scraped knees and daddy protected against bogey men? Is the truly dominant and accurate symbol of the present and the future not Sanctuary but the department store, the Pentagon, the video cassette counter, the Nautilus machine, the science lab, the supersonic jet, the "star wars" satellites? Those are not idle questions. To me they are compelling, urgent, profoundly religious.

Susannah Heschel wrote an article about her father Abraham Heschel in which she quotes a wonderfully provocative and powerful midrash in which God says, "I am God and you are my witnesses; if you are not my witnesses, then I am not God."⁵ That midrash stays with me like a ringing in my ears. The first part is a simple statement of fact, a part of which defines who I am: I am God's witness, at least that, whatever else the character of my relationship to God — child . . .heir. . .That definition of my identity helps a little to explain, or hint at explanations for, the tugs and twistings of my search for meaning in life, my wrestling with the claims of conscience and justice and need, my longing for and pursuit of freedom and peace, my hunger to love and be loved. Somehow all that, and more, is generic, as far as I can tell from my experience — a given along with the color of my eyes and the size of my nose. So, not to be a witness is not to be who I am.

But, the second part of the midrash is a definition of God — limited as all human definitions are, but highly suggestive, nonetheless, and mysteriously true, in my view. ". . .if you are not my witnesses, then I am not God." Somehow, who God is — in Him/Herself and *for me* — and what God does — in the world and *in my life* — is contingent upon my witness. Who God is is contingent upon my attempts to love, to do justice, to exercise mercy; upon my efforts to be honest with myself and others; upon my endeavors to make peace, to act with integrity — i.e., to be whole, to try to relate to others in a saving way, to provide and be and seek sanctuary, if you will.

Whatever I know of grace, of healing, of freedom, of growth; of authentic human contact and dialogue; of even tentative love and intimacy; of community, of holiness, of the kingdom; of glimpsing just fleetingly the back side of God; whatever I know of these things has come in my struggle to witness. Which is to say, my wrestling to be who I am, in the impenetrable mystery, enables God to be God — to be God for me, and thus somehow to be God for anyone, maybe everyone. Such is my experience, deepened and intensified by Public Sanctuary which has given me a new symbol to help me interpret my life and work. Sanctuary is something God and I provide for each

⁵An old midrash quoted by Susannah Heschel in her article "Heschel in Selma," HADASSAH MAGAZINE, June 1985, page 47. Reprinted by permission of Hadassah Magazine and Susannah Heschel.

other, and thus for others, and through others, for the world. Lest the "I" of that statement be misunderstood, it refers to my belief and fragments of my experience, of course, but it applies equally, if not more, to every person of faith, every community of faith.

Also, lest there be misunderstanding, my involvement in Public Sanctuary has made me unavoidably and keenly aware of my own limitations, the limitations of my witness. Those limitations press hard upon me, constantly: limitations of time, of knowledge, of faith, of talent, of wisdom, of capacity, of love. The limitations invite me to acknowledge and accept them, and so to acknowledge and accept myself. The promise of that acceptance is healing, and I am beginning, slowly, to open myself to my limitations. As limitations are accepted, hope grows. My witness will not determine what happens to the Public Sanctuary Movement. But my witness does provide a new way out of me and into the world for God, and out of the world and into me for God. It is not the limitation of my witness that prevents God from being God; it is my refusal to witness. And part of my witness is to acknowledge my limitations and to accept them. That's hard. I pray a lot these days.

One thing that helped me acknowledge those limitations was the wedding of my daughter Karen in January, 1986, and the process leading up to it. Central to that process were a series of counseling sessions we had as a family. Karen's mother and I were divorced several years ago, and the wounds never healed. In the counseling sessions, Karen and her brothers Mark, David and Tom were able to tell me their hard truth about how I had hurt them during their childhood years by my inattention, my anger, my expectations, my abandonment of them for my work. There was much grief and pain in what we shared, but curiously, there was much love and healing in it, and a new possibility for closeness between us, a new way to be sanctuary for each other. That is not a parable so much as a witness, a connection; the way of hope, a grace; perhaps even a prayer begun to be answered, more snapping twigs and shards of light.

So, I listen more now and try to sort things out, and admittedly, there are always ragged edges and pieces that just don't fit the puzzle. I am learning to be gentle, I think, and my anger is tempered with a kind of tenderness toward the world — the long ache of it, the incredible loveliness of it, the moan and the song which steal on the ear when the wind is just so. And yes, we go on, Public Sanctuary goes on, the witness goes on, because "There is no one but us [and] there never has been." But by grace there is us. Us, a limp and an undeniable Presence.

> "O Lord have mercy on us.
> Christ have mercy on us.
> Lord have mercy on us."

> Alleluia! Alleluia! Alleluia!

Note on Verdict of Sanctuary Trial

Just prior to the press date for this book, on May 1, 1986, eight of the eleven persons on trial for their involvement in Public Sanctuary were found guilty following a trial in Tucson, Arizona, lasting more than six months. Of the eight defendants, six were found guilty of conspiring to smuggle aliens from El Salvador and Guatemala into the United States, and two were found guilty of charges relating to harboring, transporting and inducing the illegal entry of refugees. The six found guilty of conspiracy were the Reverend John Fife, one of the founders of the Sanctuary Movement; Sister Darlene Nicgorski, a Catholic nun; the Reverend Ramon Dagoberto Quinones, a Catholic priest; and three church lay workers — Peggy Hutchison, Phillip Willis-Conger, and Maria del Socorro Pardo de Aquilar. The two found guilty of lesser charges were the Reverend Anthony Clark and Wendy LeWin. The three defendants found innocent were James Corbett, one of the founders of the Sanctuary Movement, Mary Kay Espinoza and Nena MacDonald.

Although at the time of this printing no detailed expert analysis of the legal aspects of the trial were available, two issues relating to it seem clear. The first is that nearly all means of defense were denied when U.S. District Court Judge Earl Carroll barred the defendants from using questions pertaining to the U.S. policies which are complicit in promoting the violence and oppression in Central America and which cause the tide of refugees; or from referring to the 1980 Refugee Act and international laws regarding refugees. (Ironically, it is those laws under which the United States *is* receiving and granting political asylum to refugees from Nicaragua — which underscores the political bias of the Administration, as well as the discriminatory application of the law by the Immigration and Naturalization Service. Additionally, it emphasizes the willful failure of the INS to adhere to its own rules by not informing refugees from El Salvador and Guatemala of their right to file for asylum or allowing them time to properly do so if they try.) Judge Carroll also hindered the defense by allowing the prosecution to admit contested evidence gathered by a paid government informer who covertly tape recorded religious services without prior court order, the first time in our nation's history that has been done. Such illegal infiltration of religious services is a clear violation of First Amendment rights.

The second issue relating to the trial is that it involved complex and difficult aspects so that, as John Fife said following his conviction, "The jury did not hear the full truth. The mixture of the verdict reflects their confusion."

Defense attorneys stated that the verdict will be appealed.

BIBLIOGRAPHY

Berryman, Phillip. *Inside Central America*. New York: Pantheon, 1985.
———. *The Religious Roots of Rebellion: Christians in Central American Revolutions*. Maryknoll, NY: Orbis Books, 1984.
———. *What's Wrong in Central America and What to Do About it*. Philadelphia: American Friends Service Committee, 1983.
Bitter and Cruel. London: Central American Human Rights Committee, British Parliament Human Rights Group, October, 1984.
Bonino, Jose Miguez. *Doing Theology in a Revolutionary Situation*. Philadelphia: Fortress Press, 1975.
Bonner, Raymond. *Weakness and Deceit: U.S. Policy and El Salvador*. New York: Times Books, 1984.
Brown, Cynthia, ed. *With Friends Like These: The Americas Watch Report on Human Rights & U.S. Policy in Latin America*. New York: Pantheon, 1985.
Carrigan, Ana. *Salvador Witness: The Life and Calling of Jean Donovan*. New York: Simon and Schuster, Inc., 1984.
Changing Course: Blueprint for Peace in Central America and the Caribbean. Washington, D.C.: Institute for Policy Studies, 1984.
Clark, Kenneth. *Civilisation: A Personal View*. New York: Harper & Row, Publishers, Inc., 1970.
Clements, Charles, M.D. *Witness to War: An American Doctor in El Salvador*. New York: Bantam Books, 1984.
Collins, Joseph, with Francis Moore Lappe, Nick Allen and Paul Rice. *Nicaragua: What Difference Could a Revolution Make?* rev. ed. San Francisco: Institute for Food and Development Policy, 1985.
Dillard, Annie. *Holy the Firm*. New York: Harper & Row, Publishers, Inc. 1977.
———. *Teaching a Stone to Talk*. New York: Harper & Row, Publishers, Inc. 1982.
Diskin, Martin, ed. *Trouble in Our Backyard: Central America and the United States in the Eighties*. New York: Pantheon, 1983.
Fuentes, Carlos. "High Noon in Latin America." *Vanity Fair* (Sept. 1983): 47.
Golden, Renny, and Michael McConnell. *Sanctuary: A New Underground Railroad*. Maryknoll, NY: Orbis Books, 1986.
Gutierrez, Gustavo. *The Power of the Poor in History*. Maryknoll, NY: Orbis Books, 1983.
———. *A Theology of Liberation*. Translated and edited by Sister Caridad Inda and John Engelson. Maryknoll, NY: Orbis Books, 1973.
Helton, Arthur C. "Political Asylum Under The 1980 Refugee Act: An Unfulfilled Promise." *Journal of Law Reform* 17:2 (Winter 1984): 253.
Heschel, Susannah. "Heschel in Selma." *Hadassah Magazine* (June 1985): 47.
LaFeber, Walter. *Inevitable Revolutions: The United States in Central America*. New York: W.W. Norton & Company, 1983.
Lernoux, Penny. *Fear and Hope: Toward Political Democracy in Central America*. New York: The Field Foundation, 1984.

MacEoin, Gary, ed. *Sanctuary: A Resource Guide for Understanding and Participating in the Central American Refugees' Struggle.* New York: Harper & Row, Publishers, Inc., 1985.

Nairn, Allan. *Endgame: A Special Report on U.S. Military Strategy in Central America.* NACLA Report on the Americas, Vol. XVIII, Number 3, May/June 1984.

Niebuhr, Reinhold. *The Children Of Light And The Children Of Darkness.* New York: Charles Scribner's Sons, 1972.

———. *Moral Man and Immoral Society: A Study in Ethics and Politics.* New York: Charles Scribner's Sons, 1932.

———. *The Nature and Destiny of Man: A Christian Interpretation.* New York: Charles Scribner's Sons, 1953.

———. *The Self and the Dramas of History.* New York: Charles Scribner's Sons, 1957.

Niebuhr, H. Richard. *Radical Monotheism and Western Culture.* New York: Harper Bros., 1960.

———. *The Responsible Self.* New York: Harper & Row, Publishers, Inc., 1963.

Oates, Stephen B. *Let the Trumpet Sound: The Life of Martin Luther King, Jr.* New York: Harper & Row, Publishers, Inc., 1982.

Tamez, Elsa. *Bible of the Oppressed.* Maryknoll, NY: Orbis Books, 1982.

Walker, Thomas, ed. *Nicaragua: The First Five Years.* New York: Praeger, 1985.

White, Richard Alan. *The Morass: United States Intervention in Central America.* New York: Harper & Row, Publishers, Inc., 1984.

The following organizations provide important information on Central America and/or the Public Sanctuary Movement:

American Friends Service Committee
1501 Cherry St.
Philadelphia, PA   19102

Americas Watch
34 West 44th St.
New York, NY   10036

Amnesty International
322 Eighth Ave., 10th floor
New York, NY   10001

Coalition for a New Foreign
   and Military Policy
712 G. St., SE
Washington, D.C.   20003

Inter-religious Task Force on
   El Salvador and Central America
475 Riverside Dr., Rm. 633
New York, NY   10115

Religious Task Force
   on Central America
1747 Connecticut Ave., NW
Washington, DC   20009

Tucson Ecumenical Council
317 West 23rd St.
Tucson, AZ   85713

Washington Office on Latin America (WO
110 Maryland Ave., NE
Washington, D.C.   20002

THE AUTHOR:
Ted Loder

TED LODER has been called many names: "free-wheeling," "emotional," "provocative," "outrageous," "courageous." They're all true. As Senior Minister of one of Philadelphia's most unusual churches — the First United Methodist Church of Germantown (FUMCOG) — he actively encourages openness to question and to change. He leads his church to the forefront of political activism and social concerns. Ted is Co-Founder and Chairman of the Board for the Metropolitan Collegiate Center (a program preparing disadvantaged youths for college and jobs); he is Co-Founder of Plowshares (a non-profit housing renovation corporation); he is also President of Metro-Ministries, Inc. (the instrument of the United Methodist Church in Easter Pennsylvania to coordinate property and personnel of the church in the city); and he is a member of the Advisory Committee for the Wholistic Health Center (a medical mission to depressed areas of the city).

Ted Loder's ministry extends beyond the Philadelphia neighborhood to world neighbors. The First United Methodist Church of Germantown declared Public Sanctuary in 1984 and now provides sanctuary for a family of Guatemalan refugees. Ted has also been a member of a Congressional Delegation on a fact-finding mission to Central America.

For many people, Ted Loder's mixture of scholarship (he received his B.D. degree from Yale Divinity School and an honorary doctorate from Willamette University) and of creativity (he was selected by the *National Observer* as one of America's Outstanding Creative Preachers for writing and staging story and drama sermons) stimulates an emerging freedom to re-connect with the church, to re-explore beliefs, and to re-discover passion.

Other books by Ted Loder include *Guerrillas of Grace: Prayers for the Battle* and *Tracks in the Straw: Tales Spun from the Manger*.

LURAMEDIA™ PUBLICATIONS

by Pat Backman
JOURNEY WITH MATTHEW
(ISBN 0-931055-03-2)

by Marjory Zoet Bankson
BRAIDED STREAMS:
Esther and a Woman's Way
of Growing
(ISBN 0-931055-05-9)

by Lura Jane Geiger
ASTONISH ME, YAHWEH!:
Leader's Guide
(ISBN 0-931055-02-4)

by Lura Jane Geiger
with Pat Backman
BRAIDED STREAMS:
Leader's Guide
(ISBN 0-931055-09-1)

by Lura Jane Geiger, Sandy Landstedt,
Mary Geckeler, and Peggie Oury
ASTONISH ME, YAHWEH!:
A Bible Workbook-Journal
(ISBN 0-931055-01-6)

by Ted Loder
GUERRILLAS OF GRACE:
Prayers for the Battle
(ISBN 0-931055-04-0)
NO ONE BUT US:
Personal Reflections on Public Sanctua
(ISBN 0-931055-08-3)
TRACKS IN THE STRAW:
Tales Spun from the Manger
(ISBN 0-931055-06-7)

by Elizabeth O'Connor
SEARCH FOR SILENCE
(ISBN 0-931055-07-5)

LuraMedia™ operates as a creative publishing forum. LuraMedia™ selects, designs, produces and distributes books, teaching manuals and cassette tapes with subject area specialization in personal growth using journaling, music, art, meditation, stories and creativity in a spiritual context.

LuraMedia™ is a company that searches for ways to encourage personal growth, shares the excitement of creative integrity, and believes in the power of faith to change lives.

HIVELY AVE. MENNONITE CHURCH
ELKHART, INDIANA

LURAMEDIA™
10227 Autumnview Lane
San Diego, California 92126-0998